ADVANCES IN MONETARY ECONOMICS

ADVANCES IN MONETARY ECONOMICS

Edited by DAVID CURRIE

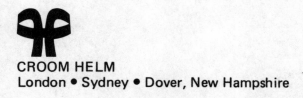

CROOM HELM
London • Sydney • Dover, New Hampshire

©1985 ESRC Money Study Group
Croom Helm Ltd, Provident House, Burrell Row,
Beckenham, Kent BR3 1AT

Croom Helm Australia Pty Ltd, Suite 4, 6th Floor,
64-76 Kippax Street, Surry Hills, NSW 2010, Australia

British Library Cataloguing in Publication Data

Advances in monetary economics.
   1. Money
   I. Currie, David A.
   332.4   HG221

   ISBN 0-7099-3443-2

Croom Helm, 51 Washington Street,
Dover, New Hampshire 03820, USA

Library of Congress Cataloging in Publication Data
Main entry under title:

Advances in Monetary Economics

   Bibliography: p.
   Contents: Policy credibility and unemployment in
the UK by David Backus and John Driffill—Debt
neutrality in disequilibrium ?6 , 38) 4-, (8,—
Fiscal policy and the real exchange rate by
Francesco Giavazzi and Jeffrey Sheen—(etc.)
1. Monetary policy—Addresses, essays, lectures.
2. Economic policy—Addresses, essays, lectures.
I. Currie, David A.
HG230.3.A38   1985   332.4   85-21304
ISBN 0-7099-3443-2

Printed and bound in Great Britain
by Billing & Sons Limited, Worcester.

CONTENTS

Contents

ACKNOWLEDGEMENTS

The production of this volume would not have been possible
without the help of a number of people. Thanks are due to the
Committee of the Money Study Group for their help in the editorial
process, particularly to Tony Courakis who organised the Conference
at Brasenose College, Oxford, where many of the papers were
presented; to Christopher Green, the Secretary of the Money Study
Group, and to Victoria Chick. Thanks are also due to Peter Sowden
of Croom Helm for his guidance in the production of the book.
However, the major debt is to Alison Finch of Queen Mary College,
who so efficiently combined typing and copy-editing, and organised
the overall production of the book with remarkable good humour
during long periods when the editor was distracted with other
matters.

Finally, the Money Study Group owes a great debt to the ESRC
for its continuing financial support and encouragement over many
years.

INTRODUCTION

The Money Study Group was formed in 1969 with two main objectives. The first is to bring together people (in the United Kingdom and abroad) who are concerned with the functioning of the British and international monetary system, whether as academic scholars, economists in the financial sector, or officials of the Bank of England and the Treasury. The second objective is to promote research into monetary economics. The Group subscribes to no particular school of thought, and takes no collective position on policy and other questions. It organises regular seminars and an annual Conference.

This volume draws together papers given at the 1984 Money Study Group Conference, held in September at Brasenose College, Oxford, and papers presented at seminars during that year. They provide a good indication of the vitality and range of the Money Study Group's activities, including papers on theoretical, empirical and institutional aspects of monetary economics.

The volume opens with a theoretical paper by Backus and Driffill which reflects current theoretical interest in the question of time-consistency and credibility of policy rules. Backus and Driffill show how these issues are naturally viewed in a game-theoretic framework, and how the explicit consideration of questions of reputation can resolve problems of time inconsistency that otherwise arise. This is because governments have an incentive to maintain their investment in reputation, and to resist, therefore, the short run temptation to renege on past policy commitments.

Rankin uses a disequilibrium framework to re-examine the debt neutrality proposition of Barro and others. He develops a model which elegantly - and in a tractable manner - combines an overlapping generations model, asset accumulation arising from government deficits, and the disequilibrium approach. In this context he demonstrates that the proposition that government bonds do not constitute net wealth is invalid, and in which bond-financed tax cuts can produce a sustained expansion of the economy.

The paper by Giavazzi and Sheen continues the analysis of bond-financed fiscal deficits, but in an open economy context, re-examining Mundell's result that a fiscal expansion with a given money supply will lead to an appreciation of the exchange rate. They show that a short-run appreciation is quite possible, but the wealth effects operating on expenditures and asset-demands may well reverse this in the longer run, leading to a depreciation. This analysis is of direct relevance to current debates on the dollar and the US fiscal deficit, and to suggestions, increasingly popular in the UK, that fiscal expansion with a tight monetary policy will deliver economic expansion, with an appreciation of the exchange rate offsetting inflationary pressures. Giavazzi and Sheen note the urgent need for more empirical work in this area.

The paper by Becker, Dwolatzky, Karakitsos and Rustem is concerned with the design of optimal policy when there is more than one available model of the economy. They propose a procedure for deriving a Pareto optimal policy, which performs reasonably well in whichever model turns out to be the true one. They illustrate this procedure using the Treasury and National Institute models as rival views of the world.

Keating describes in detail the new monetary sector of the London Business School model. This has a high level of sectoral and asset disaggregation, an approach which had tended to fall into disfavour in the UK in recent years. The approach adopted is a mean/variance one with adjustment costs added, and the main innovation in the model is the incorporation of explicit modelling of expectations concerning capital gains, using the assumption of rational expectations. This gives considerably interest to policy simulations resulting from the model, with the possibility of distinguishing the consequences of anticipated and unanticipated policy changes. Time will tell just how robust the model is for forecasting purposes; but it represents a major and significant development in monetary modelling.

Van Loo describes the banking sector of a larger, highly disagregated model of the Dutch financial system. The high degree of disaggregation permits careful analysis of the detailed instruments of monetary policy available to the monetary authorities. This paper, together with that of Keating, suggest that the structural, highly disaggregated approach to monetary modelling has much to offer.

Gallais-Hamonno uses a Markowitz risk/return framework to examine the effect of government guidelines on the portfolio decisions of French open funds. These guidelines act to limit the freedom of fund managers to diversify their portfolios internationally, as well as requiring them to hold a certain portfolio of government liabilities with the officially stated view of reducing risk. The approach identifies which guidelines have only limited effect and which severely constrain portfolio decisions. The findings suggest that the constraints have to act perversely in so far as their objective is to reduce the risk of portfolios held by the open funds.

Hoggarth and Ormerod model the determination of sales of long maturity government debt to the UK non-bank private sector. The analysis confirms earlier work concerning the importance of expectations of capital gains on gilt holdings; but also highlights the significance of expectations of capital gains on equities. Hoggarth and Ormerod also find that simple extrapolative mechanisms for expectations formulation outperform rational expectations approaches. The emphasis on monetary control and the crucial role of gilt sales in controlling monetary aggregates gives this work an important policy dimension.

Hammond and Kay compare methods of insurance regulation in the UK and Germany. This comparison is topical in view of the proposed reform of the procedures for financial regulation in the UK following publication of the Gower Report. It is also apposite in view of the contrast between the strict regulations operative in Germany and the lightly regulated system in the UK. Their study suggests that over-regulation may raise costs and prices considerably and limit innovation, while giving only limited gains by reducing the costs to consumers of fraud and insolvency.

Finally Cable and Turner provide an interesting blend of theory and institutional analysis in analysing the arguments concerning bank provision of finance for industry in the UK. They argue that credit rationing and high collateral requirements may arise from an unequal distribution of information between borrowers and lenders, and that the UK structure of banking institutions is likely to give rise to such an informational asymmetry. On this view, changes in bank lending behaviour are likely to result less from exhortation or regulation, and more from changes in the structure of institutions to integrate banks and industrial companies more closely along Japanese or German lines.

A unifying thread running through these papers is their concern with policy in the monetary sphere, both in terms of broad macroeconomic questions of monetary and fiscal management and the issues of policy at the microeconomic level towards financial institutions and markets. What they demonstrate is the importance and relevance of monetary economics to crucial and widely debated policy issues. The Money Study Group is pleased to be able to advance the debate by making these papers generally available. The Group looks forward to playing a continuing and influential role in analysing problems of monetary policy and in advancing the understanding of those issues more widely in the policy community.

CONTRIBUTORS

David Backus is Assistant Professor at Queen's University, Kingston, Canada and Visiting Lecturer at the University of Southampton.

Robin Becker is Senior Analyst Programmer in the Department of Electrical Engineering at Imperial College of Science and Technology.

John Cable is Senior Lecturer in Economics at the University of Warwick.

David Currie is Professor of Economics at Queen Mary College, University of London, and Treasurer of the ESRC Money Study Group.

John Driffill is Lecturer in Economics at the University of Southampton.

Barry Dwolatzky is a Research Associate in the Department of Electrical Engineering at Imperial College of Science and Technology.

Georges Gallais-Hamonno is Director of the Institut Orléanais de Finance, Université d'Orléans, France.

Francesco Giavazzi is Associate Professor at the Università di Venezia, Italy.

Elizabeth Hammond is a Research Officer at the Institute for Fiscal Studies, London.

Glenn Hoggarth is Senior Economic Analyst at the Henley Centre for Forecasting, London.

Contributors

Elias Karakitsos is a Research Fellow in the Department of Electrical Engineering at Imperial College of Science and Technology.

John Kay is Director of the Institute for Fiscal Studies, London.

Giles Keating is Senior Research Officer at the Centre for Economic Forecasting, London Business School.

Peter D. van Loo is a senior economist in the Econometric Research and Special Studies Department of de Nederlandsche Bank NV, Amsterdam.

Paul Ormerod is Director of Economic Research at the Henley Centre for Forecasting, and Visiting Professor of Economics at Queen Mary College, University of London.

Neil Rankin is Lecturer in Economics at Queen Mary College, University of London.

Berc Rustem is SERC Advanced Research Fellow in the Department of Electrical Engineering at Imperial College of Science and Technology.

Jeffrey Sheen is Lecturer in Economics at the University of Essex.

Paul Turner is Lecturer in Economics at the University of Southampton.

POLICY CREDIBILITY AND UNEMPLOYMENT IN THE U.K.

David Backus and John Driffill

INTRODUCTION

The fall in the rate of inflation that we witnessed over the past few years was accompanied in the UK by the highest rates of unemployment since the 1930's. Manufacturing output fell in 1980 by 13 per cent in real terms and unemployment rose from 5 per cent in 1979 to 12 per cent five years later. We argue that part of this foregone output should be attributed to public scepticism over the government's commitment to disinflation, that is, to credibility problems. This scepticism led the private sector to demand wage increases larger than the rate of inflation turned out to be, thus magnifying the severity of the policy-induced recession. In a second version of our theory, this effect is compounded by private sector resistance to smaller nominal wage increases.

In the absence of such credibility effects, we find the extent of the UK unemployment difficult to explain. Keynesians of a decade ago might disagree, arguing simply that the Phillips curve is flat. Arthur Okun's (1978) survey and interpretation of Phillips curve estimates falls into this category. The crucial issue is where the "stickiness" embodied in the Phillips curve comes from. One view, exemplified by the work of Stanley Fischer (1977) and John Taylor (1980), is that sluggishness in nominal wages and prices results from long-term wage contracts. In this case, gradual disinflation is possible with no fall in output if government policy is credible (Taylor (1983)). Faster disinflation is also possible, but the predicted output loss is much smaller than we have seen (Fischer (1984)). In our opinion the high levels of unemployment observed in the UK are a puzzle that has yet to be explained.

The standard approach to the credibility problem facing government policymakers rests on the notion of time inconsistency: the "optimal" policy involves promises of future policy which the government will not find advantageous to fulfill when the future arises. Such a policy has an obvious credibility problem! In an economy with long-term contracts, the "optimal" plan calls for lower inflation in the future. But to be successful, wage-setters must be convinced that inflation will be lower (as promised) at the end of the

3

contract than at the start. The time inconsistency of this policy gives the private sector reason for doubt.

We examine explicitly this issue of policy credibility. But rather than base our argument on time-inconsistency in a dynamic model, we use the static model of Robert Barro and David Gordon (1983a, b) and focus our attention on the dynamics induced by the government's reputation for fighting inflation. The analysis of reputation is based closely on work by David Kreps and Robert Wilson (1982).

2. THE BARRO-GORDON MODEL

The essence of the credibility/time-inconsistency problem is the government's inability to precommit its future actions. Barro and Gordon take a model from an earlier paper by Finn Kydland and Edward Prescott (1977) and collapse this argument into a single period. In their economy inflation and output are related by a Phillips curve with the natural rate property:

$$y = y_n + (x - x^e)$$

where y is output, y_n is the natural rate, and x and x^e are the actual and expected rates of inflation.

The commitment problem is best seen by viewing policy as a game between the government and the private sector. Suppose the government dislikes inflation but likes output, even beyond the natural rate. A utility function with this property is:

$$U_g (x, x^e) = -x^2 + a(y - y_n)$$
$$= -x^2 + a(x - x^e)$$

where $a > 0$ is a parameter. The public may also like output and dislike inflation, but individual agents are too small to affect these aggregates. Instead they simply try to avoid expectational errors:

$$U_p (x, x^e) = -(x - x^e)^2$$

Consider now the Nash equilibrium to the game with these utility functions in which the government chooses x and the public x^e. The solution is

$$x = x^e = a/2$$

In short, the equilibrium involves a positive rate of inflation even though the economy has a vertical Phillips curve and the government dislikes inflation.

Barro and Gordon argue persuasively that the source of the

difficulty is the government's inability to commit its policy ahead of time. Suppose, for example, that the government could do this by going first. Then the government would choose the inflation rate to maximize its utility, given its knowledge that the public will follow by choosing $x = x^e$. The equilibrium in this case is $x = x^e = 0$, which yields a higher level of government utility. Clearly everyone prefers this outcome ($U_p = 0$ in both cases), but what happens when the government cannot guarantee its policy of zero inflation? The private sector realizes that if it expects zero inflation, the government has an incentive to inflate in order to raise output above the natural rate. Without precommitment, therefore, the government's "optimal" policy of zero inflation is not credible and will lead to a recession because the private sector expects inflation.

We believe this model captures the essential features of the government's credibility problem in a static context. We turn now to dynamic aspects of government policy and reputation.

3.   CREDIBILITY AND GOVERNMENT POLICY

The Barro and Gordon model leaves one with the impression that inflation is the inevitable outcome of government policy. Below we argue that public uncertainty about government preferences (about the parameter a, for example) or behaviour changes the situation considerably. This uncertainty is only temporary, however, as the public eventually learns the truth from the government's behaviour. Thus a severe anti-inflationary policy, such as that practised by Mrs Thatcher, produces an initial period of high unemployment. But as the public learns that her promises (threats?) of low inflation are credible, the cost eventually disappears.

Without imperfect information, such results are impossible. If we consider the Barro-Gordon model as a game played a finite number of times, then the only subgame perfect equilibrium is one in which the rate of inflation is a/2. The static Nash equilibrium is repeated in each play of the game, as we show with a standard recursive argument. A subgame perfect equilibrium is one in which at each stage in the game, each player plays his best move given the state of the game at that stage, and knowing that subsequent play will be conducted in the same way. This has the effect of ruling out the use of incredible threats and promises to support a particular outcome of the game. It means that the solution can be computed recursively, by solving first the game in the final period given the state of the economy at that time and, having done that, solving the game in the penultimate period given the conditions ruling at the start of that period, and so on.

In the Barro-Gordon game, this procedure is particularly simple because the model itself has no dynamics. In the Nash equilibrium for the last period of play (period T, say) the government maximizes $-x_T^2 + a(x_T - x_T^e)$, taking x_T^e as given, and the private sector maximizes $-(x_T - x_T^e)^2$, taking x_T as given. Therefore they play

$x_T = x^e_T = a/2$. These last-period moves are independent of anything that happened before in the game. Neither side can credibly use its last-period play as a threat to manipulate earlier play by the other side. In the penultimate period, therefore, the government maximizes $- x^2_{T-1} + a(x_{T-1} - x^e_{T-1})$ and the private sector maximizes $- (x_{T-1} - x^e_{T-1})^2$. Again the outcome is $x_{T-1} = x^e_{T-1} = a/2$. And so it continues for earlier periods. For any finite number of repetitions, the unique subgame perfect equilibrium is $x_t = x^e_t = a/2$ for all times t. This solution is clearly inferior to the Pareto efficient outcome ($x_t = x^e_t = 0$, all t), but it is dynamically consistent. Neither side ever has any incentive to depart from it unilaterally.

The analysis of the subgame perfect solution to the game does however pose some questions. Suppose, for example, that the government finds itself stuck with a Pareto-inefficient outcome. In informal discussions of this situation, one might imagine that the government would try to "take the lead" and play $x = 0$ in the hope that its example would induce the private sector to play $x^e = 0$ in subsequent plays of the game. However, the formal analysis above allows no room for this: rational players with full knowledge of the payoff matrices can compute the optimal play, in which the event $x_t = 0$ should never be observed. More importantly, the model predicts that the private sector will not change its behaviour even if it observes $x = 0$ for several periods.

A formalization which does allow us to introduce these possibilities is provided by Kreps and Wilson (1982) in their analysis of the chain-store paradox. For simplicity we set $a = 2$, so that the Pareto optimal outcome of the game is $x = x^e = 0$ and the Nash equilibrium is $x = x^e = 1$. Furthermore, we restrict the choices of the two players so that x and x^e are either zero or one. Ruling out other actions and restricting the players to binary choices simplifies the analysis considerably while preserving the essential features of the game.

How should the private sector respond to the "impossible" event $x_t = 0$? The central feature of the analysis is the private sector's uncertainty about how the government will play the game. "Impossible" events will lead the private sector to modify its belief that the game is played according to the Barro-Gordon rules. To be specific, let us say that at the start of period t, the private sector attaches probability p_t to the possibility that the government is committed irrevocably to playing the no-inflation policy, $x_t = 0$. The number p_t characterizes completely the government's reputation. The irrevocably committed government was designated "hard-nosed" in a previous paper (Backus and Driffill (1984a)) and the rational government was designated "wet". Payoff matrices which rationalize such behaviour are:

		public	
		$x^e = 0$	$x^e = 1$
wet government	$x = 0$	0	-2
	$x^e = 0$	1	-1
hard-nosed government	$x^e = 0$	0	0
	$x = 1$	-1	-1

The payoff matrix for the wet government comes from the objective function on page 4. The payoffs for the hard-nosed government can be derived by setting $a = 0$.

Suppose now that the game is played a finite number of times from $t = 1$ to $t = T$. The game begins at $t = 1$ and the government has some initial reputation p_1 which is exogenous to the analysis, lies strictly between zero and one and is known to both players. This reputation changes the game radically, since it allows the government to pretend to be hard-nosed even if it is not. In each period the private sector will attempt to maximize its expected utility given its beliefs about the probabilities of the two events $x = 1$ and $x = 0$. If $x = 1$ is more likely to occur than $x = 0$, then the private sector should choose to play $x^e = 1$ and vice versa. If they are equally likely, the private sector is indifferent and may randomize between them choosing $x = 0$ with probability z between zero and one.

The probability with which the event $x = 0$ occurs is non-zero for two reasons. First, the probability p_t that the government always plays $x = 0$ (that it is a <u>hard-nosed</u> government) is generally non-zero. Second, it may now be advantageous for a wet government to play $x = 0$ with positive probability in order to persuade the private sector that it is hard-nosed. The probability of observing $x_t = 0$ is thus $p_t + (1 - p_t)y_t$ where y_t is the probability with which a wet government plays $x_t = 0$.

Consider how the government's play affects its reputation. If the event $x_t = 0$ actually occurs, then the private sector will revise its beliefs about the probability that it faces a hard-nosed government. By Bayes' theorem

prob (govt. is hard-nosed|$x_t = 0$)
   = prob (govt. is hard-nosed)/prob ($x_t = 0$)

or

$$p_{t+1} = p_t/[p_t + (1 - p_t)y_t].$$

Thus the reputation of the government is enhanced ($p_{t+1} > p_t$) if a wet government is taking a risk and playing $x_t = 0$ with probability y_t less than one. If a wet government were to play $x_t = 0$ with

7

probability one, then the observation $x_t = 0$ gives no further information about the kind of government and the reputation would not change. If the event $x = 1$ occurs then, since only a wet government ever plays $x = 1$, the private sector can infer that it surely faces a wet government and sets $p_{t+1} = 0$. After this has occurred nothing the government does can recoup its reputation. In subsequent periods, the outcome will be $x = x^e = 1$, the complete information perfect equilibrium.

Consider now the behaviour of the government. A hard-nosed government always plays $x_t = 0$. A wet government plays $x_t = 0$ with probability y_t. y_t is chosen so as to maximize its expected utility arising from current and subsequent plays of the game, and is chosen to balance the risk of conceding (large y_t) against the larger reputation that risk promises (large p_{t+1}). The lower is y_t, the higher is its expected utility arising from the current round of the game. Also, the lower is y_t, the greater will be its reputation on entering the next stage of the game if $x_t = 0$ and, if the expected utility derived from playing the game is positively related to reputation at the start of the game, the higher is the utility to be enjoyed in the future. But against that, lower y_t increases the probability of playing $x_t = 1$ and so blowing the reputation ($p_{t+1} = 0$) and achieving a lower level of expected utility in the future. Balancing these two considerations leads to a well-defined optimal value of y_t for the government.

It turns out that the optimal value of y_t in each stage of the game depends on the reputation on entering it. In this case the critical reputation is $p_t^* = (\frac{1}{2})^{T-t}$. If $p_t \geq (\frac{1}{2})^{T-t}$, then the wet government optimally plays $x_t = 0$ with probability 1 ($y_t = 1$). If $p_t < (\frac{1}{2})^{T-t}$ the wet government optimally plays $x_t = 0$ with probability:

$$y_t = \frac{p_t}{1-p_t} \cdot \frac{1 - (\frac{1}{2})^{T-t}}{(\frac{1}{2})^{T-t}} ,$$

which lies strictly between zero and one.

There are two interesting features of this result. First, the critical reputation p_t^* diminishes as the distance $(T-t)$ to the terminal period increases. If the terminal date is a long way off, p^* is very small indeed, so even a small reputation will enable a government to pursue a zero-inflation policy with probability one. Second, we can use it to describe the solution to the game. We start with an initial reputation p_1. Until the time is reached when the initial reputation is less than the critical reputation $p_s^* = (\frac{1}{2})^{T-s}$, the government plays $y_t = 1$, so $x_t = 0$ with probability 1. In this interval of time, $t = 1, 2, \ldots s - 1$, the private sector plays $x_t^e = 0$ also with probability one. So we have full employment ($y = y_n$) with zero inflation.

After this critical time, the government randomizes between playing zero inflation and inflation equal to one, so that in each period its reputation is just good enough to induce the public to expect inflation with probability $\frac{1}{2}$, and thus to be indifferent between expecting zero inflation and inflation. The public in this case randomizes between the two possibilities with equal probability. This goes on until the government's randomization leads it by chance to play $x_t = 1$. During this interval, we have actual inflation equal to zero, but expected inflation equal to one half the time and zero at other times. There is a 50% chance of a recession each period. If we allowed the private sector a continuous range of choices for x^e, then the more natural interpretation of $x^e = \frac{1}{2}$ and a small recession with certainty applies.

Once the government plays $x = 1$, its reputation for being tough goes to zero. In the period in which this occurs, we get higher output than we otherwise would, with inflation equal to one. After this event occurs, we have inflation equals one and full employment until the end of the game.

Figure 1 illustrates these general properties with a specific example. Suppose the initial reputation of government, p_1, lies between $(\frac{1}{2})^7$ and $(\frac{1}{2})^8$. Before $T - 7$, the outcome is zero expected and actual inflation with certainty ($x_t = x_t^e = 0$). We also have full employment ($y_t = y_n$). At $T - 7$, the government's actual reputation, which is still unchanged, is too small and it finds it optimal to randomize between inflating and holding out. In the scenario illustrated, we assume that the government actually ends up holding out ($x_{T-7} = 0$), with its reputation enhanced next period.

In periods $T - 6$ to $T - 4$ the government is randomizing optimally between inflating and holding out, and we assume for the purpose of illustration that it actually ends up holding out in these three periods, with its reputation enhanced in each successive period. But in these periods the private sector believes that inflation could occur with probability $\frac{1}{2}$. Therefore they choose randomly between expecting inflation ($x = 1$) and no inflation ($x^e = 0$). The equilibrium probabilities are $\frac{1}{2}$ each. So there is a 50% chance that each of the three periods will be a recession, with $x = 0$, $x^e = 1$, and $y < n$.

Suppose that in period $T - 3$, the toss of the coin is such that the government inflates in that period. The private sector's randomization means that we get a boom ($x = 1$, $x^e = 0$, $y > y_n$) or full employment ($x = 1$, $x^e = 1$, $y = y_n$), each with probability $\frac{1}{2}$. After period $T - 3$, the government's reputation is ruined and we get full employment with inflation until the end of the game - the perfect information equilibrium.

Figure 2 plots the path of expected output over time, given the actual path of government expenditure in the illustrative scenario of

Figure 1. It shows the recession that occurs in T - 6, T - 5, T - 4, and the boom in T - 3 when the government finally inflates.

The model captures the idea that credibility of government policy is crucial to its effectiveness, but it can be extended in a number of ways. As an example, consider what happens if we introduce uncertainty about private sector behaviour. Assume as before that the private sector believes at the start of period t that there is a probability p_t that it faces a hard-nosed government, as before, which will never cause inflation, and a probability $1 - p_t$ that it faces a "wet" government. But now replace the previous assumption that the government knows with certainty the payoffs of the private sector, and replace it with the assumption that it believes that there is a probability q_t that it faces an "intransigent" private sector which will never reduce its expectations of inflation from $x_t^e = 1$ to $x^e = 0$. The government believes that with probability $(1 - q_t)$ it faces a private sector whose payoff matrix results from costs of expectational errors as before and, in addition, that this private sector pays a once-and-for-all cost c in the period when it first moderates its expectations from $x^e = 1$ to $x^e = 0$. This assumption is a way of representing the idea that when there is a fall in the rate of inflation, the first groups of persons to cut wages or prices (relative to what they would have been) suffer a temporary fall in real income. This occurs if, for example, wage setting takes place in an environment of staggered long-term contracts.

The game begins with the private sector and government having some initial reputations, f and g. The analysis of the game is carried out in detail in Backus and Driffill (1984b) and leads to the following behaviour. The game is played with each side choosing the optimal randomization between concession and fighting on.

Fighting means the private sector plays $x^e = 1$ and the government plays $x^e = 0$. If, by a given stage of the game, neither side has conceded, each side's reputation for toughness is enhanced as before, according to Bayes' rule. If the government concedes, then its reputation goes to zero at once. In all subsequent rounds of the game, we have inflation and full employment: $x = x^e = 1$, $y = y_n$. In the period of time until one side or the other has conceded, we find the government causing zero inflation $x = 0$, but the private sector acting as if it is expecting positive inflation, $x^e = 1$. (It may, for example, continue to set wages based on the expectation expectation of accommodating monetary policy.) This leads to a recession $(y < y_n)$ until someone concedes. The expected length of this period of recession depends on the initial reputations of the two players. In the case where the government actually is hard-nosed, and the private sector is not intransigent, we show that the expected length of time until the private sector concedes is greater the worse is the initial reputation of the government.

The analysis of the model with uncertainty on both sides of the game is in principle the same as the one-sided uncertainty case, but the details become more complex. In Backus and Driffill (1984b), where these results are derived, we follow Kreps and Wilson (1982) in going from a discrete-time to a continuous-time formulation to keep the analysis as simple as possible. The development of the game as it is played is illustrated in Figures 3 and 4. If the initial reputations are (f, g), then the private sector initially makes a choice between conceding and fighting so that its reputation jumps on to the curve in Figure 3 if it actually fights. While both players fight, their reputations grow through time along the curve. If the private sector concedes at date t*, then at that point its reputation goes to zero. Figure 4 illustrates the associated paths of output and the actual and expected inflation. Again the economy suffers a recession until one side gives in.

4. IMPLICATIONS OF THE THEORY

The results shed light on a number of puzzles. Let us look first at recent experience in the UK. Figure 5 presents inflation and unemployment since 1978, which we argue look much as the theory predicts. Mrs Thatcher was elected in May 1979, and began formulating her policies. As with any new government, there was a degree of uncertainty about what these policies would be. The first two years, in fact, did little to raise any reputation she had for resisting inflation. The rate of inflation rose from a year-over-year 8 per cent in 1978 to over 16 per cent in 1980. One reason was that large wage increases for public sector employees, agreed to by the previous Labour government, were implemented soon after she took office. Another was the 7 per cent increase in the value-added tax in late 1979, a condition for joining the EEC, which raised measured retail prices by about 4 per cent. See Willem Buiter and Marcus Miller (1981(a), 1983) for details. At the same time, the Thatcher government was implementing an extremely tight macroeconomic policy, both monetary and fiscal. Although the rate of growth of sterling M3, the Bank of England's preferred aggregate, has declined fairly slowly over the past 5 years, the growth rates of both M1 and the monetary base fell precipitously. Real M1 actually fell by 11 per cent in 1980.

Partly as a result of these policies, inflation moderated and has been in the neighbourhood of 5 per cent per annum since early in 1983. Unemployment rose from 5.0 per cent in late 1979 to 10.8 per cent just two years later, and has yet to return to pre-1980 levels. As we said in the introduction, we think that part of this unemployment is the result of public scepticism over the government's disinflationary program. Without such a credibility problem the observed output-inflation tradeoff is difficult to explain. However, the fact that employment has failed to grow, as it did in the United States, remains a puzzle.

The theory also resolves some theoretical difficulties. Note that the solution concept resolves the problem of dynamic inconsistency. In most of the plays of the finitely-repeated game, the equilibrium outcome has the government sticking to an ex-ante optimal policy of causing zero inflation. The loss of reputation imposes a cost of playing the inflation policy and reduces even its short term attractiveness to zero. There is a unique equilibrium policy for the government to pursue and, given the information structure of the game, any deviation from it will give no higher value for the government's objective function.

Finally, the analysis explains why one would expect to find the Phillips curve relation unstable over time and across countries. The length of time needed to cut expected inflation to zero and thus the output cost associated with disinflation depends on the reputations of the players. A credible announcement of future anti-inflationary policy, or a pre-commitment, will cut inflation more rapidly than an irresolute policy stance. Since the stance and perception of policy are difficult to measure, econometric studies are unlikely to capture stable relationships.

An example is the comparison between the UK and US in the period 1979 - 1984, when inflation fell more rapidly and with less unemployment in the US than in the UK. Two possible explanations accord with the theory: (i) the independence of the Federal Reserve from the rest of government in the US that lent credibility to its planned tight money policy; and (ii) the initially contradictory signals about actual UK monetary policy that were put out by having monetary targets in the UK consistently exceeded, even though the exchange rate rose strongly until the end of 1980.

5. CONCLUSION

Our theory is essentially a parable, and some aspects of it work less well than others. We noted, for example, that an explanation for continued high rates of unemployment must be found elsewhere. Nevertheless, we think our story captures some elements of recent UK experience. And given observed clashes between government, trade union, and employers, the combative features of our second model strike a familiar note.

On the theoretical side, we think it is useful to regard macroeconomic policy as a game. Doing so enables us to formalize issues of policy credibility and to resolve the problem of dynamic inconsistency.

ACKNOWLEDGEMENT

David Backus thanks the SSHRC of Canada for financial support.

Figure 1

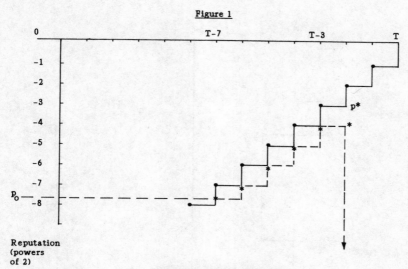

Reputation
(powers
of 2)

Illustrative path of the game

p_0 lies between 2^{-7} and 2^{-8}

Up to and including T – 8: $x = x^e = 0$ with certainty

T–7	government randomizes, and plays $x = 0$	private sector plays $x^e = 0$
T–6 to T–4}	government randomizes, plays $x = 0$	private sector plays $x^e = 0$ and $x^e = 1$ each with probability ½.
T–3	government randomizes but plays $x = 1$	private sector randomizes, with probability ½ of playing $x^e = 0$ and $x^e = 1$
T–2 to T }	The government's reputation is now zero. It plays $x = 1$ and the private sector plays $x^e = 1$ with certainty.	

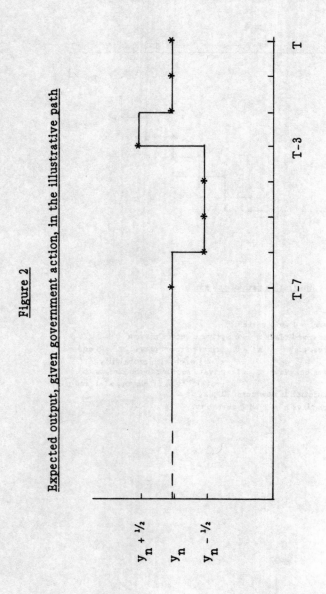

Figure 2

Expected output, given government action, in the illustrative path

14

Figure 3

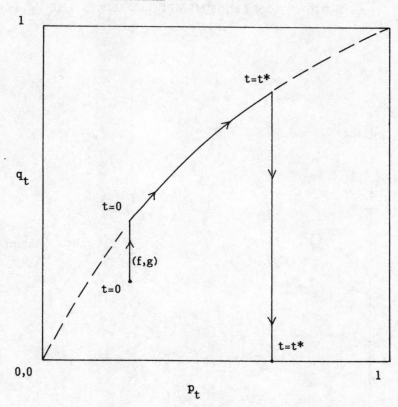

output

Figure 4

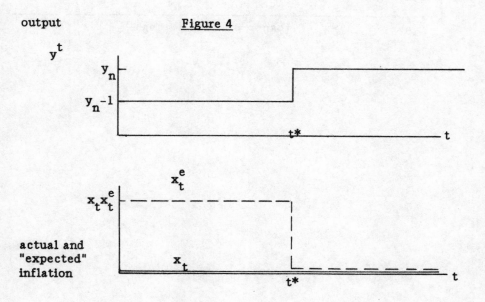

actual and
"expected"
inflation

Figure 5: INFLATION AND UNEMPLOYMENT IN THE UK 1978-1984

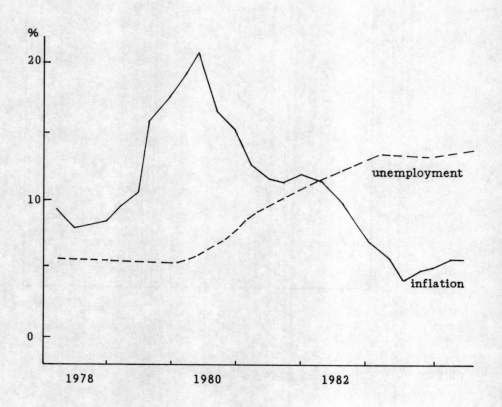

DEBT NEUTRALITY IN DISEQUILIBRIUM

Neil Rankin

INTRODUCTION

It is now quite widely recognised (see, for example, Hahn (1980), Begg (1982)) that the crucial condition in demonstrating the neutrality of money is perfectly flexible prices and hence a continuous state of market equilibrium, and not the assumption of rational expectations, or, in a non-stochastic context, perfect foresight. Sticky prices, and hence market disequilibrium, therefore provide the most likely basis for a Keynesian theory of the non-neutrality of money, and there is now a large "disequilibrium" literature demonstrating monetary policy effectiveness under such circumstances (classic references being Barro and Grossman (1971), Benassy (1975) and Malinvaud (1977)). However, historically the Keynesian school has laid more emphasis on fiscal than on monetary policy effectiveness, and for an effective fiscal policy the crucial element is not the non-neutrality of money but the non-neutrality of government debt. A pure fiscal policy change is taken to be a change in spending or taxation or both, with the change in the deficit, if any, being financed by borrowing. The key question is whether issuing extra debt in order to finance a tax cut or subsidy has any effect on the real economy: if not, then borrowing is equivalent to taxation, and the most commonly considered fiscal policy change, an increase in government spending, has a multiplier equal only to the balanced budget one.

Debt neutrality is an issue which has received much less attention in the disequilibrium literature, and the object of this paper is to help fill the gap. However, it is useful to start by briefly reviewing the conclusions of other approaches to this subject. Two strongly contrasting results stand out: the first is that of Barro (1974), who re-asserts the proposition, originally associated with Ricardo, that government debt is neutral, on the basis of a model of overlapping generations with bequests. The second is that of Blinder and Solow (1973) (to take only one representative of this approach – others being Ott and Ott (1965), Christ (1968), Tobin and Buiter (1976)), who use a dynamic version of the IS-LM model to show that a bond-financed spending increase can have a long-run multiplier much greater than the balanced budget one. The difficulties which arise in reconciling these two results intuitively are, first, that Blinder and Solow's model has no explicit microeconomic foundations, unlike Barro's; and second that Barro's model uses instantaneously-clearing markets whereas Blinder and Solow - at least, implicitly - are describing a world of fixed prices and thus disequilibrium.

In pursuing the Keynesian approach, the task is therefore to construct a model based on fixed prices and disequilibrium but with clear microeconomic foundations. The object is to determine whether this results in debt non-neutrality analogous to the money non- neutrality found in earlier disequilibrium models. It is worth noting that Barro's model, interpreted literally, completely begs the question with regard to the short-run effectiveness of fiscal policy - the question in which macroeconomists are most interested - since the market-clearing assumption together with a fixed capital stock and an exogenous labour supply imply that short-run output is exogenous whether debt is neutral or not. The disequilibrium framework, on the other hand, allows conclusions to be drawn which are directly relevant to short-run macroeconomic management.

The plan of the paper is as follows. In section 2 a model of overlapping generations with no bequests is used to suggest the most likely microeconomic foundations for the non-neutrality result of Blinder and Solow (1973). Its static and dynamic behaviour is analysed, with the assumption of perfect foresight being universally employed. It is indeed found that such a model reproduces more or less exactly Blinder and Solow's conclusions. More generally, it provides a very close microfoundations equivalent to the traditional IS-LM model, enabling analysis of short- and long-run effects of both fiscal and monetary policy of various types, without relying on arbitrary expectations assumptions or specifications of structural relationships.

However, as a demonstration of debt non-neutrality, it is open to Barro's objection that it ignores the possibility of bequests between generations which might cancel out the government's attempt to stimulate demand and hence output, by borrowing from future generations to subsidise current ones. Hence in section 3, Barro-type bequests are implicitly introduced - "implicitly", because in fact what are assumed are infinitely-lived individuals. This provides a polar case to be contrasted with section 2; in reality, there are considerable doubts as to whether bequests can ever generate exact equivalence to an infinitely-lived individual, and to the extent that they cannot, this casts further doubt on Barro's result (see Tobin (1980), Buiter (1980), Gale (1983 Ch. 1.8)). Given this equivalence, it is found that Barro's objection is upheld: debt becomes completely neutral despite a state of permanent market disequilibrium. Thus disequilibrium alone is not sufficient to generate non-neutrality of debt, unlike non-neutrality of money. The intuitive reason for this is the one given by Barro: with infinite lives and perfect foresight, bonds are not perceived as net wealth. However, this is not a complete explanation, since with fixed prices, the possibility of equilibrium becoming indeterminate arises, as Gale (1983 Ch. 1.10) has shown. This means that the neutral outcome of a bond-financed tax cut is only one possibility; Keynesian expansionary responses might also be entirely consistent with the model. Section 3 shows that the indeterminacy found by Gale disappears when money as well as bonds are present, ensuring that the neutral outcome is the only possible one.

Finite lives, or the failure of the Barro bequest mechanism, are therefore an important example of a possible escape route from debt neutrality, in disequilibrium as well as equilibrium. An alternative such escape is considered in section 4: this is the possibility that bonds provide "liquidity services" in the same way as money, which can be represented by including them in the utility function. It can be argued that the neutrality result of section 3 is the consequence of an arbitrary asymmetry in the conventional treatment of the two assets, whereby money is assumed to provide liquidity services and bonds are not. Removing this asymmetry is shown to restore non-neutrality despite the assumption of infinite lives, with a bond-financed tax cut producing convergence to a higher long-run level of output not dissimilar to that of the section 2 model, provided that money and bonds are sufficiently strong substitutes. Moreover, this is an example of debt being non-neutral despite the fact that government bonds are not "net wealth", as usually understood.

2. A MODEL WITH FINITE LIVES

(i) Overview

The economy has four commodities: goods, labour, money and bonds. Bonds are of one-period maturity, i.e. promises of one unit of money in one period's time, with a current price q_t. The interest rate (r_t, say) is thus $1/q_t - 1$. The price, P, and money wage, W, are exogenous, and are assumed constant over time. This latter is undoubtedly a very crude assumption relative to assuming, for example, that P and W respond to previous excess demands, but it represents the extreme case of disequilibrium, enabling its implications to be seen fully. Such an assumption is also implicit in the IS-LM approach of Blinder and Solow (1973). The bond price, q_t, is determined by assuming instantaneous clearing of the money market. The economy has three types of agent: consumers, firms and the government, whose individual behaviour we now describe.

(ii) Consumer behaviour

In any period there are two generations of consumers - "young" and "old" - each of which is taken to be represented by a single individual. Consumers live for two periods, obtaining utility from consumption in each period. They work only when young, and therefore have to save for retirement. There is no utility of leisure, so the young's labour supply (which may be rationed) equals their exogenous time endowment, L. Besides their labour income, the young also receive the profits of firms, which we assume are immediately distributed. To save for old age, the consumer may either accumulate money or bonds. Since money pays no interest, the demand for it will be zero unless it performs functions apart from being a store of value. These are modelled by assuming real balances provide utility, for example as a result of reducing the sacrifice of time involved in making transactions. Such an assumption is the one adopted in the money-and-growth literature - see, for example, Sidrauski (1967), Brock (1974).

Consider first the problem of the young. Note that the young's income is always exogenous to them, and in fact equal to aggregate income y_t, because profit income is exogenous, while labour income is wL ($w \equiv W/P$) when unrationed in the labour market, or $w\ell_t$ when rationed by the quantity constraint $\ell_t < L$. Thus so long as there is no consumption rationing, their problem may be written:

$$\text{maximise } u(c_t^t, m_t, c_{t+1}^t) \tag{1}$$

$$\text{subject to } y_t - \tau_t = c_t^t + m_t + q_t b_t \tag{2}$$

$$m_t + b_t = c_{t+1}^t \tag{3}$$

or, combining (2) and (3) to eliminate b_t,

$$y_t - \tau_t = c_t^t + q_t c_{t+1}^t + [1-q_t] m_t \tag{4}$$

where c_t^t, c_{t+1}^t = consumption of generation born in period t

τ_t = lump-sum tax

$m_t \equiv M_t/P_t$ = end-of-period real money balances

$B_t \equiv b_t/P_t$ = end-of-period real redemption value of bonds

Maximising (1) subject to (4) clearly results in the young's consumption and money demand functions:

$$c_t^t = c(y_t - \tau_t, q_t) \tag{5}$$

$$(+) \quad (+)$$

$$m_t = m(y_t - \tau_t, q_t) \tag{6}$$

$$(+)\quad(+)$$

The signs under variables indicate what would be the "familiar" ones for the partial derivatives. $c_y, m_y > 0$ is implied by all goods being "normal" (and together with the "adding up" constraint, this also implies $c_y < 1$). $c_q, m_q > 0$ requires rather stronger assumptions: note that from (4), a rise in q raises the "price" of future consumption and lowers the "price" of money. Thus if all are net substitutes and if substitution effects dominate, $m_q > 0$ is assured; but to get $c_q > 0$ we further require current consumption to be a closer substitute (in a loose sense) for future consumption than for money. These signs will be used to derive comparative static results, although they are not always necessary for them.

When there is excess demand for goods, the arbitrary but simple rationing scheme adopted will be that the old get priority. Thus, except under extreme excess demand, the young have no need to anticipate future goods rationing. When faced with a current goods ration of c_t, their maximisation problem must be re-worked in the usual way, and this results in the constrained money demand function:

$$m_t = m^c(y_t - \tau_t, q_t, c_t) \tag{7}$$

$$(+)\quad(+)\ (-)$$

The new variable, c_t, has a negative influence, given the assumptions of normality and net substitutability.

Considering secondly the problem of the old in period t, it is clear that their behaviour is entirely predetermined, so that they simply consume an amount equal to their outstanding stocks of money and bonds: $c_t^{t-1} = m_{t-1} + b_{t-1}$.

(iii) Firm behaviour

There is a single representative firm whose only variable input is labour, with the production function $y = f(\ell)$, $f' > 0$, $f'' < 0$. When unrationed, its profit-maximising labour demand and goods supply functions are:

$$\ell_t = \ell^d(w) \quad (\equiv f'^{-1}(w)) \tag{8}$$

$$(-)$$

$$y_t = y^s(w) \quad (\equiv f(f'^{-1}(w))) \tag{9}$$

$$(-)$$

21

When rationed to y_t or ℓ_t these become:

$$\ell_t = \ell^{cd}(y_t) \quad (\equiv f^{-1}(y_t))$$ (10)

$$(+)$$

$$y_t = y_t^{cs}(\ell_t) \quad (\equiv f(\ell_t))$$ (11)

$$(+)$$

(iv) <u>Government behaviour</u>

The government makes purchases of output g_t and redeems maturing bonds b_{t-1}, financing this by a lump-sum tax on the consumer τ_t and issuing new bonds to the value $q_t b_t$:

$$g_t + b_{t-1} = \tau_t + q_t b_t$$ (12)

($m_t - m_{t-1}$) would in general enter on the R.H.S., but since the concern is with fiscal policy, this has been set to zero.)

(v) <u>Short-run equilibrium</u>

The equilibrium concept employed is the familiar fix-price one defined by Benassy (1975), so that the equilibrium trades (y_t, ℓ_t) are such as to equal the minimum of demand and supply in their respective markets, and also such as to ensure, given the rationing scheme, that perceived quantity constraints equal actual ones. q_t, as noted above, moves to clear the money market. This allows four configurations of rationing, or regimes, in principle, but only three in practice, since the simple model of the firm rules out the case where it is rationed in both markets. Thus, as in the simple models of Barro-Grossman (1971) and Malinvaud (1977), the three regimes are:

Keynesian unemployment (K): excess supply of goods and labour

Repressed inflation (R): excess demand for goods and labour

Classical unemployment (C): excess demand for goods, excess supply of labour

The comparative statics of regimes R and C are of small intrinsic interest since output is there independent of fiscal (and monetary) policy variables: in R, employment is supply-determined and thus equal to L, with output consequently f(L); in C, output is supply-determined, where the supply function is (9), and thus depends

22

only on w. Thus we shall concentrate on the comparative statics of regime K. For reference, the defining equations for R and C are in the appendix.

Output and employment are demand-determined in K, so that the equilibrium, (y_t, ℓ_t, q_t) is defined by:

$$\ell_t = \ell^{cd}(y_t)$$

$$y_t = c(y_t - \tau_t, q_t) + m_{t-1} + b_{t-1} + g_t \qquad \text{"IS"} \qquad (13)$$

$$m_t = m(y_t - \tau_t, q_t) \qquad \text{"LM"}$$

Note that the system (13) has a convenient recursive structure, whereby the "IS" and "LM" equations can be solved independently for (y_t, q_t), with ℓ_t being determined "residually", knowing y_t. In this respect the model conforms more than usually closely to the textbook IS-LM model - although it should be clear that this structure depends on the rather specific assumptions made earlier - and the motivation for labelling the equations "IS" and "LM" should be apparent. "IS" may be slightly misleading insofar as there is no investment in the model, but a consistent extension to include this may readily be made (for example, in Rankin (1984)).

This recursive structure allows us to draw the familiar "IS-LM" diagram, which, with the sign assumptions made above, has the conventional appearance:

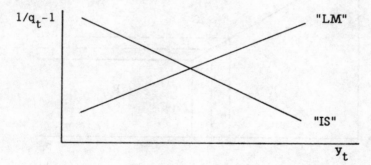

Figure 1

Increases in g_t and m_t shift the "IS" and "LM" curves to the right, respectively. Of particular importance for dynamic behaviour is the "net wealth effect" of a rise in the initial bond stock, b_{t-1}. From (13), this acts identically to a rise in g_t, therefore unambiguously raising output. Intuitively, this is because only the old hold initial stocks of bonds, and they spend these entirely on consumption. If they too had a positive demand for money, this would introduce a wealth effect into money demand which would counteract the wealth effect on consumption and make the net wealth effect on output ambiguous, as in Blinder and Solow (1973).

The most significant difference from the traditional IS-LM model arises in the response to a tax cut. From (13), this stimulates money demand as well as consumption, i.e. shifts not only the IS but also the LM curve, making the net effect prima facie ambiguous. Differentiation reveals that the condition for y_t to increase is $c_y m_q - m_y c_q > 0$, a sufficient condition for which to hold is that the utility function be weakly separable between c_{t+1}^t and (c_t^t, m_t). This is not a strong requirement, so that the orthodox sign for the tax multiplier may be assumed to hold overall. The presence of τ_t in the money demand function also has the consequence that the balanced budget multiplier is unity, unlike in the traditional IS-LM model where the addition of the money market to the elementary income-expenditure model depresses the balanced budget multiplier below unity. (These results are shown in the appendix.) Since the balanced budget multiplier is just the sum of spending and tax multipliers, this further implies that with a negative tax multiplier, the spending multiplier must be greater than unity, ensuring no "crowding out" of private by public spending.

A summary view of short-run equilibria in this model may be obtained from the regime diagram, indicating the regime in which the economy lies for different values of (b_{t-1}, w) (with $g_t, \tau_t, m_t, m_{t-1}$ given):

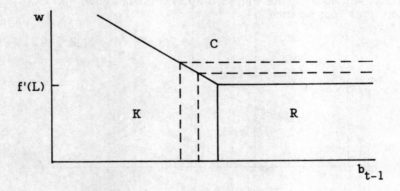

Figure 2

Broken lines are loci of equal output and employment. This is very similar to the classifications obtained in comparable models elsewhere (for example Barro and Grossman (1976)), so we shall not discuss the details of its properties.

(vi) Long-run behaviour

By virtue of the non-zero tax multiplier, debt is clearly non-neutral in the short-run in this model. It remains to be seen whether any expansionary effect is neutralised in the long run. A "step" increase in spending or cut in taxes, from an initial position of budget balance, produces a deficit causing the bond stock to rise over time with consequent effects on output as seen in the previous section. Some automatic mechanism for closing the deficit is necessary if the economy is to converge, and as in Blinder and Solow (1973), this may be provided by assuming an income tax, such that $\tau_t = \alpha + \beta y_t$. Note that such a tax is still "lump-sum" from the individual's point of view, since y_t is exogenous to him, and so creates no microeconomic distortions.

The simplest way to analyse the dynamics is to draw a diagram for the government deficit:

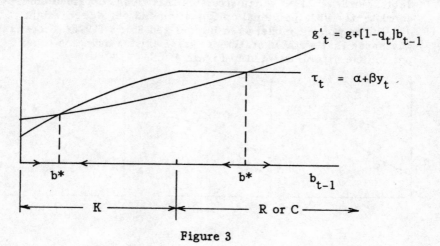

$$g'_t = g+[1-q_t]b_{t-1}$$

$$\tau_t = \alpha+\beta y_t$$

Figure 3

The shape of the tax locus depends on how y_t varies with b_{t-1}: above, it was seen that y_t increases with b_{t-1} in K, but is independent of it in R or C. g'_t is the "outlay" locus, i.e. government spending plus debt interest, and it is upward-sloping and upward-curving, since q_t decreases with b_{t-1} in all regimes. Figure 3 is drawn for a given value of w (and of $m' = m_{t-1} = m_t$), and it is this which determines whether the economy enters regime R or regime C as b_{t-1} increases. (Figure 3 may be imagined as a vertical slice through a three-dimensional diagram whose base is the regime diagram of Figure 2). The vertical distance $g'_t - \tau_t$ measures the deficit to be financed by increasing the bond stock, $q_t[b_t-b_{t-1}]$ (cf. (12)), and therefore where this is positive the economy moves right, where negative, left.

As drawn, there exists a stable stationary state in regime K and an unstable one in R or C. Starting from a stationary state in regime K an increase in g shifts the g'_t locus up and the τ_t locus left (since – in K only – g raises y_t at given b_{t-1}). Assuming the net effect is a

25

deficit, over time the bond stock will increase, and the economy converges on a new stationary state with a higher b* and a higher value of τ, implying output must also have risen. This is exactly the behaviour obtained by Blinder and Solow (1973). (In the unlikely event of the net effect being a surplus the model will oscillate: see the appendix for a rigorous analysis.) To show more explicitly the non-neutrality of debt, we should consider a tax cut rather than a spending increase. A cut in α shifts the τ_t locus down and the g'_t locus up (since it reduces q_t), similarly resulting in convergence over time to a higher b* and a higher value of τ, which latter again implies output must have risen (see also the appendix). The model therefore clearly demonstrates long-run as well as short-run neutrality of debt. Moreover, it is worth stressing that this is obtained completely consistently with individual optimisation and perfect foresight.

In the present model as in Blinder and Solow (1973), there is no guarantee that a stable stationary state exists, and some other possibilities are illustrated in Figure 4:

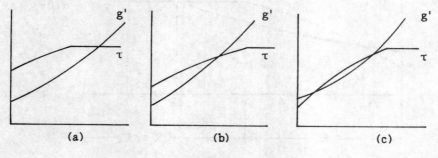

| (a) | (b) | (c) |

Figure 4

In (a), no stationary state exists in K at all. In (b), one exists, but is unstable, so that a tax cut from an initial stationary state leads to a divergent expansion of the economy. In (c), K contains both stable and unstable stationary states. A general observation which may be made is that stable stationary states can only exist in regime K. A similar result was originally discovered for money-financing by Bohm (1978). This adds to the possible arguments for saying that K is the regime most likely to be observed: in Figure 3, for example, the economy will converge on K for a wide range of initial positions.

A simple solution to instability in regime K was proposed by Tobin and Buiter (1976), and can easily be illustrated using the present approach. The problem in such a case is that, although tax revenue rises over time as income rises, debt interest rises even faster, so that the deficit widens. The answer is to hold total outlay, i.e. spending plus debt interest, $g'_t \equiv g_t + [1-q_t]b_{t-1}$, constant over time, rather than spending alone. The g' locus then becomes horizontal, and any stationary state in regime K must be stable, as Figure 5 shows:

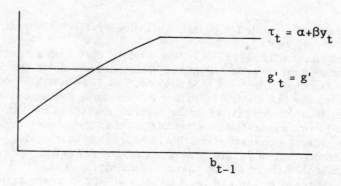

Figure 5

Moreover, in this case, from the budget balance condition, $g' = \alpha + \beta y$, the long-run multiplier of g' or of α on output is simply plus or minus the reciprocal of the marginal propensity to tax, $1/\beta$. In the previous case, the exact expression for the multiplier is less convenient, and is derived in the appendix.

3. A MODEL WITH INFINITE LIVES

(i) Introduction: the Barro critique

Although the previous section provides quite plausible microeconomic foundations for the model described by Blinder and Solow (1973), it exposes it to the argument put forward by Barro (1974): that debt non-neutrality depends on the assumption that individuals have finite lives. Because of this, the government is able to shift the burden of debt onto future generations by cutting taxes and increasing borrowing, financing this by higher taxes on future generations. In a Walrasian world, with an initially given capital stock and exogenous labour supply, this would not affect current output, but it would raise current consumption at the expense of current investment, and thus reduce the long-run capital stock and hence output. (The classic formalisation of this non-neutrality of debt, in the growth context, is by Diamond (1965).) If, however, individuals had infinite lives (combined with perfect foresight and perfect capital markets), this intertemporal reallocation of taxation would not affect their behaviour, which would be based on the unchanged present value of their disposable income to infinity. The tax cut would simply cause them to save more to repay the higher future taxes. Barro's (1974) contribution was to point out that the same neutralising mechanism could operate if finitely-lived overlapping generations were allowed to make bequests to the succeeding generation, based on the latter's utility being an argument of the former's. There are considerable doubts as to whether this equivalence of an overlapping-generations dynasty to a single infinitely-lived individual can ever be perfect (see Tobin (1980), Buiter (1980), Gale (1983 ch. 1.8)), but here we accept this as true, and ask whether "introducing bequests" into the

27

the model of section 2, i.e. infinitely-lived individuals, restores the neutrality of debt.

At an intuitive level, it is less obvious that such a change will restore neutrality than it is in the Walrasian world. In the fix-price, Keynesian unemployment model of section 2, although a tax cut increases the tax burden on future generations, it does not end up by making them worse off, as in the market-clearing case. In fact it makes future generations better off, so that the higher consumption of the current generation is achieved together with, not at the expense of, that of future generations. The reason for this is evidently that there are permanently unemployed resources which the initial increase in demand calls forth, and this increase in demand is perpetuated by the rise in the stock of bonds which occurs over time. Given this it would appear paradoxical that introducing bequests should eliminate any rise in income, because by making a bequest the current generation would then have made the future generations (and themselves) worse off, rather than better off as occurs in the Walrasian world.

However, there is a tension between this argument and the earlier observation that, with infinitely-lived individuals whose behaviour therefore depends only on the present value of their disposable income to infinity, a tax cut financed by borrowing must be neutral because it leaves this present value unchanged. The value of the tax cut must be equalled by the discounted present value of extra future taxation, unless the government is to violate its intertemporal budget constraint, which imposes that the discounted present value of spending must equal the discounted present value of taxation. If income increases, it cannot therefore be because the tax cut has raised lifetime wealth, it must simply be because the economy has moved from one equilibrium to another, i.e. equilibrium must be non-unique. This is an important observation which has been made by Gale (1983 ch. 1.10). It means, in particular, that the neutral outcome must always be a possible one, even if there are others. If there are, then the Keynesian story must be that the tax cut simply acts as a trigger for a self-fulfilling change in expectations: individuals' expectations of income in all future periods increase, hence they increase demands, which causes the very same changes in income in all periods as was expected. At best this can be a weak form of non-neutrality, because anything which stimulates expectations will work as well as a tax cut; and without a psychological theory of expectation-formation, there is no guarantee that a tax cut will work.

A model of non-unique equilibrium in a fix-price, Keynesian unemployment world with overlapping generations and Barro-type bequests has been constructed by Gale (1983 ch.1.10). The stationary state of such an economy is consistent with a continuum of values of y over a given range. However, this economy contains only one asset – bonds. The extension of the model of section 2 to infinite lives which is made below continues to involve both money and bonds, and it is shown that the presence of money removes the non-uniqueness of the Gale model. The only possible outcome of a tax cut is then the neutral one, so it is concluded that Barro-type bequests do destroy the non-neutrality of the model of section 2.

(ii) The revised consumer model

The only change made to the model of section 2 concerns the consumer. The consumer is now an infinitely-lived individual with perfect foresight, obtaining utility from consumption and real money balances in each period. In each period he has a time endowment L, which, continuing to assume no utility of leisure, thus equals his exogenous labour supply. His income, which as before comprises profit and labour income, is thus exogenous to him whether rationed or not in the labour market. The presence of money in the utility function continues to represent the liquidity services it is assumed to provide, in addition to being, like bonds, a store of value. Formally, the problem is:

maximise $\sum_{t=0}^{\infty} [1+\delta]^{-t} u(c_t, m_t)$ $\qquad\qquad \delta > 0$ $\qquad\qquad$ (14)

subject to $b_{t-1} + m_{t-1} + y_t - \tau_t = c_t + m_t + q_t b_t$ $\quad t = 0...,\infty$ $\qquad$ (15)

Combining the single-period constraints in (15), by successively eliminating b_0, b_1, b_2,..., between periods,

$$b_{-1} + \sum_{t=0}^{\infty} [y_t - \tau_t][q_0 q_1 \cdots q_{t-1}] = \sum_{t=0}^{\infty} [c_t + m_t - m_{t-1}][q_0 q_1 \cdots q_{t-1}] \qquad (16)$$

where $[q_0 q_1 \cdots q_{t-1}] \equiv 1$ when $t = 0$, and variables are defined as previously.

Maximising (14) subject to (16) results in demand functions for current consumption and money whose arguments are the consumer's lifetime wealth, given by the term on the L.H.S. of (16), together with all current and future bond prices (i.e. interest rates, recalling $q_t = 1/[1+r_t]$), which determine the "prices" of consumption and money in different periods, as the R.H.S. of (16) shows. However, rather than examine the behaviour of the model by using these functions, a neater approach is to work directly with the first-order conditions for the solution of the consumer's problem. These are derived by the usual Lagrange procedure: letting λ be the Lagrange multiplier and setting the partial derivatives of the Lagrangean with respect to (c_t, b_t) $(t=0,...,\infty)$ to zero, we have,

$$[1+\delta]^{-t} u_c - \lambda[q_0 q_1 \cdots q_{t-1}] = 0 \qquad\qquad t = 0,...,\infty \qquad (17)$$

$$[1+\delta]^{-t} u_m - \lambda[1-q_t][q_0 q_1 \cdots q_{t-1}] = 0 \quad t = 0,...,\infty \qquad (18)$$

From the conditions (17) for periods t and t+1,

$$u_c(c_{t+1}, m_{t+1})/u_c(c_t, m_t) = [1+\delta]q_t \tag{19}$$

and from (17) and (18) for the same period, t,

$$u_m(c_t, m_t)/u_c(c_t, m_t) = 1-q_t \tag{20}$$

(19) and (20) are of direct use in determining the properties of the model, as will be seen below.

(iii) The stationary state under Keynesian unemployment

In section 2 it was noted that output in regimes R and C was independent of monetary and fiscal variables, and this result is clearly not affected by the above modification of consumer behaviour. Any effect of debt on output can therefore only arise in regime K, and thus in this section we confine attention to situations where the economy is in all periods in the interior of this regime.

Since the equilibria dealt with involve perfect foresight, which in this model is the rather demanding requirement that all future values of y_t, τ_t and q_t be correctly predicted by the consumer, we cannot solve for short-run equilibrium without also solving for the complete time path of the economy. (The reason for this difference from the previous model is that there the individual did not need to predict any future endogenous variables: he merely had to "predict" the future price level, which was exogenous.) Moreover, since there is an infinite time horizon, there will in general be an infinite number of perfect foresight time paths starting from any arbitrary initial position, i.e. value of b_{-1}. This is a general property of infinite-horizon, perfect foresight models, and the convention for determining a unique path which has generally been adopted is to select the convergent path (see Begg (1982)). In the present context, where the consumer's planning horizon is also infinity, such a convention can be justified by appealing to the transversality condition for dynamic optimisation over an infinite horizon (see Dixit (1976 ch. 10)). However, to establish that a unique convergent path exists, the stability properties of the model must be examined, and analytically it is more convenient to do this after first studying the stationary state to which the economy converges, assuming it converges at all.

Under Keynesian unemployment, output and employment are demand-determined. Therefore if the desired stationary level of consumption can be determined by looking at the consumer's behaviour alone, the equilibrium output level follows simply as $y=c+g$, and the equilibrium employment is then fixed as $\ell = \ell^{cd}(c+g)$. Now, setting $c_t = c_{t+1} = c$ in (19), and $m_t = m_{t+1} = m'$, where m' is the exogenous money supply, it follows that the stationary state bond price must equal $1/[1+\delta]$ (i.e. the stationary state interest rate equals the subjective time preference parameter, δ). Turning to (20), and again setting $c_t = c_{t+1} = c$, $m_t = m_{t+1} = m'$, and using the result

$q = 1/[1+\delta]$, we obtain:

$$u_m(c,m')/u_c(c,m') = \delta/[1+\delta] \tag{21}$$

This gives an equation for determining c. It is immediate that stationary state consumption, and thus output, is quite determinate, unlike in Gale's model referred to above. It is also immediate that debt is neutral in the stationary state in this model, since neither bonds nor taxation enter (21). This latter of course would be expected to follow from determinacy, given the intuitive argument that bonds and taxation must cancel out of the model.

(iv) Behaviour outside the stationary state

Given that bonds have no real effects in the model, in any period there are no "predetermined" variables whose evolution jointly determines the time path of the economy. This means that the only state variable is consumption, i.e. all perfect foresight time paths of the economy can be completely described by a difference equation in consumption alone. Such a difference equation may be obtained by combining (19) and (20) to eliminate q_t, and setting $m_t = m_{t+1} = m'$, as before:

$$u_c(c_{t+1},m') = [1+\delta][u_c(c_t,m') - u_m(c_t,m')] \tag{22}$$

The non-uniqueness of perfect foresight paths, referred to earlier, is indicated by the fact that the model provides no obvious initial condition for fixing c_0. As mentioned, this problem is conventionally solved by choosing c_0 to ensure a convergent path. In the present case of a single difference equation, an obvious such path is the one in which c_t starts and remains at its stationary state value, defined by (21). For this to be unique, it is then necessary that the stationary state be unstable, i.e. that for any $c_0 \neq c$, the path of consumption does not converge on c. Local stability of the stationary state requires that $-1 < dc_{t+1}/dc_t < 1$, and from (22) we have:

$$dc_{t+1}/dc_t = [1+\delta][1 - u_{mc}/u_{cc}] \tag{23}$$

$u_{cc} < 0$ is necessary for the concavity of u(.), while u_{mc} will in general be positive ($u_{mc} < 0$ implies that consumption is "inferior" for some relative prices). Therefore $dc_{t+1}/dc_t > 1$, the stationary state is unstable, and the unique perfect foresight path of the economy must be taken to be the stationary one. The observations about debt neutrality made in the previous sub-section can be taken to apply to the short run as well as the long run.

(v) Summary

The "IS-LM" model with infinite lives generalises Barro's result to
the case of market disequilibrium. A tax cut financed by borrowing
has no effect on output; while a spending increase financed by
borrowing (since spending does not enter (21)) has a short- and
long-run multiplier of unity on output - the value of the traditional
balanced budget multiplier. Thus the finite lives of the previous
section, or the failure in some sense of Barro's bequest mechanism,
have a very important role to play in generating non-neutrality of
debt. This generalisation of Barro's result should be more directly
worrying for Keynesians than the result in its original
market-clearing context, since in the present model where output is
demand-constrained there is a clear motive for attempting demand
management in the first place.
    Why does the indeterminacy found by Gale, which, as argued
above, is the only way a weak form of non-neutrality might be
preserved in the present context, not arise in this model? The cause
is undoubtedly the presence of money. If money was abolished, then
of the two conditions (19) and (20) determining consumer behaviour,
(20) would disappear. The remaining condition (19) is inadequate to
tie down the stationary state consumption level, so this becomes
indeterminate. By removing money, no fewer endogenous stationary
state variables result, but an equilibrium condition is lost, and this
creates the extra degree fo freedom which produces indeterminacy.

4.   LIQUIDITY SERVICES OF BONDS

(i) Introduction

Even if Barro bequests produce the perfect equivalence to an
infinitely-lived individual which we have assumed, there are other
ways in which government debt may be non-neutral. Looking again
at (21), it is evident that money is not neutral even though debt is.
Simple differentiation yields:

$$dc/dm = [\delta u_{cm} - [1+\delta]u_{mm}]/[[1+\delta]u_{mc} - u_{cc}]$$

This is positive, assuming u_{cc}, $u_{mm} < 0$, $u_{mc} > 0$. The marked
difference from bonds is clearly a result of assuming that money
enters the utility function whereas bonds do not. Such an assumption
is conventional in the money-and-growth literature (Sidrauski (1967),
Brock (1974)), but it is surely unjustifiably asymmetric. In reality,
money is not unique amongst assets in providing services other than
being a store of value, and hence there is a strong case for assuming
bonds provide liquidity services too. Thus in this section the
preceding model is revised by assuming both money and bonds enter
the consumer's utility function; in all other respects it is unchanged.

(ii) The revised consumer model

The consumer's problem is:

maximise $\sum_{t=0}^{\infty}[1+\delta]^{-t} u(c_t, m_t, b_t)$ $\qquad\qquad$ $\delta > 0$ $\qquad$ (24)

subject to $b_{t-1} + m_{t-1} + y_t - \tau_t = c_t + m_t + q_t b_t$ $\qquad$ $t = 0,...,\infty$ $\qquad$ (25)

In this case the problem cannot be solved by first consolidating the single-period constraints (25) into the lifetime constraint, because this eliminates the choice variables b_1, b_2,..., which appear in the utility function. Thus it must be treated as a multiple constraint one, by letting λ_t ($t = 0,...,\infty$) be the Lagrange multiplier for each of the constraints in (25). The first-order conditions may then be written,

$$[1+\delta]^{-t} u_c + \lambda_t = 0 \qquad\qquad (26)$$

$$[1+\delta]^{-t} u_m + \lambda_{t+1} - \lambda_t = 0 \qquad\qquad (27)$$

$$[1+\delta]^{-t} u_b + \lambda_{t+1} - q_t \lambda_t = 0 \qquad\qquad (28)$$

Using (26) to substitute out λ_t from (27) and (28), we obtain:

$$u_c(c_{t+1}, m_{t+1}, b_{t+1}) = [1+\delta][q_t u_c(c_t, m_t, b_t) - u_b(c_t, m_t, b_t)] \qquad (29)$$

$$u_c(c_{t+1}, m_{t+1}, b_{t+1}) = [1+\delta][u_c(c_t, m_t, b_t) - u_m(c_t, m_t, b_t)] \qquad (30)$$

Note that (30) is equivalent to (22); (29) is the equivalent of (19), except that it now contains u_b as well.

(iii) The stationary state under Keynesian unemployment

For the same reasons as before, we confine attention to equilibria entirely within regime K, and start by considering the stationary state. Once again it is convenient to work directly with the first-order conditions from the consumer's problem. However, since bonds now have real effects by virtue of entering the utility function, we need to add in a specification of the government's financing policy before the equilibrium values of stationary state variables can be determined. This we shall take to be as in section 2, with taxation being a linear function of income. The government's budget constraint is then:

$$g + b_{t-1} = \alpha + \beta y_t + q_t b_t \qquad\qquad (31)$$

Now setting $c_t = c_{t+1} = c$, $b_t = b_{t+1} = b$, and $m_t = m_{t+1} = m'$,

33

where m' is exogenous, (29), (30) and (31) become:

$$u_c(c,m',b) = [1+\delta][qu_c(c,m',b) - u_b(c,m',b)] \tag{32}$$

$$u_c(c,m',b) = [1+\delta][qu_c(c,m',b) - u_b(c,m',b)] \tag{33}$$

$$g + [1-q]b - \alpha - \beta[c + g] = 0 \tag{34}$$

These three equations define the equilibrium stationary state values (c,q,b). It is clear that, since the fiscal variables g, α and β now enter the equations, c will in general not be independent of these. Thus, as would be expected, government debt is no longer neutral. However, there is a special case in which neutrality still holds. If $u(.)$ is weakly separable between (c_t, m_t) and b_t, i.e. has the form $u(v(c_t, m_t), b_t)$, then the marginal rate of substitution between consumption and money, u_m/u_c, is independent of b_t. (33), slightly rearranged, then becomes identical to (21) of the previous model, so that once more c depends only on m'.

Leaving this case aside, to see under what conditions consumption responds positively to a tax cut, we may differentiate (32)-(34) totally, obtaining:

$$\frac{dc}{d\alpha} = \frac{-[\delta u_{cb} - [1+\delta]u_{mb}]}{\beta[\delta u_{cb} - [1+\delta]u_{mb}] + [1-q][\delta u_{cc} - [1+\delta]u_{mc}] + b\phi} \tag{35}$$

where $\phi \equiv \{ [\delta u_{cb} - [1+\delta]u_{mb}] [u_{cc}[1-[1+\delta]q] + [1+\delta]u_{bc}]$

$-[\delta u_{cc} - [1+\delta]u_{mc}] [u_{cb}[1-[1+\delta]q] + [1+\delta]u_{bb}] \}/[1+\delta]u_c$

To sign the denominator, we appeal to the "correspondence principle": that stability of the stationary state (without which the multiplier is meaningless) requires it to be either positive or negative. To determine the required sign, and how likely it is to come about, necessitates a direct investigation of non-stationary state behaviour. Below, it will be shown that the required sign is positive. For (35) to have a conventional negative sign, it must thus have a negative numerator.

An extreme case generating a negative numerator and positive denominator is where money and bonds are perfect substitutes. To see this, note that the utility function can then be written $u(c_t, m_t + b_t)$, whence $u_m = u_b$. From (32) and (33), $u_m = u_b$ implies $q = 1$ (i.e. the price of bonds is then forced to equal, as might be expected, the "price" of money). Furthermore the special form of $u(.)$ evidently implies $u_{mm} = u_{bb} = u_{mb}$ and $u_{cb} = u_{cm}$. Using these results in (35), ϕ is readily shown to be zero, and both numerator and denominator then have the common factor $\delta u_{cb} - [1+\delta]u_{mb}$. This is positive, since $u_{mb} = u_{bb} < 0$ by concavity, and the unique cross-partial, $u_{cb} (= u_{cm}) > 0$ if consumption is not inferior (cf. the

34

discussion of the sign of (26)). Thus the numerator is negative and the denominator positive, and when the common factor is cancelled the resulting multiplier is $-1/\beta$, the familiar reciprocal of the marginal propensity to tax. It follows that, more generally, a sufficiently high degree of substitutability between money and bonds will ensure stability and a negative tax multiplier.

(iv) <u>Behaviour outside the stationary state</u>

To elucidate the implicit difference equations which drive the economy, consider the following three equations, which are the necessary conditions (29) and (30) from the consumer's problem (having set $m_t = m_{t+1} = m'$), and the government's budget constraint (31):

$$u_c(c_{t+1},m',b_{t+1}) = [1+\delta][q_t u_c(c_t,m',b_t) - u_b(c_t,m',b_t)] \qquad (36)$$

$$u_c(c_{t+1},m',b_{t+1}) = [1+\delta][u_c(c_t,m',b_t) - u_m(c_t,m',b_t)] \qquad (37)$$

$$\alpha + \beta[c_{t+1}+g] + q_{t+1}b_{t+1} = g + b_t \qquad (38)$$

(37) and (38) would enable us to go from (c_t,b_t) to (c_{t+1},b_{t+1}), if only q_{t+1} were known. Now, since the L.H.S.'s of (36) and (37) are identical, by equating their R.H.S.'s, and re-writing the equation for period t+1, we have the following expression for q_{t+1} as an implicit function of (c_{t+1},b_{t+1}):

$$[1-q_{t+1}]u_c(c_{t+1},m',b_{t+1})=u_m(c_{t+1},m',b_{t+1})-u_b(c_{t+1},m',b_{t+1}) \qquad (39)$$

This, together with (37) and (38), enables us to solve for (c_{t+1},b_{t+1}) given (c_t,b_t).

The local stability of this system is examined by first obtaining a linear approximation about the stationary state, (c,b). This is a mechanical exercise in differentiation (performed in the appendix), resulting in a system of the form:

$$\begin{bmatrix} \Delta c_t \\ \Delta b_t \end{bmatrix} = C \begin{bmatrix} c_t - c \\ b_t - b \end{bmatrix} \qquad (\Delta x_t \equiv x_{t+1}-x_t) \qquad (40)$$

where C is a (2×2) matrix of partial derivatives evaluated at (c,b). The stability of such a system depends on how many of the two eigenvalues of C are "stable". In a perfect foresight economy, what is required for a unique convergent path is not "complete" stability, but as many stable eigenvalues as there are predetermined variables (see, e.g., Begg (1982)). Since b_t is a predetermined variable, the "stability" requirement alluded to earlier becomes, more precisely, the need for one stable and one unstable eigenvalue. The usual condition for this, (though, as noted in the appendix, not a strictly necessary one in discrete time models) is that one eigenvalue be positive and one negative, so that their product, which is equal to the determinant of C, must be negative. Det (C), however, equals the denominator of (35) multiplied by a negative factor (see appendix) so that the condition for a unique, convergent, perfect foresight path implies that this denominator must be positive, as asserted earlier. The essential reason why the determinant of C reappears in the denominator of the long-run multiplier is that this is also the Jacobean determinant in the comparative statics of the stationary state, as may be seen by setting the L.H.S. of (40) to zero.

To evaluate the short-run tax multiplier, we need to solve explicitly for the convergent path. However, such an exercise does not reveal very much in general terms beyond what is known once it is established that a unique convergent path exists, and hence is not undertaken here. Numerous illustrations of the general procedure exists for other perfect foresight contexts, e.g. Begg (1980).

(v) Summary

Although it is not surprising to discover that if bonds have functions other than as a store of value they are no longer neutral, it does not follow from this alone that bond-financed tax cuts can necessarily operate to produce a long-run convergent expansion of the economy. The above demonstration that there exist plausible conditions under which this can occur may therefore provide some reassurance for Keynesians. Note also that the proposition that bonds are neutral if they are not perceived as net wealth, i.e. if they are equalled by the discounted present value of future tax liabilities in the lifetime budget constraint of the individual, breaks down in this model. In the less conventional sense they are of course net wealth, as a result of directly providing utility.

5. CONCLUSIONS

An asymmetry has been observed between the factors resulting in the non-neutrality of money and those resulting in the non-neutrality of government debt. Price rigidity alone is not sufficient to generate the latter, and must be accompanied by some other feature, of which we have examined two. One might be generically termed "finite lives", including under this heading any failures of the bequest mechanism to make a sequence of finitely lived generations equivalent to an infinitely-lived individual. A second is the "liquidity services" provided by government bonds, which are often ignored by monetary theorists, but have been seen to have a potentially crucial role. The importance of non-neutrality of debt in making fiscal policy an effective tool of macroeconomic management has been clearly demonstrated in these cases.

Despite the fact that price rigidity and hence market disequilibrium has been seen not to result in debt non-neutrality without further qualifications, it is clearly the sine qua non for a meaningful theoretical analysis of short-run macroeconomic management issues. The approach pioneered by Barro and Grossman (1971, 1976), Benassy (1975) and Malinvaud (1977), as well as many others, has been shown to provide a very natural microeconomic basis for the traditional Keynesian IS-LM model and its dynamic extension by Blinder and Solow (1973). In this respect it may be hoped that some further evidence has been provided for the usefulness of "disequilibrium" theory.

APPENDIX

Repressed inflation and classical unemployment equilibria

$$\ell_t = L$$

$$y_t = y^{cs}(\ell_t) \qquad\qquad \text{Repressed inflation}$$

$$m_t = m^c(y_t - \tau_t, q_t, y_t - m_{t-1} - b_{t-1} - g_t)$$

$$\ell_t = \ell^d(w)$$

$$y_t = y^s(w) \qquad\qquad \text{Classical unemployment}$$

$$m_t = m^c(y_t - \tau_t, q_t, y_t - m_{t-1} - b_{t-1} - g_t)$$

Note: the third argument of $m^c(.)$ is c_t, which has been substituted out using the income-expenditure identity.

Short-run comparative statics with finite lives

Totally differentiating the "IS" and "LM" equations in (13),

$$\begin{bmatrix} 1-c_y & -c_q \\ -m_y & -m_q \end{bmatrix} \begin{bmatrix} dy_t \\ dq_t \end{bmatrix} = \begin{bmatrix} -c_y & 1 \\ -m_y & 0 \end{bmatrix} \begin{bmatrix} d\tau_t \\ dg_t \end{bmatrix}$$

Hence, by Cramer's rule,

$$\frac{dy_t}{dg_t} = \frac{-m_q}{-[1-c_y]m_q - m_y c_q}, \quad \frac{dy_t}{d\tau_t} = \frac{c_y m_q - m_y c_q}{-[1-c_y]m_q - m_q c_q}$$

whence also $dy_t/dg_t + dy_t/d\tau_t = 1$.

Stability and long-run comparative statics with finite lives

The government budget constraint is:

$$\Delta b_{t-1} = [g + [1-q_t]b_{t-1} - \alpha - \beta y_t]/q_t \tag{A1}$$

Evaluating at the stationary state,

$$d\Delta b_{t-1}/db_{t-1} = [1 - q + kb[1-\beta]m_y/m_q - k\beta]/q$$

$$\qquad\qquad\qquad (+) \qquad\qquad (+) \qquad\qquad (+)$$

where k is the short-run spending multiplier. For stability this must lie between -2 and 0. Positive values are quite possible; values less than -1 mean a bond stock increase creates a budget surplus, and are thus very unlikely.

The stationary state (y,q,b) is defined by the "IS" and "LM" equations and the budget constraint (A1), with all variables set to stationary values. Totally differentiating as for the short-run multipliers, we have:

$$\frac{dy}{dg} = \frac{-k}{[1 - q + kb[1 - \beta[m_y/m_q - k\beta]/q}$$

$$\frac{dy}{d\alpha} = -\frac{dy}{dg}\{1 + [1-q]c_y + [b+[1-q]c_q]m_y/m_q\}/q$$

$$\qquad\qquad\qquad\qquad (+)$$

These are clearly positive and negative (respectively) if the stationary state is stable.

Stability of the model with utility of bonds

To obtain a linear approximation of the model, totally differentiate (37) and (38),

$$\begin{bmatrix} u_{cc} & u_{cb} \\ \beta + b\partial q_{t+1}/\partial c_{t+1} & q + b\partial q_{t+1}/\partial b_{t+1} \end{bmatrix} \begin{bmatrix} dc_{t+1} \\ db_{t+1} \end{bmatrix}$$

$$= \begin{bmatrix} [1+\delta][u_{cc}-u_{mc}] & [1+\delta][u_{cb}-u_{mb}] \\ 0 & 1 \end{bmatrix} \begin{bmatrix} dc_t \\ db_t \end{bmatrix}$$

where, from (39),

$$\partial q_{t+1}/\partial b_{t+1} = [[1-q]u_{cc}+u_{bc}-u_{mc}]/u_c$$

$$\partial q_{t+1}/\partial c_{t+1} = [[1-q]u_{cb}+u_{bb}-u_{mb}]/u_c$$

Note all partial derivatives are evaluated at (c,q,b). The linear approximation is then obtained by replacing dc_t by c_t-c and db_t by b_t-b. Write the resulting system in the matrix form:

$$Ax_{t+1} = Bx_t \qquad\qquad (A2)$$

where $x'_t = [c_t-c \quad b_t-b]$ and A,B are the corresponding matrices above. From this,

$$x_{t+1} = A^{-1}Bx_t \qquad\qquad (A3)$$

$$\Delta x_t = [A^{-1}B - I]x_t = A^{-1}[B-A]x_t \qquad\qquad (A4)$$

This is the system given above by (40).

When written in the conventional form for a difference equation system (i.e. (A3)), "saddlepoint" stability requires that one eigenvalue of $A^{-1}B$ should lie inside and the other outside, the unit circle (see, e.g. Chiang (1974)). Since both must be real for this to occur, an equivalent condition is that one eigenvalue of $A^{-1}B - I$ should lie inside and the other outside, the interval $(-2,0)$. This means that their product, which equals $\det(A^{-1}B - I)$, could strictly speaking be either negative or positive. To justify the usual procedure of insisting on a negative sign, note that in the positive case divergent paths would be oscillatory, and although this is irrelevant if the economy is only ever on a convergent path, divergent paths do play a part in the solution to perfect foresight models when a policy change is announced in advance (see, e.g., Wilson (1979)). Thus the most plausible approach is first to seek cases where such potentially extravagant behaviour does not arise, and this means starting with the "usual" negativity condition.

Stability of the sort discussed thus imposes $\det(A^{-1}[B-A]) < 0$. However the matrix whose determinant is directly relevant to the comparative statics of the stationary state is $B-A$, as may be seen by setting $x_{t+1} = x_t = x$ in (A2) and solving for x. (Direct computation of $\det(B-A)$ confirms its equality to the denominator of (32).) To obtain a sign condition on $\det(B-A)$, which equals $\det(A^{-1}[B-A]).\det(A)$, we must therefore determine the sign of $\det(A)$. Multiplying out,

$$\det(A) = [qu_{cc}-\beta u_{cb}] + b[u_{cc}[u_{bb}-u_{mb}] - u_{cb}[u_{bc}-u_{mc}]]$$

The sign of the term in b is thoroughly ambiguous, and its importance to the overall sign in any case depends on the initial level of the bond stock. The first term is most likely to be negative, since $u_{cc} < 0$ by concavity and the cross-partial u_{cb} is most naturally assumed to be positive. Thus it is most likely that $\det(A) < 0$, whence stability implies $\det(B-A) > 0$.

ACKNOWLEDGEMENTS

This paper is based on part of my D.Phil thesis, "Fiscal Policy in Quantity-Constrained Equilibrium", submitted at the University of Oxford, June 1984. For valuable discussions and comments I am particularly grateful to my supervisor, John Muellbauer,and to Douglas Gale, Claudio Borio, Jim Mirrlees and David Currie, while of course being solely responsible for all errors and opinions.

FISCAL POLICY AND THE REAL EXCHANGE RATE

Francesco Giavazzi and Jeffrey Sheen

INTRODUCTION

The extent of fluctuations in real exchange rates over the last decade of flexible exchange rates has puzzled international commentators and has stimulated a large literature to explain the phenomenon. Perhaps the most influential paper was Dornbusch's (1976) overshooting model where short run fluctuations in the real exchange rate originate from the assumption of sticky prices. Others have focussed on the role of "news" in asset markets (e.g. see Frenkel (1980)) whilst another section of this literature has concerned itself with the implications of time-consuming portfolio readjustments (e.g. see Dornbusch and Fischer (1980), Kouri (1976), Branson (1976), Branson and Buiter (1983)). Our work continues in the spirit of this last approach, demonstrating that fiscal policy can be a source of real exchange rate fluctuations.[1]

We wish to challenge one of the most enduring results produced by Mundell (1963) which is that fiscal expansion always leads to a real exchange rate appreciation. Higher (potential) interest rates generate (incipient) capital inflows forcing the exchange rate down to restore external equilibrium through trade deficits. A further result of Mundell was that exports would be crowded out and fiscal policy would therefore be ineffective under flexible exchange rates with perfect capital mobility. This latter result has already been challenged by a number of authors in that it depends on the assumption that the money market is independent of the exchange rate (see for example Branson and Buiter (1983), Sachs (1980)). Mundell's analysis has been criticised for ignoring long run portfolio equilibrium and for never introducing perfect foresight. We make these two amendments, but also introduce the possibility of government budget imbalance financed by bond issues.

We construct a simple fixed output model that abstracts altogether from the presence of money, concentrating only on real variables. We permit the existence of real short-term assets issued by the government and by foreign agents. Models of bond-financed deficits have typically exhibited instability (or are likely to) because the issue of debt (usually) does not reduce the deficit. Blinder and Solow (1973), Tobin and Buiter (1976) et al. require bond issues to generate wealth effects sufficient to raise (output and) the tax-take more than the extra service. In a survey of this literature, Christ (1979) suggests that the problem of instability can be overcome if the government adjusts its deficit by a proportion of outstanding debt greater than the rate of interest.[2] We study, therefore, macromodels that incorporate very simple stabilizing reaction functions.

In our open economy model, we find that stability depends on four factors: i) whether the above fiscal adjustment exceeds the rate of interest, ii) whether extra wealth implies dissavings, iii) whether the simple Marshall-Lerner condition holds, and iv) the degree of asset substitutability.

We show that, if the economy is stable, an unanticipated fiscal expansion need not lead to an appreciation in the short or long run. With tax stabilization, tax cuts must lead to a long run depreciation, while a rise in (bond or tax-financed) government expenditure may cause a long run depreciation and always crowds out private expenditure. The results are symmetrical if government expenditure is used to stabilise.

In the model we present, fiscal policy affects the real exchange rate through two separate channels: wealth effects on expenditure and imperfect asset substitutability. We build the basic model in Section 1, allowing only the first channel to operate. We show that the Mundell result will occur in the short run, but not necessarily in the long run.

In Section 2, we concentrate on the role of imperfect asset substitutability assuming that expenditure is a function only of current income, hence excluding wealth effects. We show that the Mundell result can be reversed in both the short and long run.

Announcement effects are an important element of the dynamic response of the economy to changes in fiscal policy because there is always a lag between the announcement and the implementation. In section 3 we use numerical analysis to investigate this issue, and we show that the announcement of a future fiscal expansion is immediately expansionary while the effects on the exchange rate depend on the degree of asset substitutability.

1. FISCAL POLICY, THE REAL EXCHANGE RATE AND WEALTH EFFECTS

1.1 The Model

Consider a small open economy, facing a fixed foreign real rate of interest, r*, and foreign goods prices. Assume that real domestic government bonds are held only by domestic residents who also hold real foreign bonds, f. The outstanding stock of domestic bonds varies when the government budget is not balanced, while foreign bonds can only change via the current account. There is perfect capital mobility and, in the analytical part of this section, the two assets are perfect substitutes in portfolios. The domestic country is specialised in fixed production, q_0, of its goods which are imperfectly substitutable in consumption for foreign goods. The real exchange rate, λ, is the relative price of foreign goods (assets) to domestic ones; it is completely flexible.

The Government Budget Constraint

The government issues real bonds, b, and raises taxes, τ, to finance its expenditures, g. Since there is an inherent instability problem with bond issues because of bond service, rb, (except when interest rates are negative) assume that the government recognises the problem and adjusts taxes and/or government expenditure in proportion to the stock of outstanding bonds.[3] Denote these fiscal adjustments as $\alpha_g b$ and $\alpha_\tau b$. Hence

$$g = g_0 - \alpha_g b \tag{1}$$

$$\tau = \tau_0 + \alpha_\tau b \tag{2}$$

$$\dot{b} = (r - \alpha)b + g_0 - \tau_0 \tag{3}$$

where $\alpha = \alpha_g + \alpha_\tau$ and g_0 and τ_0 are the exogenous components of fiscal policy. For the sake of exposition, we shall develop the case where $\alpha_g = 0$ and $\alpha = \alpha_\tau$ (except at the end of the discussion of long run equilibrium).

Balance of Payments

Assuming flexible exchange rates, the capital account must match the current account, the latter comprising the service and trade accounts:

$$\lambda \dot{f} = r^* \lambda f + t \tag{4}$$

where t is the trade account and is negatively related to expenditure and positively to the real exchange rate.

$$t = t(\lambda, c) \tag{5}$$

where $t_\lambda > 0$; $-1 < t_c < 0$.

An exchange rate depreciation is assumed to improve the trade account; in fact, this simple Marshall-Lerner condition turns out to be necessary for stability.
    It is useful to remember that a partial equilibrium instability problem similar to the one discussed for bond-financed fiscal deficits

arises in the foreign asset accumulation process because of the need to service foreign assets.[4] In the reduced form of this model, however, the trade account is not necessarily independent of the level of f, and may have the capacity to overcome the need to service. It will be seen below that f_f will be negative under static expectations if higher wealth generates dissaving but that under perfect foresight the trade account is, ceteris paribus, independent of the level of f.

Private Sector

Private sector financial wealth, w, is given by

$$w = b + \lambda f \tag{6}$$

and disposable income[5] is given by:

$$y = q_0 - \tau_0 - \alpha b \tag{7}$$

Private sector expenditure on domestic and foreign goods is:

$$c = c(r, y, w) \tag{8}$$

$$c_r < 0, 0 < c_y < 1, c_w > 0$$

It is useful to define:

$$c_f = \lambda c_w > 0 \tag{8'}$$

$$c_\lambda = f c_w > 0$$

$$c_b = -\alpha c_y + c_w \gtrless 0$$

The interest rate effect on expenditure is assumed to have the conventional negative effect. An increase in foreign bonds or a real depreciation raises expenditure because of higher wealth and income. We deliberately assume that domestic bonds constitute positive net wealth (although see page 49 for a discussion of the implications of Ricardian neutrality). A rise in domestic bonds raises financial wealth but lowers income on account of the tax stabilisation policy. For the sake of exposition, we shall assume that c_b is positive.

1.2 Temporary Goods Market and Asset Market Equilibrium

At every moment in time the domestic goods market clears and is given by:

$$q_0 = c + g_0 + t \tag{9}$$

Using (6) to (9), one can establish the relationship between r and λ that maintains temporary goods market equilibrium. An increase in the rate of interest (by assumption) lowers expenditure, creating excess supply and requiring a real depreciation to raise demand through normal substitution effects and the additional channel of upvalued foreign assets. This positive relationship is shown in Figure 1 as the GG curve whose slope is given by:

$$\frac{\delta r}{\delta \lambda} = \frac{t_\lambda + (1+t_c)c_\lambda}{-c_r(1+t_c)} \tag{10}$$

The real rates of return on domestic and foreign real bonds are always equal apart from expected changes in the real exchange rate, μ, and a risk premium γ, which depends positively on $\frac{b}{\lambda f}$ (and on the level of risk and the degree of risk aversion).

$$r = r^* + \mu + \gamma \tag{11}$$

$$\gamma = \gamma(b/\lambda f)$$

$$\gamma' \gtreqqless 0$$

It is vital to study the implications of imperfect asset substitutibility in a model that recognizes the possibility of real exchange rate fluctuations. These fluctuations induce negative correlation in r and r* which is a precondition for diversification. In section 2, we shall focus specifically on the implications of imperfect substitutibility. In this section, from here on assume that $\gamma = 0$.

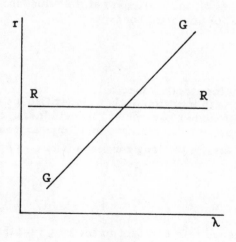

Figure 1

In Figure 1, asset market equilibrium is shown as the RR line and is horizontal because the real exchange rate does not affect the capital market for given expected changes in that rate. Higher g_0, b and f or lower τ_0 will raise spending on domestic goods implying an upward shift of the GG schedule and a real exchange rate appreciation. If μ (or r^*) increases, the RR schedule shifts upward and will actually cause λ to depreciate. Hence an increase in expected depreciation will be associated with an actual depreciation as we move up the GG curve. This property will be important in the perfect foresight model. Note that if $t_c = -1$, the GG curve is vertical and λ will only change if g does.

The temporary equilibrium described in Figure 1 can be obtained from the solution of (9) and (11) assuming that exchange rate expectations are exogenous and can be written as

$$\lambda = \lambda(b, f; g_0, -\tau_0, \mu) \tag{12}$$

$$r = r(b, f; g_0, -\tau_0, \mu) \tag{13}$$

where[6]

$$\lambda_b < 0, \ \lambda_f < 0, \ \lambda_{g_0} < 0, \ \lambda_{-\tau_0} < 0, \ \lambda_\mu > 0$$

$$r_b = 0, \ r_f = 0, \ r_{g_0} = 0, \ r_{-\tau_0} = 0, \ r_\mu = 1$$

1.3 Long Run Equilibrium

In the long run or stationary state, all real assets and their prices are constant. Setting $\dot{b} = 0$ in (3), the stationary state value (shown with a "—" above the variable) of domestic bonds is:

$$\bar{b} = \frac{g_0 - \tau_0}{\alpha - \bar{r}} \tag{14}$$

where $\alpha > \bar{r}$ is necessary for stability (see below).

This result accords with intuition in that higher fiscal deficits should be associated with higher government indebtedness. It is however important to note that an increase in autonomous taxes, τ_0, leads to lower overall taxes in the long run since it causes a reduction in government debt, i.e.

$$\frac{d\bar{\tau}}{d\tau_0} = 1 - \frac{\alpha}{\alpha - \bar{r}} = \frac{-\bar{r}}{\alpha - \bar{r}} < 0$$

With the real exchange rate constant in the long run, the rate of interest is:

$$\bar{r} = r^* \tag{15}$$

Given perfect substitutability, the long run rate of

interest is independent of fiscal policy or the value of foreign assets. In Figure 2 (which bears a resemblance to Figure 1) the capital market equilibrium curve is shown as the KK curve.

Current account equilibrium implies:

$$r^* \bar{\lambda} \bar{f} + \bar{t}(\bar{\lambda}, \bar{c}) = 0 \tag{16}$$

or that the service account surplus is matched by a trade deficit. The long run domestic goods market equilibrium is given by:

$$q_0 = \bar{c} + g_0 - r^* \bar{\lambda} \bar{f}$$

which, using (8) and (14), becomes

$$\bar{r} = \Theta (\bar{\lambda} \bar{f}; g_0, -\tau_0) \tag{17}$$

where

$$\Theta_1 = \frac{(c_w - r^*)}{-(c_r - \sigma \bar{b})} > 0$$

$$\Theta_2 = \frac{1 - \sigma}{-(c_r - \sigma \bar{b})} > 0$$

$$\Theta_3 = \frac{(c_y - \sigma)}{-(c_r - \sigma \bar{b})} > 0$$

$$\sigma = -c_b / (\alpha - \bar{r}).$$

These signs on Θ_1, Θ_2, Θ_3 are satisfied if

(i) $c_y > \sigma$

(which is true for $c_w > \bar{r}, \alpha > \bar{r}$)

(ii) $\sigma > \dfrac{c_r}{\bar{b}}$

(which implies a lower limit on the policy variable α in excess of $\bar{r}$).

These assumptions ensure that autonomous fiscal expansion (which leads to larger holdings of government debt) generates excess demand for goods requiring a higher long run rate of interest, given fixed foreign assets; they also turn out to be necessary conditions for stability of the equilibrium (see appendix).

In Figure 2a, (17) is shown as the IS curve with the slope Θ_1. Higher foreign assets (for stability reasons) generate net spending thus requiring a higher interest rate to maintain long run goods market equilibrium.

The intersection of the two curves establishes the solution for the rate of interest and the value of foreign assets independently of

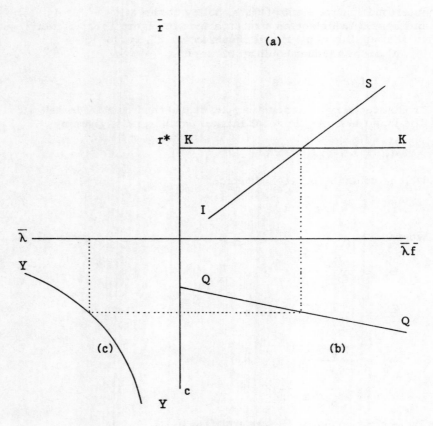

Figure 2

the real exchange rate. Before finding the solution for the latter, one needs to solve for long run private spending. Since $t = -r^* \lambda f$

$$\bar{c} = q_0 - g_0 + r^* \bar{\lambda} \bar{f} \qquad (9')$$

Once the solution to $\bar{\lambda} \bar{f}$ is known, $\bar{c}$ can immediately be obtained from (9)' depicted in Figure 2b as the QQ curve. Higher income from abroad permits greater domestic spending.

The goods market equilibrium can also be written as:

$$q_0 = \bar{c} + g_0 + t(\bar{\lambda}, \bar{c}) \qquad (9'')$$

implying a negative relationship between private expenditure and the real exchange rate, i.e.

$$\frac{d\bar{\lambda}}{d\bar{c}} = \frac{-(1+t_c)}{t_\lambda} < 0$$

and is depicted in Figure 2c as the YY curve. With fixed output, higher domestic spending will require an appreciation of the real exchange rate to worsen the trade account.

1.4 Long Run Effects of Fiscal Policy

A Tax Cut

Consider a cut in taxes, τ_0. With perfect asset substitutes, the only curve to shift in Figure 2 is the IS curve which moves up because aggregate demand is stimulated and would require a higher rate of interest (at unchanged $\lambda \bar{f}$) to restore equilibrium. $\lambda \bar{f}$ must fall, consumption following suit. The real exchange rate must, however, depreciate [7] to create an incremental trade surplus to match the service deficit.

In particular, with $\bar{r} = r^*$, using (17), (9') and (9")

$$\frac{d(\lambda\, \bar{f})}{-d\tau_0} = -\frac{\Theta_3}{\Theta_1} = -\frac{(c_y - \sigma)}{(c_w - r^*)} < 0$$

$$\frac{dc}{-d\tau_0} = \frac{-r^* (c_y - \sigma)}{(c_w - r^*)} < 0$$

$$\frac{d\lambda}{-d\tau_0} = \frac{(1 + t_c)\, r^*}{t_\lambda} \qquad \frac{(c_y - \sigma)}{c_w - r^*} > 0 \qquad (18)$$

Hence a tax cut does not benefit consumers in the long run. Rather it worsens their situation, all the benefits being distributed abroad through higher exports and lower domestic ownership of foreign assets.

We should, however, point out that if Ricardian neutrality were assumed so that domestic bonds do not constitute positive net wealth (and if asset income were included in disposable income), σ would become equal to c_y and the tax cut would not affect $\bar{\lambda}$, $\bar{f}$ or $\bar{c}$. This result obviously follows from the well-known application of the Modigliani-Miller theorem to the financing of government expenditure - taxes and debt issue are equivalent.

An Increase in Government Spending

An increase in Government spending will cause a greater upward shift of the IS curve ($\Theta_2 > \Theta_3$ because $c_y < 1$) for the usual reason that taxes act on aggregate demand in the first instance through the marginal propensity to spend out of income. The value of foreign assets falls (to A_1) and this will have to be brought about by current account deficits. The QQ curve also shifts towards the origin (see Figure 3) because the intercept is lowered. The result is that consumption is crowded out by more than 100% by an increase in government expenditure. This occurs because the sustainable level

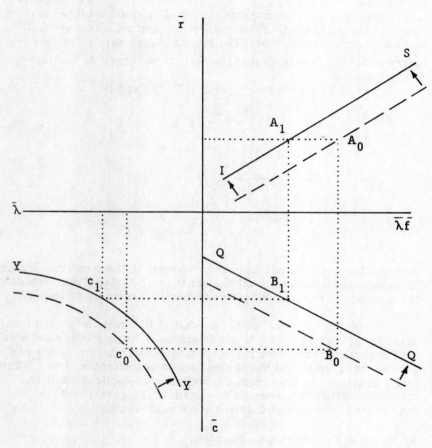

Figure 3

of foreign asset holdings falls, reducing income. Domestic bond income does increase but taxes have to rise by more for stability of the stationary equilibrium. Finally the YY curve shifts inwards towards the origin (a vertical shift in excess of that of the QQ curve). The net effect on the exchange rate is indeterminate although we show a depreciation in Figure 3. Differentiating (17), (9') and (9") in turn gives:

$$\frac{d(\bar{\lambda f})}{dg_0} = \frac{-\theta_2}{\theta_1} = \frac{-(1-\sigma)}{(c_w - \bar{r})} < 0$$

$$\frac{d\bar{c}}{dg_0} = -1 + r^* \frac{d(\bar{\lambda f})}{dg_0} = -1 - \frac{r^*(1-\sigma)}{(c_w - \bar{r})} < 0$$

$$\frac{d\bar{\lambda}}{dg_0} = \frac{1 + (1+t_c)\frac{d\bar{c}}{dg_0}}{-t_\lambda} = \frac{1+(1+t_c)(-1 - \frac{r^*(1-\sigma)}{(c_w - \bar{r})})}{-t_\lambda}$$

$$= \frac{(1+t_c)\frac{r^*(1-\sigma)}{c_w - \bar{r}} + t_c}{t_\lambda} \qquad (19)$$

$$\gtrless 0$$

The ambiguous effect of government expenditure on the real exchange rate arises from the fact that crowded out private spending falls on domestic and foreign goods.[8] If the private sector only purchased foreign goods ($t_c = -1$), imports would take the full brunt of higher g and a real appreciation (to the tune of $-1/t_\lambda$) would be required to raise net imports. If instead, at the other extreme, only domestic goods were purchased ($t_c = 0$), the real exchange rate would have to depreciate so that exports improve sufficiently to counteract the deteriorated service account income. Hence the more 'open' is the economy, the more likely that a stable long run Mundell fiscal policy result is obtained. These results are only marginally affected if debt is assumed neutral, i.e. if σ rises to become equal to c_y. Indeed, it is government expenditure and not its financing that matters under neutrality.

Since this indeterminacy arises in a model which specifically contrives stability with bond financing, it is useful to observe $d\bar{\lambda}/dg$ across the range of the stabilization parameter, α. Since α only enters the derivative through σ (which is $-(c_w-\alpha c_y)/(\alpha - \bar{r})$), it can be seen that σ approaches c_y as α approaches ∞. Since the discounted wealth effect exceeds the income effect on expenditure ($c_w/\bar{r} > c_y$) as $\alpha \to \bar{r}$ from above (below) $\sigma \to -\infty$ ($+\infty$). From (19), the unstable Mundell result can be obtained for $\alpha = 0$ since $\bar{\lambda f}$ in fact rises by $1/\bar{r}$ and so current account surpluses would be needed but could not be generated. It is worth noting that the ambiguity remains as $\alpha \to \infty$; but the closer it is to the necessary and sufficient condition on it for stability (see appendix) the more likely is a depreciation.[9]

A Balanced Budget Expansion

A balanced budget expansion where $dg = d\tau_0 = dx$ generates similar results to an increase in g but the movement in all variables is less. This is because an autonomous tax rise does not amount to the same thing as an accumulation of government debt. Hence,

$$\frac{d\bar{\lambda f}}{dx} = \frac{\theta_3 - \theta_2}{\theta_1} = \frac{-(1 - c_y)}{(c_w - r^*)} < 0$$

and

$$\frac{d\bar{\lambda}}{dx} = \frac{(1+t_c)r^*(1-c_y)/(c_w - r^*) + t_c}{t_\lambda} \lessgtr 0$$

but less than $\dfrac{d\bar{\lambda}}{dg}$ because $\sigma < c_y$.

The ambiguity on the long run real exchange rate exists here independently of the size of the stabilization parameter, α. Bond financing is irrelevant for the long run in this case, provided the equilibrium is stable.

Stabilization with Government Expenditure

It is important to realize that the above results change if $\alpha_g = \alpha$, $\alpha_\tau = 0$. In the same way as before, it can easily be seen that

$$\frac{d\bar{g}}{dg_0} = \frac{-\bar{r}}{(\alpha - \bar{r})} < 0$$

and that

$$\frac{d(\bar{\lambda f})}{dg_0} = \frac{-1}{(\alpha - \bar{r})} < 0$$

$$\frac{d\bar{c}}{dg_0} = 0$$

$$\frac{d\bar{\lambda}}{dg_0} = \frac{-r^*}{t_\lambda(\alpha - \bar{r})} < 0$$

Private sector expenditure and wealth is unaffected by government expenditure changes although the spending mix will move toward imported goods because the real exchange rate appreciates. Thus the pure Mundell result is obtained unambiguously only in this case. But note that long run government expenditure has in fact fallen.

A tax cut, as one might anticipate, now has an ambiguous effect on the real exchange rate, the ambiguity depending on the openness of the economy. In fact

$$\frac{d\bar{\lambda}}{-d\tau_0} = \frac{1}{t_\lambda} \frac{\alpha}{(\alpha - \bar{r})} - (1+t_c) \frac{1+r^*(1-c_y)}{(c_w - r^*)} \lessgtr 0$$

If $t_c = -1$, the exchange rate must depreciate. Therefore a non-Mundellian result is more likely, here, for more open economies. Finally, it is easy to show that long run consumption is increased by a tax cut.

1.4 Stability and Dynamics

Static Expectations

Under static expectations, (3) is independent of f and conditions for stability of the long run equilibrium are that a higher stock of foreign assets should worsen the current account and that a higher stock of domestic assets should improve the government's borrowing requirement, i.e. $\alpha > r$. The latter is true by assumption, whilst from (4) – (8) and (12), it can be shown that

$$\dot{f}_f = r^* + \frac{1}{\lambda} (t_c c_f + (t_\lambda + t_c c_\lambda - \frac{t}{\lambda}) \lambda_f)$$

which about the stationary state (where $t = -r^* \lambda f$) becomes:

$$\dot{f}_f = \frac{t_\lambda (r^* - c_w)}{t_\lambda + (1 + t_c) c_\lambda} \tag{20}$$

For this to be negative, we need to assume that

(i) $t_\lambda > 0$

(ii) $c_w - r^* > 0$

These assumptions require extra wealth to cause expenditure to rise more than income (that is, dissavings)[10] and that the standard simple Marshall-Lerner elasticities condition holds. These are reasonable conditions to impose. To understand this, note that if (i) is zero, then $f_f = 0$; any increase in f leads to an equiproportionate fall in λ, and so neither the service account nor the trade account is affected (i.e. $\frac{f}{\lambda} \lambda_f = -1$). With $t_\lambda > 0$, a smaller proportionate fall in λ occurs causing the trade account to worsen more than the service account improves.

The current account moves when domestic bonds are issued because expenditure and imports rise and because of the appreciation induced.

$$\dot{f}_b = \frac{1}{\lambda}\left[t_c c_b + (t_\lambda + t_c c_\lambda - \frac{t}{\lambda}) \lambda_b \right]$$

which, using (12) and (8) reduces to

$$\dot{f}_b = \frac{-c_b}{\lambda}\left[\frac{-t_c t_\lambda + (1 + t_c) r^* f}{t_\lambda + (1 + t_c) c_\lambda} \right]$$

around the stationary state. If the country is a net creditor, the effect of extra domestic bonds on the current account is negatively correlated with its effect on expenditure. Since we have assumed that expenditure will rise, we shall consider that $\dot{f}_b < 0$

A phase diagram can be drawn in b and f space using (3) and (4) with b and f set to zero. The BB curve (b = 0) will be horizontal in Figure 4 since it is independent of f under static expectation.

The FF curve ($\dot{f} = 0$) is negatively sloped because stability demands that an increase in f worsens the current account. Any point to the right (left) of the FF curve represents a current account deficit (surplus) whilst any point above (below) the BB curve represents a government budget surplus (deficit).

As an example, consider a tax cut. The exchange rate immediately appreciates (see Figure 1). The BB curve in Figure 5 shifts up since a higher stock of bonds (for given f) will be required for budget balance. The FF curve shifts to the left because the trade deficit is worsened (due to the appreciation and the stimulus to import spending). The economy moves northwest to a new equilibrium in Figure 4 (shown as point E_1) achieving a portfolio redistribution from foreign to domestic assets. In the course of this process, exchange rate depreciation occurs until an overall depreciation is achieved between long run equilibria.

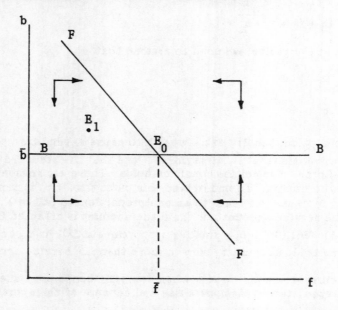

Figure 4

1.5 Perfect Foresight

With perfect foresight about changes in the real exchange rate, equation (11) becomes

$$\frac{\dot{\lambda}}{\lambda} = \mu = r - r^* \tag{11'}$$

where λ is a non-predetermined variable which must assume values that ensure continuous capital market equilibrium.

In temporary equilibrium, the rate of interest is now obtained from goods market equilibrium (9) (for given values of the state variables, λ. b and f). Hence:

$$r = r(\lambda, f, b) \tag{21}$$

where $r_\lambda, r_f, r_b > 0$ (see appendix).

A real depreciation or higher assets stimulates the demand for goods requiring a higher interest rate to restore equilibrium. This equation for the rate of interest can then be considered with the dynamic equations (11'), (3) and (4).

The dynamic system can be represented by a linear approximation about the stationary state in the following way:

$$\begin{bmatrix} \dot{\lambda} \\ \dot{f} \\ \dot{b} \end{bmatrix} = \begin{bmatrix} \Omega \end{bmatrix} \begin{bmatrix} \lambda - \bar{\lambda} \\ f - \bar{f} \\ b - \bar{b} \end{bmatrix} \tag{22}$$

where

$$\begin{bmatrix} \Omega \end{bmatrix} = \begin{bmatrix} \bar{\lambda} r_\lambda & \bar{\lambda} r_f & \bar{\lambda}_b \\ \dfrac{t_\lambda + (1+t_c)r^*\bar{f}}{\bar{\lambda}(1\,t_c)} & r^* & 0 \\ \bar{b} r_\lambda & \bar{b} r_f & r-\alpha-\bar{b} r_b \end{bmatrix} = \begin{bmatrix} + & + & + \\ + & + & 0 \\ + & + & - \end{bmatrix}$$

In the appendix we show that the determinant of Ω is given by

$$\Delta = \frac{(\alpha - r)\,\bar{\lambda} t_\lambda\,(c_w - r^*)}{(-c_r)\,(1 + t_c)} \tag{23}$$

Hence the matrix Ω can have one positive and two negative roots provided (i) the simple Marshall-Lerner condition holds ($t_\lambda > 0$), (ii) extra wealth generates dissaving ($c_w > r^*$) and (iii) the government's stabilizing response in the bond market (α) is sufficiently large. The equilibrium of the model, therefore, will then exhibit saddlepoint stability, with one non-predetermined variable, λ, free to make discrete jumps when 'news' becomes available.[11]

An important aspect of the dynamic model under perfect foresight is that the "foreign exchange" market equilibrium is a regular saddlepoint even if the government does not systematically intervene in the bond market. To see this, assume the government balances its budget continuously and that there is a constant stock of government debt outstanding. The dynamic system (22) simplifies to:

$$\begin{bmatrix} \dot{\lambda} \\ \dot{f} \end{bmatrix} = \begin{bmatrix} \Omega_1 \end{bmatrix} \begin{bmatrix} \lambda - \bar{\lambda} \\ f - \bar{f} \end{bmatrix} \tag{24}$$

where

$$\begin{bmatrix} \Omega_1 \end{bmatrix} = \begin{bmatrix} \bar{\lambda} r_\lambda & \bar{\lambda} r_f \\ \dfrac{t_\lambda + (1+t_c) r^* \bar{f}}{\bar{\lambda}(1\, t_c)} & r^* \end{bmatrix} = \begin{bmatrix} + & + \\ + & + \end{bmatrix}$$

Taking the determinants of the matrix in (24), one obtains, using (A2) in the appendix:

$$\Delta = \frac{-\bar{\lambda} t_\lambda (c_w - r^*)}{(-c_r)(1 + t_c)}$$

so that Ω_1 has one positive and one negative root if the above conditions (i) and (ii) hold. Then the saddlepoint equilibrium and dynamics can be depicted as in Figure 5 where the $\dot{\lambda} = 0$ schedule must be steeper than the $\dot{f} = 0$ schedule.

Integrating (24) for the convergent paths gives

$$(\lambda(T) - \bar{\lambda}) = \frac{\lambda \bar{r}_f}{(\mu - \bar{\lambda} r_\lambda)} (f_0 - \bar{f}) e^{\mu T}$$

$$(f(T) - \bar{f}) = (f_0 - \bar{f}) e^{\mu T} \tag{25}$$

where μ is the negative root of Ω_1 and f_0 an initial condition. From (25) it can be seen that an overshooting impact appreciation occurs (when $T \to 0$) given a long run appreciation and a long run decline in foreign assets.

The exchange rate is a non-predetermined forward-looking asset price which moves instantaneously to the stable arm (in Figure 5) of the saddlepoint equilibrium after an exogenous shock. The model, therefore, displays the property (in common with Kouri (1976), Dornbusch and Fischer (1980) and Branson and Buiter (1983)) of a negative association between the movements in the exchange rate and the current account.[12]

Consider a balanced budget expansion. For the same reasons as

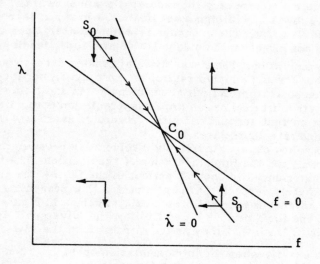

Figure 5

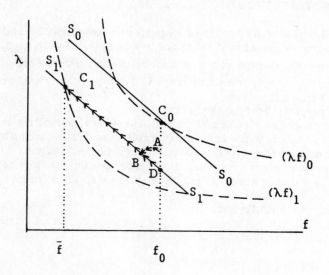

Figure 6

before, the long run effect on $\bar{\lambda}$ is indeterminate, though $\bar{\lambda} \bar{f}$ must fall. In Figure 6 (where only the saddlepaths are shown) the economy falls on to a lower iso-foreign asset line and a long run depreciation is presumed to occur. The exchange rate immediately appreciates to D and then converges on the unique stable arm to C_1 leading to a long run depreciation. The fiscal stimulus creates excess goods demand, thus forcing a higher rate of interest and an impact appreciation so as to crowd out goods demand. In addition, since foreign assets must decline, an impact appreciation is required to bring about current account deficits. As foreign assets are divested, the exchange rate depreciates.

Fiscal policy changes invariably involve a lag between the announcement and the implementation of the decision. If a fiscal stimulus is announced to occur T periods in the future, the exchange rate immediately depreciates in anticipation thus preventing any future instantaneous but predictable capital gains. In Figure 6, λ falls to A, and for T periods λ and f follow the "divergent" dynamics governed by C_0 such that they arrive at point B on the new saddlepath exactly when the implementation occurs.[13] Thenceforth, convergence is identical to the unanticipated case.

2. FISCAL POLICY, THE REAL EXCHANGE RATE AND IMPERFECT ASSET SUBSTITUTABILITY

We now consider the contribution of imperfect asset substitutability, when wealth effects are absent from the consumption function, i.e. we set $\frac{\partial c}{\partial w} = 0$ in (8), assume $\gamma' > 0$ and include asset income in disposable income. Re-tracing our steps in Section 1, we shall briefly indicate the changes involved.

The RR schedule becomes negatively sloped because a depreciation lowers the risk premium and, therefore, permits a lower domestic rate of interest for temporary capital market equilibrium. Also the GG curve is flatter because a depreciation no longer generates a wealth effect. Expansionary fiscal policy can now raise the rate of interest (for given μ) and thus cause a smaller impact appreciation.

In the long run equilibrium

$$\bar{r} = r^* + \gamma \left[\frac{\bar{b}}{\bar{\lambda} \bar{f}} \right]$$

so that, using (14)

$$\bar{r} = \phi (\bar{\lambda}\bar{f}; g, -\tau_0)$$

where

$$\phi_1 = \eta/(\lambda f)$$

$$\phi_2 = \phi_3 = -\eta/(g - \tau_0)$$

where

$$\eta = \cfrac{\gamma' \bar{b}/\overline{\lambda f}}{\cfrac{\gamma' \bar{b}/\overline{\lambda f}}{(\alpha - \bar{r})} - 1}$$

which is negative if $\gamma' \dfrac{\bar{b}}{\overline{\lambda f}} < (\alpha - \bar{r})$, i.e. if the degree of imperfect substitutability is not too large.

The KK curve in Figure 2a becomes negatively sloped if an increase in foreign assets lowers the risk premium thus requiring a lower interest rate in the long run.

Long run goods market equilibrium becomes

$$q_0 + r^*\bar{\lambda}\bar{f} = \bar{c}(\bar{r}, \bar{y}) + g$$

$$\bar{r} = \hat{\Theta}(\bar{\lambda}\bar{f} : g, -\tau_0)$$

where

$$\hat{\Theta}_1 = \frac{-(1 - c_y)r^*}{(-c_r)} < 0$$

$$\hat{\Theta}_2 = \frac{(1 - c_y)}{(-c_r)} > 0$$

$$\hat{\Theta}_3 = 0$$

With this Keynesian expenditure function, the IS curve takes on the conventional negative slope in Figure 2a and tax cuts have no effect on this curve. An autonomous tax cut induces non-autonomous tax increases such that disposable income is unchanged. Long run disposable income is $q_0 - g + r^* \bar{\lambda} \bar{f}$.

A tax cut only affects the KK curve; it shifts upward if $\eta < 0$ and, with a more negatively sloped IS curve, causes a fall in $\bar{\lambda} \bar{f}$. Consumption falls for two reasons – the drop in disposable income and the rise in the real interest rate. Hence the real exchange rate depreciates in the long run. It is worth noting that reverse results occur if the KK curve is steeper than the IS curve, or if γ' is sufficiently large.

An increase in government spending shifts IS and KK upwards and, hence, has an ambiguous effect (as before) on the real exchange rate. But the reasons are slightly different. Due to the endogeneity of the domestic rate of interest, the change in $\bar{\lambda} \bar{f}$ cannot be unambiguously predicted. The important point is that the imperfect substitutability channel can generate similar long run results to the wealth-expenditure channel.

Concerning stability, the first thing to appreciate is that our model is globally unstable with the Keynesian expenditure function and perfect asset substitutability. The relationship between foreign asset increments and savings becomes $r^*(1-c_y) > 0$ (instead of $r^* - c_w < 0$). Thus (20) would be positive and the static expectations model is unstable. Similarly, the determinant Δ of the perfect foresight matrix of (23) would become negative.

Introducing sufficient imperfect substitutability can make $\dot{f}_f$ negative; after some manipulation (20) becomes

$$\dot{f}_f = \frac{t_\lambda \, r^*(1 - c_y - \frac{\gamma'M}{r^*})}{t_\lambda + 1 + t_c)(c_\lambda + \gamma'M)} \tag{20'}$$

where

$$M = -c_r (1 + t_c) \frac{\bar{b}}{\lambda^2 \bar{f}^2}$$

The numerator of (20)' becomes negative for sufficiently large γ'. An increment in f lowers the risk premium and thus the interest rate, encouraging expenditure on imports.

Similarly, under perfect foresight, the negative value of Δ can be overcome with sufficiently large γ'. After some manipulation, the determinant becomes

$$\Delta = \frac{(\alpha - r) \bar{\lambda} \, t_\lambda \, r^* (1 - c_y)}{(- c_r) (1 + t_c)} + \gamma'N \tag{23'}$$

where

$$N = \frac{\bar{b}}{(1+t_c)(-c_r)\bar{\lambda}\bar{f}^2} \left[(\alpha - \bar{r}) \, t_\lambda (-c_r + \bar{b} \, c_y) + r^*\lambda f t_\lambda (1-c_y) \right] > 0$$

The second term in (23'), if sufficiently large, can make Δ positive as desired.

Finally, the system restricted to the foreign exchange market in (24) is mildly modified. Decreasing substitutability can be shown to flatten the $\lambda = 0$ schedule.

Since the long run is so indeterminate, it is quite possible to generate an impact depreciation after a fiscal expansion. This unusual outcome may occur if the degree of asset substitutability is so low that the rising rate of interest bears more than the whole burden of maintaining instantaneous goods market equilibrium. Further depreciations must also be registered as is apparent from considering Figure 1 with a downward sloping RR curve.

3.   DYNAMIC EFFECTS OF FISCAL POLICY

Since the dynamics of the three dimensional system cannot be adequately described graphically or analytically, we illustrate the dynamic effects of fiscal policy using numerical analysis.[14] We consider the "tax stabilisation" model with perfect and imperfect asset substitutability and without financial income in disposable income. The last assumption is quite innocuous.

The simulation model can be summarized thus:

$$\frac{\dot{\lambda}}{\lambda} = r - r^* - \gamma \left(\frac{b}{\lambda f} - v \min \right)$$

$$\lambda \dot{f} = r^* \lambda f + t$$

$$\dot{b} = (\alpha_\tau - r) b + g_0 - \tau_0$$

$$t = x_0 \lambda^{\epsilon_1} - t_0 \lambda^{-\epsilon_2} c$$

$$q_0 = c + g_0 + t$$

$$c = a_1 (q - \tau_0 - \alpha b) - a_2 r + a_3 (b + \lambda f)$$

Values of Parameters and Constants

$$r^* \quad = 0.04$$
$$\gamma \quad = 0.0 \text{ or } 0.01$$

$$v \min = 3.0$$

$$\alpha_\tau \quad = 0.2$$
$$g_0 \quad = 35.8$$
$$\tau_0 \quad = 26.2$$
$$x_0 \quad = 8.95$$
$$t_0 \quad = 0.15$$
$$q_0 \quad = 100.0$$
$$\epsilon_1 \quad = 0.7$$
$$\epsilon_2 \quad = 0.2$$
$$a_1 \quad = 0.9$$
$$a_2 \quad = 100.0$$
$$a_3 \quad = 0.16725$$

We undertake four different numerical experiments:

(a)   A tax cut: $\Delta \tau_0 = -3.0$

(b)   A government expenditure rise: $\Delta g_0 = 3.0$

(c)   A balanced budget expansion: $\Delta g_0 = \Delta \tau_0 = 3.0$

(d)   An announcement of a tax cut in the future: $\Delta \tau_0 = -3.0$
        from period 3 onwards.

Each of these four are studied for perfect and imperfect asset substitutability.

The results of these experiments are shown in Table 1.[15] In every unanticipated fiscal expansion experiment, the exchange rate appreciates (discretely) on impact[16] to reach a new stable manifold and current account deficits are henceforth incurred in association with actual (and expected) real exchange rate depreciation. Bond financed government expenditure increases have the greatest impact. In the long run, however, tax cuts always lead to an overall real depreciation, whilst government expenditure increases may or may not cause a long run depreciation whether financed by bond issues or tax rises. We have contrived parameter values (especially t_0) so that higher bond financed government expenditure generates a real depreciation with perfect asset substitutability. Fiscal policy always creates exchange rate overshooting or else 'perverse shooting'. In all of the experiments, private sector expenditure is crowded out in the long run, but tax cuts do cause a short term stimulus as one would expect. Fiscal expansion always initially forces up the real rate of interest because of the extra demand in the goods market. This in turn requires expected depreciation of the exchange rate to maintain asset market equilibrium. This model therefore can exhibit the same property as well-known monetary models (see Dornbusch (1976)) in that an expected depreciation requires an overvalued exchange rate after an unexpected shock.

Imperfect Asset Substitutes

The implications of imperfect asset substitutability for the dynamics of the real exchange rate (when wealth effects on expenditure are included) is simply that its time path in all experiments becomes flatter. That is, a smaller impact appreciation and a smaller (larger) long run depreciation (appreciation) occurs. However, the overshooting or reverse shooting still takes place. The cumulative current account deficits are substantially reduced, whereas the cumulative government borrowing requirement is substantially increased. If assets are perfect substitutes, expansionary bond financed fiscal policy leads to a substitution in portfolios of domestic for foreign assets. Otherwise the domestic rate of interest bears a large burden, increasing to maintain asset market equilibrium. Finally, private expenditure suffers marginally less from crowding out as assets become imperfectly substitutable.

TABLE 1

Period	λ	f	b	$\dot{\lambda}$	r	c
Initial Long Run Equilibrium for all experiments						
0.0	1.000	20.000	60.000	0.000	0.040	65.000
A) Tax cut [perfect substitutes]						
1.0	0.928	20.000	60.000	0.009	0.049	66.513
2.0	0.937	18.388	63.289	0.008	0.049	66.328
3.0	0.945	16.923	66.070	0.007	0.048	66.159
10.0	0.985	9.705	76.326	0.004	0.044	65.314
121.0	1.039	0.610	78.878	0.000	0.040	64.226
Tax cut [imperfect substitutes]						
1.0	0.952	20.000	60.000	0.013	0.055	66.011
2.0	0.964	19.027	63.674	0.011	0.056	65.754
3.0	0.974	18.281	66.909	0.009	0.057	65.541
10.0	1.006	16.604	81.047	0.002	0.060	64.876
121.0	1.004	17.737	90.345	0.000	0.060	64.916
B) Government expenditure rise [perfect substitutes]						
1.0	0.897	20.000	60.000	0.009	0.050	63.610
2.0	0.906	18.202	63.343	0.009	0.050	63.412
3.0	0.914	16.567	66.170	0.008	0.049	63.232
10.0	0.958	8.501	76.564	0.005	0.045	62.321
121.0	1.017	-1.666	78.751	0.000	0.040	61.132
Government expenditure rise [imperfect substitutes]						
1.0	0.924	20.000	60.000	0.014	0.057	63.021
2.0	0.937	18.970	63.791	0.012	0.058	62.754
3.0	0.947	18.184	67.136	0.010	0.059	62.533
10.0	0.981	16.461	81.888	0.002	0.062	61.847
121.0	0.979	17.801	91.749	0.000	0.063	61.897
C) Balanced budget expansion [perfect substitutes]						
1.0	0.968	20.000	60.000	0.001	0.041	62.114
2.0	0.969	19.861	60.042	0.001	0.041	62.099
3.0	0.969	19.732	60.074	0.001	0.041	62.085
10.0	0.973	19.054	60.151	0.000	0.040	62.013
121.0	0.978	18.036	59.999	0.000	0.040	61.906
Balanced budget expansion [imperfect substitutes]						
1.0	0.971	20.000	60.000	0.001	0.042	62.046
2.0	0.972	19.934	60.088	0.001	0.042	62.034
3.0	0.972	19.879	60.165	0.000	0.042	62.023
10.0	0.974	19.668	60.484	0.000	0.042	61.982
121.0	0.975	19.586	60.669	0.000	0.042	61.964
D) Announcement of tax cut [perfect substitutes]						
1.0	0.963	20.000	60.000	-0.009	0.031	65.778
2.0	0.952	19.024	59.393	-0.012	0.027	66.002
3.0	0.939	17.695	58.994	0.008	0.049	66.278
10.0	0.982	10.016	74.055	0.005	0.045	65.360
121.0	1.039	0.632	78.753	0.000	0.040	64.226
Announcement of tax cut [imperfect substitutes]						
1.0	0.979	20.000	60.000	-0.006	0.035	65.439
2.0	0.971	19.448	59.649	-0.009	0.032	65.590
3.0	0.962	18.661	59.551	0.012	0.056	65.784
10.0	1.006	16.276	78.150	0.002	0.060	64.875
121.0	1.004	17.824	90.306	0.000	0.060	64.916

Announcement Effects

An announcement of a fiscal expansion to take place at a date T in the future causes an immediate discrete exchange rate appreciation. Until time T, the economy is governed by the original dynamic forces and therefore moves off the original stable manifold. The immediate appreciation is therefore followed by further appreciation and current account deficits. A further immediate effect of an announced tax cut is a fall in the rate of interest. This occurs to maintain capital equilibrium because of the actual (and expected) appreciation (till T) ($\dot{\lambda} < 0$). With a lower interest rate, expenditure is stimulated (in advance) and government's borrowing requirement is seen to improve initially. When time T arrives, the economy finds itself at a slightly different point on the stable manifold to that when an unexpected tax cut takes place: the real exchange rate is higher, and the levels of both assets are lower.

4. CONCLUSION

We have used a simple fixed output model to show that different types of bond-financed fiscal policy can generate non-Mundellian results on the real exchange rate. If assets are sufficiently substitutable, anticipated or unanticipated expansions do lead to a short run appreciation but, for stable configurations, wealth effects via an expenditure channel or a portfolio channel, will reverse the short run impact. A long run real depreciation can occur, depending upon which fiscal element is assigned to the role of stabilization, upon the degree of asset substitutability and upon the extent of the openness of the economy. The long run Mundell result of an appreciation only occurs if government expenditure is raised initially but falls eventually as part of the stabilization programme. The conclusion is that the relationship between fiscal policy and the exchange rate can only be determined empirically. Indeed, there is a marked scarcity of empirical work in this area.

Perhaps the most obvious extension to the model in this paper is to allow for price inertia and short run output endogeneity. These amendments would have no long run implications but the short run effects on the exchange rate and the interest rate will be accordingly muted.[17]

The exchange rate implications of fiscal policy are also importantly dependent on the consumption/investment mix. An explicit analysis of capital accumulation will exhibit fiscal non-neutralities.

APPENDIX: PERFECT FORESIGHT AND PERFECT ASSET SUBSTITUTION

From the goods market equilibrium where

$$q_0 = c(r, y, w) + g_0 + t(\lambda, c) \tag{A1}$$

one can obtain the temporary equilibrium solution for the rate of interest as

$$r = r(\lambda, f, b) \tag{A2}$$

$$r_f = -\frac{(t_\lambda + (1 + t_c)\, c_\lambda)}{(1 + t_c)c_r} > 0 \tag{A3}$$

$$r_f = -\frac{c_f}{c_r} > 0 \tag{A4}$$

$$r_b = -\frac{c_b}{c_r} > 0 \tag{A5}$$

The three differential equations driving the system are

(i) $\quad \dot{\lambda} = (r - r^*)\,\lambda \tag{A6}$

where about the stationary state $(r = r^*)$

$$\dot{\lambda}_\lambda = \lambda r_\lambda; \quad \dot{\lambda}_f = \lambda r_f; \quad \dot{\lambda}_b = \lambda r_b \tag{A6'}$$

(ii) $\quad \dot{f} = r^*f + \frac{1}{\lambda}t\,(\lambda, c) \tag{A7}$

where about the stationary state $(t = -r^*\lambda f)$

$$\dot{f}_\lambda = \frac{1}{\lambda}(t_\lambda + t_c c_\lambda + t_c c_r r_\lambda - \frac{t}{\lambda}) = \frac{1}{\lambda(1+t_c)}\; (t_\lambda + (1+t_c)r^*f) > 0$$

$$\dot{f}_f = r^* + \frac{t_c}{\lambda} \cdot (c_f + c_r r_f) = r^* \tag{A7'}$$

$$\dot{f}_b = \frac{t_c}{\lambda} \cdot (c_b + c_r r_b) = 0$$

and

(iii) $\dot{b} = (r - \alpha)\,b + g - \tau_0 \tag{A8}$

where

$$\dot{b}_\lambda = br_\lambda; \quad \dot{b}_f = br_f; \quad \dot{b}_b = r - \alpha + br_b \tag{A8'}$$

(A6'), (A7') and (A8') provide the elements of Ω in (22).

To establish that Ω has one positive and two negative roots, we compute the determinant (which represents the product of the three roots) and the trace (which gives the sum). The determinant

$$\Delta = (r - \alpha + br_b)(r^* \bar{\lambda} r_\lambda - \frac{r_f}{(1 + t_c)}(t_\lambda + (1 + t_c) r^*f))$$

$$+ \frac{br_f}{(1 + t_c)} r_b (t_\lambda + (1 + t_c) r^*\bar{f})$$

$$- br_\lambda \bar{\lambda} r_b r^*$$

Around the stationary state $(r = r^*)$, this reduces to

$$\Delta = (r - \alpha)(r^* \bar{\lambda} r_\lambda - \frac{r_f}{(1 + t_c)}(t_\lambda + (1 + t_c) r^*\bar{f}))$$

which using (A3), (A4) and (A5) becomes[18]

$$\Delta = \frac{(\alpha - r).t_\lambda.\bar{\lambda}.(c - r^*)}{-c_r.(1 + t_c)} \tag{A9}$$

In order that two roots are negative and one positive, the determinant must be positive. Necessary conditions for this are:

(i) $\quad \alpha > r$

(ii) $\quad t_\lambda > 0$

(iii) $\quad c_w > r^*$

which are identical to the necessary and sufficient conditions for stability with static expectations.

However, the above three conditions are not sufficient because the determinant could be positive if all three roots were positive. If in addition the sum of the roots were negative, the system must exhibit the required saddlepath stability.

The trace is $r - \alpha + br_b + r^* + \bar{\lambda} r_\lambda$ which is negative if

$$\alpha > r + bc_b / (-c_r) + r^* + \bar{\lambda} r_\lambda$$

Since $r^* + \bar{\lambda} r_\lambda > 0$, it must be true that $\alpha > r + bc_b/(-c_r)$. This latter condition is nothing but $\sigma > c_r / \bar{b}$ which is condition (ii) on page 47.

ACKNOWLEDGEMENTS

This paper originated from joint work with Charles Wyplosz. It was written under the auspices of an ESRC grant, HR 8019. We wish to thank Luigi Guiso for invaluable research assistance.

NOTES

1. There are three recent contributions in this area. The first by Sachs and Wyplosz (1984) is very similar in spirit to ours, but concentrates more on the issue of imperfect asset substitutability. Buiter (1984) and Giovannini (1984) study the correlation of fiscal policy with the real exchange rate in a model where savings and investment derived from optimal intertemporal choices by finitely lived households and infinitely lived firms.

2. In fact, Christ's suggestion was to amend the Tobin-Buiter definition of government expenditure to include after tax bond service (which did not generate stability) by including, instead, bond services gross of tax. This is equivalent to our statement.

3. In making the tax adjustment, the government does not divulge its motives, and merely changes, say, tax thresholds. Otherwise, the implicit real rate of return on bonds would be different from r and may be negative. Even if the tax adjustment were empirically detectable, bonds are most likely held by a different group to those that pay the bulk of taxes. The idea that the government is rational enough to recognise the stabilization problem and introduces a perpetual adjustment is rather strong. Instead, one could easily model a process whereby the government intervenes when bonds (or an appropriate ratio) hit a ceiling or floor. The ceiling or floor will then describe the stationary state.

4. See Branson (1976).

5. The absence of asset income in disposable income is unimportant for the results obtained in this section. It is introduced in Section 2 because, there, c_w is set to zero.

6. The exact solutions for the partial derivatives are:

$$\lambda_b = -(1+t_c)\, c_b\, /\, x; \quad \lambda_f = -(1+t_c)\, c_f\, /\, x$$

$$\lambda_{g_0} = -1\, /\, x; \quad \lambda_{-\tau_0} = -(1+t_c)c_y\, /\, x; \quad \lambda_\mu = -(1+t_c)c_r\, /\, x$$

where $x = t_\lambda + (1+t_c)\, c_\lambda > 0.$

7. If a fixed target wealth saving function were instead used, long run wealth and consumption and hence, from (9"), the exchange rate would be unaffected by the tax cut.

8. We have also assumed that the government only purchases domestic goods. Obviously, the indeterminancy will be affected by different government propensities.

9. Introducing allocative effects of government expenditure

between productive and unproductive uses, may reverse these conclusions. An increase in public investment raises output, q_0, causes the curves in Figure 3 to reverse their shifts, thereby increasing the likelihood of an appreciation.

10.   This assumption is well rooted in tradition - see, for example, Metzler (1951).

11.   We ignore the problem of the multiplicity of perfect foresight paths and assume that the economy always finds the unique path that leads to the steady state.

12.   Branson and Buiter (1983) analyse a similar model with money and conclude that the sign of $\dot{f}_f$ is an empirical matter. Dornbusch and Fischer (1980) pointedly <u>assume</u> that higher foreign assets worsen the current account; obviously one obtains different results since the $\dot{f} = 0$ curve is positively sloped in the Dornbusch and Fischer model.

13.   See Wilson (1975) for an analysis of the effects of anticipated future stocks in a monetary model.

14.   We make use of NAG routines: D02RAF to solve the two point boundary problem and C05NAF to solve the non-linear simultaneous equation problem. The former uses a deferred correction technique and Newton iteration developed by V. Pereyra to solve systems of non-linear differential equations with general boundary conditions. The latter uses a hybrid method due to M.J.D. Powell.

15.   The period in Table 1 may be considered as almost a year if one assumes r* = 0.04 approximates average annual real rates of interest.

16.   Although it is theoretically feasible to obtain an impact depreciation, we were unable to find parameter patterns which generated numerical convergence.

17.   The role of sticky goods prices is investigated by Sachs and Wyplosz (1984).

18.   It can be easily checked that Δ will be identical if instead α_g was used rather than α_τ by the government.

OPTIMAL POLICY UNDER MODEL UNCERTAINTY

Robin Becker, Barry Dwolatzky, Elias Karakitsos
and Berc Rustem

INTRODUCTION

This paper examines the problems posed for macroeconomic policy
design by the existence of rival models of the economy. These
problems can be dealt with by designing policies that are acceptable,
in varying degrees, to all models. This paper examines a procedure
for doing this. We also assume that all rival models fit the data
reasonably well and that statistical inference cannot reject any one
model in favour of its rivals. We propose an algorithm for dealing
with the existence of rival models, which computes policies on all
rival models simultaneously. Nevertheless, it is designed to be
efficient and relatively modest in its storage requirements. A
minimax extension of the algorithm is also used to generate policies
which are invariant whichever model eventually turns out to
represent the economy.

To illustrate the proposed procedures, numerical experiments are
reported which use the UK models of HM Treasury and the National
Institute of Economic and Social Research, as rival models. The
optimal policies computed simultaneously on both models are
discussed along with minimax policies.

1. THE METHOD FOR "PARETO OPTIMAL POLICIES" FOR RIVAL MODELS

Consider the two nonlinear models of the same system:

$$F_1 (Y_1, U, X_1) = 0, \quad F_2 (Y_2, U, X_2) = 0 \tag{1}$$

where F_1, Y_1, X_1, F_2, Y_2, X_2 are the nonlinear model equations,
endogenous variables and exogenous variables associated with models
1 and 2 respectively. The exogenous variables X_1 and X_2 are <u>fixed</u> at
their historical values prior to any optimization or model simulation
considered hereafter. The variable U is the vector of policy

instruments common to both models. Let the cost functions associated with each model be

$$J_1(Y_1, U) = \tfrac{1}{2}[(U - U_1^d)^T Q_1^u (U - U_1^d) + (Y_1 - Y_1^d)^T Q_1^y (Y_1 - Y_1^d)] \qquad (2a)$$

$$J_2(Y_2, U) = \tfrac{1}{2}[(U - U_2^d)^T Q_2^u (U - U_2^d) + (Y_2 - Y_2^d)^T Q_2^y (Y_2 - Y_2^d)] \qquad (2b)$$

where the superscript d denotes the desired values of the variables associated with each model. The weighting matrices Q_1^y, Q_2^y are symmetric positive semidefinite and the matrices Q_1^u, Q_2^u are symmetric positive definite. In the exercises discussed below, it is assumed that $Y_1^d = Y_2^d$, $U_1^d = U_2^d$, $Q_1^y = Q_2^y$ and $Q_1^u = Q_2^u$. This is to maintain the consistency of policy objectives irrespective of the model being utilised. In general, however, such a consistency is not required by the method.

The combined cost function used in the simultaneous optimization of the two models is given by

$$J(Y_1, Y_2, U) = \alpha J_1(Y_1, U) + (1 - \alpha) J_2(Y_2, U) \qquad (3)$$

where the scalar α is chosen prior to entering the simultaneous optimization algorithm and reflects the relative importance attached to each model. In the experiments discussed below, J_1 corresponds to the model of HM Treasury (HMT), and J_2 corresponds to the National Institute (NI) model of the UK economy. The scalar α is initially assigned the value 0.5 for the exercises presented in Section 2. The selection of α using a minimax characterization is discussed in Section 3.

The simultaneous optimization algorithm (see Rustem, 1983) solves the problem

$$\min\{J(Y_1, Y_2, U) \mid F_1(Y_1, U, X_1) = 0, \ \ F_2(Y_2, U, X_2) = 0\} \qquad (4)$$

The set of instrument trajectories, U, which solves this minimization problem will be referred to as the "Pareto optimal policy".

It is assumed that given the values of X_1, X_2 and the policy instrument vector U, both models can be solved independently from each other for their respective endogenous variables Y_1 and Y_2. Let the mappings between X_1, U and Y_1 and X_2, U and Y_2 be denoted by g_1 and g_2 respectively. Thus, given the model solution programs and X_1, X_2, U, we can calculate

$$Y_1 = g_1(U, X_1) \qquad (5a)$$

$$Y_2 = g_2(U, X_2) \qquad (5b)$$

Substituting (5) in (3), we can reformulate (4) as the unconstrained optimization problem

$$\min\{J(g_1(U, X_1), g_2(U, X_2), U)\} \tag{6}$$

which can be solved using a Gauss-Newton algorithm. The algorithm is discussed in detail in Rustem (1983) along with methods for overcoming the difficulty of the a priori specification of the parameter α. The essential feature of the algorithm is that at any point U_k, $(k = 0, 1, ...)$ it computes iteratively a descent direction given by

$$d_k = - H_k^{-1} \nabla J (g_1(U_k), g_2(U_k), U_k) \tag{7}$$

where H_k is a Hessian approximation, and a stepsize τ_k which determines U_{k+1}, given by

$$U_{k+1} = U_k + \tau_k d_k \tag{8}$$

such that J at U_{k+1} is sufficiently less than J at U_k. How the algorithm works is explained later on.

The two models employed in this study are the forecasting models of HM Treasury and the National Institute of Economic and Social Research, used here for the period 1978:1 to 1984:4. Full listings of these models are, of course, available (NIESR (1983): HMT (1982)).

2.   THE PROBLEM OF MODEL UNCERTAINTY AND THE PARETO OPTIMAL POLICY

The details of the objective function in terms of which the optimal policy mix for each model is obtained, are given in Table 1. Three ultimate targets are included: inflation, P, unemployment, U, and the current account of the balance of payment, CB.

To optimize the objective function, fiscal and monetary policy is used. We consider fiscal policy as operating through two instruments: real government expenditure, G, and the standard rate of income tax, t. Monetary policy works through the short term interest rate on government bonds, r, the Treasury Bill Rate. The first difference of each of these instruments, ΔG, Δt, Δr is also included as targets in the objective function to avoid large fluctuations in their usage between quarters. For the policy instruments we assume that their desired values are the same as in the base - or "do-nothing" run (see below); hence, there is no incentive in changing policy other than satisfying the ultimate targets. The desired path for inflation is zero, unemployment 500,000 and current account zero. To compare the optimization results, a base run is needed. This is described as a "do-nothing" case, i.e. a simulation of the model over the 7-year planning horizon (1978: 1 - 1984: 4) in which the policy instruments are not actively used but remain fixed. The values which the instruments assume are: $G = 6000$, $t = 30$, $r = 10$. To facilitate comparisons between the HMT and NI models, the latter is adjusted so that both models produce the same "do-nothing" trajectories in terms of the target variables. This is done as a simple 4-target 4-instrument optimization problem. The residual variable in the equations for each of the four targets is used as an instrument in the NI model to track the corresponding values of the target variables from the HMT model. The results appear in Table 2.

Since the HMT model offers a much more detailed disaggregation of government spending by type of asset and sector than the NI model, a common set of instruments is found by standardizing them to the level of aggregation offered by the NI model. The proportion of a particular category of spending to the total is then used to allocate changes in total to the particular category of spending. Both models have common instruments for monetary policy, the Treasury Bill Rate and, for direct taxation, the standard income tax rate.

The starting point is an evaluation of the seriousness of the model uncertainty problem. The two models considered here are not generally regarded as being very different. If the effects of model uncertainty on the design of economic policy turn out to be important for these two models, one can conjecture that it would be even more serious for models representing polar views on how the economy works. In spite of the similarities of the HMT and NI models, differences in dynamics, long run properties and the role of intermediate targets are the main reasons for the fact that the derived optimal policies differ between the two models. The optimal policy for each model is given in the upper and lower blocks of Tables 3A and 3B.

The optimal policy mix in the HMT model is expansionary fiscal policy (as measured by the cyclically adjusted real PSBR, which is 1.5% higher, on average, than the common "do-nothing" case), together with a contractionary monetary policy implying higher interest rates, 1.8% on average above the "do-nothing" case. In the NI model, the optimal policy mix is the same but less pronounced. The cyclically adjusted real PSBR is up by 1.1% (compared with 1.5% in the HMT model) and interest rates are higher by only 0.3% (compared with 1.8% in the HMT model).

With model uncertainty, the policymaker wishes to take into account the repercussions of basing his policy on one of the models and the "real" world turning out to be represented by the other model. The way to evaluate such potential costs, and hence the importance of ignoring model uncertainty in the design of policy, is by simulating each model with the optimal instrument trajectories of the other model. This is done in the lower and upper blocks of Tables 3A and 3B. Thus the upper blocks of Tables 3A and 3B present the payoff of basing the optimal policy on the HMT model and the real world turning out to be either HMT or NI. The reader can check for himself that the last three rows (G, t and r) of the upper blocks of Tables 3A and 3B are the same. Similarly, the lower blocks of Tables 3A and 3B provide the payoffs of basing the policy on the NI model.

Using the weights of the objective function (see Table 1) one can evaluate in terms of the objective function the overall cost associated with the optimal policies for the two models. This is done in Table 4. The figures in brackets represent the objective function cost reduction relative to the common "do-nothing" case. Thus, when the policy is based on the HMT model and the real world is as portrayed by the HMT model, the objective function cost is reduced by 39% relative to the common "do-nothing" case; but it is only reduced by 15% when the real world is represented by the NI model. On the other hand, when the optimal policy is based on the NI model, the cost is reduced by 41% if the real world is like the NI model, but it is only reduced by 5% if the real world is as portrayed by the HMT model.

On the basis of this payoff matrix, the conclusion seems to be that quite significant losses occur when the problem of model uncertainty is ignored in policy design, even with models of the same theoretical persuasion. These losses are mainly due to differences in the dynamics in the two models. Some comfort, of course, still remains because in both cases the optimal policy based on a single model is better than the "do-nothing" policy, even if the real world turns out to be like the other model.

The simultaneous optimization algorithm outlined in Section 1 is applied to the policy design problem described above. The algorithm allows us to find a Pareto optimal policy which, although sub-optimal for each of the two models, will obtain, for a given value of the scalar α, the greatest possible reduction in the objective function cost when the policymaker is uncertain about which of the models represents the real world.

The algorithm is iterative in nature and Table 5 shows how it converges to the desired Pareto optimal policy. In theory, any set of instrument values may be used as a starting point for the algorithm although, in practice, convergence is faster if we use one of the single model optimum policies as an initial point for the algorithm. In Table 5 it will be seen that in this case the algorithm was started from the NI model optimal policy. As was seen in Table 4, this policy results in an objective function cost of 3304.78 on the NI model, and 5281.97 when applied to the HMT model. (Costs are written with two decimal places in Table 5 so that the performance of the algorithm can be understood as it converges to an optimal value.) The corresponding value of the combined objective function (equation (3) with $\alpha = 0.5$) is 4293.37. The algorithm computes the value of the gradient at this initial point and finds it to be equal to 71.85. This tells us that we are quite far from the required optimum point where the gradient should be approximately zero.

The simultaneous optimization algorithm begins by numerically evaluating the Jacobian matrices for both models. It then takes a step of length one unit along this initial line and immediately finds a lower value (3815.72) for the combined objective function cost. The costs associated with the individual models corresponding to this point are 3723.28 and 3908.16 for the HMT model and NI model respectively. The gradient at this point is 23.82.

In the fourth iteration, no reduction in the combined objective function cost is obtained with a step size of 1.0. The algorithm reduces the step size and tries again. With a step size of 0.01, a cost reduction is obtained, but it is only 0.06 lower than the previous best cost obtained in iteration 3. Up to this stage, the values of the Jacobian matrices have remained unchanged from the initial values computed at the start of the algorithm. After iteration 4, the Jacobian matrices for both models are numerically re-evaluated and the algorithm finds a further cost decrease at iteration 5.

After the seventh iteration, the Jacobian matrices are again recomputed, but this time no further cost decrease can be obtained. The value 3704.42 therefore represents the required optimum for the combined objective function. By substituting the common "do-nothing" instrument trajectories into equation (3), we obtain a "combined objective function do-nothing cost", equal to 5581. The algorithm has thus reduced the combined objective function by 34% relative to this "do-nothing" cost. The Pareto optimal policy when applied to the HMT model's view of the world, corresponds to an objective function cost of 3800, and when used on the NI model, reduces the cost to 3609. These values are given in Table 4, where they can be compared against the costs associated with the single model optimizations.

The Pareto optimal policy, for $\alpha = 0.5$, results in a cost reduction of 32% relative to the "do-nothing" in the HMT model and 35% in the NI model. This policy insures the policymaker against model uncertainty at a small cost, compared with the single model optimum (7% in the HMT, 6% in the NI). It also implies substantial gains relative to the off-diagonal elements of the upper and second row of Table 4 (27% in the HMT, 20% in the NI). The upper blocks of Tables 3C and 3D present the trajectories of the Pareto policy in deviation from the common "do-nothing" case. The Pareto fiscal policy, when the real world is like the HMT model, implies a higher cyclically adjusted real PSBR of 1.1% compared with 1.5% when the policy is based on the HMT model alone, and 0.9% when based on the NI model alone. The Pareto monetary policy implies interest rates higher by 0.8% on average, compared with 1.8% and 0.3% when the policy is based on either HMT or NI respectively. The Pareto optimal policy therefore lies somewhere between the two single model policies when considered as a five-year average. The same picture emerges from the NI world. However, the dynamic adjustment of the Pareto policy does not lie everywhere between the two extremes.

3. A MINIMAX CHARACTERIZATION OF THE OPTIMAL POLICY WITH RIVAL MODELS

In the derivation of the Pareto optimal policy, α has been set equal to 0.5. This is an arbitrary choice which gives equal weighting to the objective functions of both models. Using the basic objective function with a 5-year horizon, Pareto policies were derived for α = 0.25 (i.e. policy weighted towards the NI model) and α = 0.75 (i.e. more weight given to the HMT model).

Figure 1 illustrates the values of the individual objective functions as problem (6) is solved for α = 0 (the NI model optimum), 0.25, 0.5, 0.75 and 1.0 (the HMT model optimum). Also plotted in Figure 1 is a curve representing the combination of the individual objective function values derived from equation (3). From the Figure it will be seen that at a certain value of α, i.e., α^*, the values of the individual objective functions are the same and also that the combined objective function has its maximum value. The solution to the problem

$$\min_{U} \quad \max_{\alpha \epsilon [0,1]} \quad \{\alpha J_1(Y_1,U)+(1-\alpha)J_2(Y_2,U)|F_1(Y_1,U)=0, F_2(Y_2,U)=0\} \qquad (9)$$

corresponds to the value α^*. We will call the Pareto optimal policy corresponding to $\alpha = \alpha^*$ the "robust optimal policy".

This value of α is determined by fitting two curves to the respective values of J_1 and J_2 (the individual objective functions) obtained by solving (6) for α = 0, 0.25, 0.5, 0.75, 1.0 and evaluating the intersection point. In this way we find that a^* = 0.6.

Using this value for α and the basic objective function with a 5-year horizon, the optimum policy robust to both models was derived. The results are given in the lower blocks of Tables 3C and 3D. The corresponding objective function costs for all of the values of α are given in Table 4. It will be seen that at α^* = 0.6 the effect of applying the robust policy to the HMT model is a cost of 3720, whereas applying it to the NI model it has an objective function cost value of 3717. The optimum solution of (9) for the present exercise thus occurs at $J_1 = J_2$ since, at this point, the policymaker would be indifferent as to which model turns out to be the actual world. Thus the value of α that solves (9) ensures that the chosen policy does not have an adverse effect whichever model happens to represent the economy.

4. CONCLUSIONS

The problem of ignoring model uncertainty in policy design is very important. Even for models which are not generally regarded as very different, like the HMT and NI models, there are substantial losses in terms of objective function cost reduction, if the real world turns out to be like the other model.

The solution to the problem of model uncertainty in policy design considered here is the formulation of a Pareto optimal policy. This is derived from the minimization of a cost function, which is a combination of the cost functions of the individual models, subject to the simultaneous constraints imposed by two models. In all cases considered, the Pareto policy results in substantial gains relative to the effects of the single model policy, when the other model turns out to be closer to the real world. In addition, the losses associated with the formulation of a Pareto policy are small, relative to the effects of the single model policy when that model turns out to represent the real world.

In using the simultaneous optimization algorithm to derive a Pareto optimal policy, the policymaker is free to assign weights to the individual objective functions. In the last section of the paper a method was presented whereby a robust policy is obtained. In this case, the weighting parameter α was selected by solving a minimax problem. The resultant policy was found to be robust in the sense that it obtains a reduction in the objective function cost which is the same (or as close to the same as possible) independent of which of the rival models turns out to represent the real world.

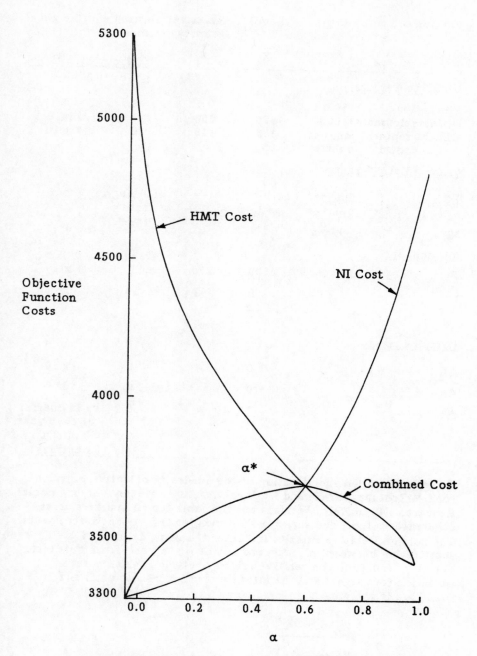

Figure 1: Variation of objective function costs with α

Variables	Units	Level X_i	Relative Priority R_i	Desired Value X^d_i	Weight q_i
Ultimate Targets					
P (Inflation)	% p.a.	13	1	0	1
U (Unemployment)	000s	1900	250	500	$.375 \times 10^{-4}$
CB (Current account)	£m, per quarter	850	125	0	$.12 \times 10^{-3}$
Intermediate Targets					
ΣCB	£m, per quarter	"do-nothing" path	–	"do-nothing" path	$.3 \times 10^{-5}$
$\dot{M}$	% p.a.	11	2.1	5	1
Instruments					
G		6100	200	6000	$.1 \times 10^{-3}$
r		9	1	10	2
t		29	2	30	1
Damping terms					
ΔG		0	–	0	$.1 \times 10^{-3}$
Δr		0	–	0	2
Δt		0	–	0	.05 in quarter 1 of each year 50 in other quarters

Table 1: Detailed specification of the quadratic objective function for HM Treasury (HMT) and National Institute of Economic and Social Research (NI) models. Weights are the same for all quarters unless otherwise stated. The variable X_i stands for targets and instruments. The column Relative Priority indicates the marginal rate of substitution between inflation and any other target. For a quadratic objective function, the relative priority between the numeraire (inflation for targets and the interest rate for instruments) and variable i is given by

$$R_i = \frac{q_n(X_n - X^d_n)}{q_i(X_i - X^d_i)}$$

Given these relative priorities, the weights, q_i, are obtained from the above equations.

COMMON DO-NOTHING

	Year 1	Year 2	Year 3	Year 4	Year 5	Year 6	Year 7	Average
U	1325	1232	1473	2286	2860	3257	3453	2269
Ṗ	8.3	12.8	20.7	14.4	8.6	4.9	5.3	10.7
CB	139	−678	700	2105	1840	1496	660	895
ΣCB	275	−1214	−1731	6617	13123	20240	24396	8815
Ṁ	18.0	15.6	11.8	11.7	7.5	7.5	6.7	11.3
G	6000	6000	6000	6000	6000	6000	6000	6000
t	30	30	30	30	30	30	30	30
r	10	10	10	10	10	10	10	10

Table 2: The common do-nothing simulation run on the two models is generated as follows:

The period covered is 1978(1) – 1984(4). Exogenous variables apart from those used as instruments assume their actual values over the historical period. The instruments are common and are standardised to assume fixed values. The target variables for both models are standardised to the HMT values. This is done as a simple 4-target 4-instrument optimisation problem. The residual variable in the equations for each of the four targets is used as an instrument in the NI model to track the corresponding values of the target variables from the HMT model.

Table 3A

HMT WORLD

	Year 1	Year 2	Year 3	Year 4	Year 5	Average
Policy based on HMT						
U	84	429	145	-235	-614	-38
$\dot{P}$	0.0	-1.1	-3.6	-1.3	3.0	0.6
CB	128	462	-373	-1507	-1506	-559
$\dot{Y}$	-0.7	-3.1	-0.6	2.4	5.1	0.6
$\dot{M}$	-1.6	-6.4	-3.8	4.4	6.0	-0.3
PSBR	-0.4	-0.1	3.1	3.0	1.7	1.5
ER	2.5	11.4	12.3	-2.7	-11.1	2.5
COMP	2.6	11.0	8.0	-9.2	-15.6	-0.6
G	-112	-492	199	433	393	84
t	1.1	-0.6	-5.1	-5.2	-4.9	-2.9
r	1.5	3.9	4.0	0.8	-1.1	1.8
Policy based on NI						
U	89	64	-242	-518	-785	-278
$\dot{P}$	-0.2	-2.1	0.4	3.5	3.0	0.9
CB	181	-354	-812	-463	-477	-385
$\dot{Y}$	-0.9	-0.5	2.3	4.0	5.3	2.0
$\dot{M}$	-6.6	-0.1	6.1	4.4	5.1	1.8
PSBR	0.2	1.1	2.4	0.4	0.5	0.9
ER	10.6	2.9	-7.6	-7.6	-10.6	-2.5
COMP	10.8	1.5	-10.3	-7.9	-7.4	-2.7
G	-62	131	494	396	642	320
t	0.1	-0.4	-2.9	-0.9	-1.3	-1.1
r	5.1	0.6	-2.0	-0.6	-1.5	0.3

Table 3B

NI WORLD

	Year 1	Year 2	Year 3	Year 4	Year 5	Average
Policy based on HMT						
U	56	352	218	51	15	138
$\dot{P}$	0.0	-1.8	-6.2	-5.2	-3.8	3.4
CB	92	890	1045	-439	-964	125
$\dot{Y}$	-0.6	-3.0	-1.0	0.3	0.4	-0.8
$\dot{M}$	-1.0	-8.6	-12.4	-4.4	0.0	-5.3
PSBR	-0.4	-0.6	2.0	2.9	2.6	1.3
ER	0.9	11.5	28.0	35.4	44.4	24.0
COMP	0.7	7.1	13.0	11.7	13.2	9.1
G	-112	-492	199	433	393	84
t	1.1	-0.6	-5.1	-5.2	-4.9	-2.9
r	1.5	3.9	4.0	0.8	-1.1	1.8
Policy based on NI						
U	53	105	-91	-205	-378	-103
$\dot{P}$	-0.8	-3.6	-4.0	0.0	1.6	-1.3
CB	363	864	-223	-1521	-1702	-444
$\dot{Y}$	-0.6	-1.1	1.4	1.7	2.7	0.8
$\dot{M}$	-7.2	-6.4	2.4	2.9	4.5	-0.8
PSBR	-0.2	0.7	2.0	1.2	1.7	1.1
ER	7.0	19.1	19.2	12.7	8.0	13.2
COMP	4.7	9.5	5.6	1.2	-0.2	4.2
G	-62	131	494	396	642	320
t	0.1	-0.4	-2.9	-0.9	-1.3	-1.1
r	5.1	0.6	-2.0	-0.6	-1.5	0.3

Table 3C

HMT WORLD

	Year 1	Year 2	Year 3	Year 4	Year 5	Average
Pareto Optimal Policy ($\alpha = 0.5$)						
U	234	332	−33	−495	−868	−166
$\dot{P}$	−0.3	−1.8	−2.9	1.8	3.5	0.1
CB	223	322	−658	−1207	−1178	−500
$\dot{Y}$	−1.7	−2.4	1.0	4.1	6.2	1.4
$\dot{M}$	−3.1	−5.3	−2.6	3.9	5.8	0.8
PSBR	−0.6	0.2	3.0	2.0	0.7	1.1
ER	4.6	10.5	1.5	−4.8	−11.7	0
COMP	4.6	9.2	−3.4	−9.5	−12.9	−2.4
G	−324	−279	355	550	677	196
t	0.8	0	−5.1	−3.9	−2.3	−2.1
r	2.1	2.9	0.2	0.4	−1.4	0.8
Robust Policy with $\alpha^* = 0.6$						
U	204	353	13	−476	−888	−159
$\dot{P}$	−0.2	−1.7	−3.3	1.6	3.6	0
CB	224	348	−631	−1262	−1261	−516
$\dot{Y}$	−1.6	−2.6	0.6	4.0	6.3	1.4
$\dot{M}$	−3.1	−5.9	1.9	4.0	6.2	0.6
PSBR	−0.6	0.2	3.1	2.2	0.8	1.1
ER	4.8	11.6	2.8	−4.3	−11.9	0.6
COMP	4.8	10.5	−2.1	−9.3	−13.5	−1.9
G	−275	−304	338	581	717	212
t	1.2	0	−4.9	−3.7	−2.3	−2.0
r	2.3	3.4	0.6	0.6	−1.4	1.1

Table 3D

NI WORLD

	Year 1	Year 2	Year 3	Year 4	Year 5	Average
Pareto Optimal Policy ($\alpha = 0.5$)						
U	174	318	97	−157	−313	24
$\dot{P}$	−0.2	−3.0	−5.3	−2.2	0.0	−2.1
CB	222	948	421	−1149	−1505	−213
$\dot{Y}$	−1.6	−2.5	0.3	2.0	2.4	0.1
$\dot{M}$	−2.7	−8.8	−4.3	0.0	3.2	−2.5
PSBR	−0.7	−0.2	2.2	2.3	2.2	1.2
ER	2.5	14.4	22.4	20.8	20.1	16.0
COMP	1.8	8.2	8.6	5.0	4.4	5.6
G	−324	−279	355	550	677	196
t	0.8	0	−5.1	−3.9	−2.3	−2.1
r	2.1	2.9	0.2	0.4	−1.4	0.8
Robust Policy with $\alpha* = 0.6$						
U	150	326	129	−132	−289	37
$\dot{P}$	−0.1	−3.0	−5.8	−3.0	−0.8	−2.5
CB	214	1005	561	−1049	−1428	−139
$\dot{Y}$	−1.4	−2.6	0	1.8	2.3	0
$\dot{M}$	−2.6	−9.6	−5.7	−0.9	2.7	−3.2
PSBR	−0.7	−0.3	2.2	2.5	2.3	1.2
ER	2.4	15.3	25.1	25.2	26.8	19.0
COMP	1.7	8.8	9.9	6.7	6.7	6.8
G	−275	−304	338	581	717	212
t	1.2	0	−4.9	−3.7	−2.3	−2.0
r	2.3	3.4	0.6	0.6	−1.4	1.1

Objective function costs

Policy	Objective function	Horizon	Common "do nothing"	HMT World	NI World
Based on HMT	Basic	5 years	5581	3429(39%)	4746(15%)
Based on NI	"	"	"	5282(5%)	3305(41%)
Pareto optimum with (α=0.5)	"	"	"	3800(32%)	3609(35%)
Pareto optimum with (α = 0.25)	Basic	5 years	5581	4122(26%)	3422(39%)
Pareto optimum with (α = 0.5)	"	"	"	3800(32%)	3609(35%)
Robust i.e. (α* = 0.6)	"	"	"	3720(33%)	3717(33%)
Pareto optimum with (α = 0.75)	"	"	"	3583(36%)	4005(28%)

Table 4: Objective function costs obtained by applying various policies to HMT and NI models. Numbers in parentheses show the cost reduction achieved as a percentage of the common "do-nothing" case.

Iteration	Step size	Gradient	HMT cost	NI cost	Combined cost
Start at NI optimum		71.85	5281.97	3304.78	4293.37

Numerical evaluation of Jacobian matrices for both models

Iteration	Step size	Gradient	HMT cost	NI cost	Combined cost
1	1.0	23.82	3723.28	3908.16	3815.72
2	1.0	5.91	3854.94	3708.53	3781.74
3	1.0	7.97	3838.62	3655.09	3746.86
4	1.0	–	3755.93	3837.83	3796.88
	0.1	–	3828.85	3665.44	3737.14
	0.01	7.75	3837.58	3656.01	3746.80

Numerical re-evaluation of Jacobian matrices for both models

Iteration	Step size	Gradient	HMT cost	NI cost	Combined cost
5	1.0	2.23	3796.57	3612.89	3704.73
6	1.0	–	3814.19	3596.05	3705.11
	0.1	1.73	3798.58	3610.50	3704.54
7	1.0	–	3814.14	3595.32	3704.73
	0.1	1.50	3799.93	3608.90	3704.42**

Numerical re-evaluation of Jacobian matrices to confirm the optimum

Iteration	Step size	Gradient	HMT cost	NI cost	Combined cost
8	1.0	–	3793.17	3630.37	3711.77
	0.1	–	3798.92	3610.54	3704.72
	0.01	–	3799.88	3609.06	3704.47

** Optimum

Table 5: Iteration steps in simultaneous optimisation algorithm.
Basic objective function with 5-year horizon and $\alpha = 0.5$.
Combined cost reduction from "do-nothing" = 34%.

THE FINANCIAL SECTOR OF THE LONDON BUSINESS SCHOOL MODEL

Giles Keating

1. INTRODUCTION

This paper presents a disaggregated financial model, in the spirit of
the proposals of Brainard and Tobin (1968) but ambitious in its
considerable disaggregation among sectors and assets; in its
derivation and estimation of explicit optimising behaviour using a
modified version of Parkin's (1970) mean-variance framework; in its
calculation of explicitly market clearing asset prices by inversion of
demand curves; in its assumption of rational expectations both during
estimation and during forecasts and simulation; in its provision of a
very wide range of government monetary policy instruments,
including money, bills, bonds, foreign currency intervention and
equity sales; in its structural allowance for rationing and resulting
spillover effects, and in its complete integration with the full LBS
macro-econometric model of the UK economy (see Budd et al.
(1984)).
    There have been many attempts to estimate similar systems,
each including only some of the features noted above. For example
Backus et al. (1980) and Green (1984) estimate large-scale
Brainard-Tobin models and make explicit allowance for rationing,
although not based on structural parameters. Spencer and Mowl
(1978) estimate a disaggregated model that is linked to a full
macro-econometric model (that of HM Treasury) and which offers a
wide range of government monetary policy instruments, but is not
based on explicit optimising behaviour. Parkin (1970) derives and
estimates a portfolio choice model based on explicit optimising
behaviour, but covers only a single sector.
    The model reported in this paper relies on four main
foundations. First, the portfolio choice behaviour of private
non-bank domestic and overseas agents is assumed to be based on
optimising behaviour in a modified Parkin-style mean-variance
framework, and the cross-equation restrictions implied by this
framework are imposed during estimation. Second, the government is
assumed to set its monetary policy by choosing supplies of various
financial assets. A wide range of policy regimes is possible. One of
the main cases considered here assumes that short term interest

rates and the supply of bonds are chosen, and the government then supplies the combination of money and bills needed to clear all markets. The third foundation is the behaviour of banks and building societies. In contrast to the non-bank and overseas sectors, no explicit optimising behaviour is derived. However, it is argued that the assumed interest-rate setting is not inconsistent with the action of monopolists maximising profit (or other objectives) subject to the market-clearing short-term rate over which the banks and building societies have no control. The fourth foundation is the derivation of market-clearing asset prices and the assumption of rational expectations. Inverting the demand equations to derive full analytic solutions for the prices is impractical, but I show that instead partially-solved expressions for the asset prices can be derived and then solved numerically, using Gauss-Seidel techniques.

The reported simulation results indicate that under the assumption of rational expectations, the asset prices derived by the model have the conventional characteristics suggested by capital market theory, jumping in response to new information and, in the case of the real exchange rate, overshooting beyond the equilibrium level in reaction to monetary disturbances in line with the model of, for example, Buiter and Miller (1981b).

The layout of this paper is as follows. Section 2 describes the assumed disaggregation among sectors and assets, and outlines the model's structure. Section 3 derives the form of the asset demand functions for domestic non-bank private agents and overseas, and Section 4 presents the estimation results. Section 5 explains the derivation of market-clearing asset prices and presents some simulation results.

2. OUTLINE OF THE MODEL STRUCTURE

The financial model described in this paper assumes that the UK economy is divided into nine sectors. These are: the personal sector; industrial and commercial companies; pension funds and insurance companies; banks; building societies; unit and investment trusts; remaining financial institutions; public sector; and overseas.[1] The financial assets and liabilities available to these sectors are divided into thirteen types: bonds (gilts); equities; Treasury and local authority bills and bank certificates of deposit, hereafter referred to as 'bills';[2] bank time deposits; bank sight deposits; loans for house purchase; other bank loans; notes and coin; National Savings certificates; building society shares; hire purchase loans; foreign currency short-term assets; and foreign currency long-term assets.[3] I assume that not all of these are available to all sectors. The personal sector is assumed to have the widest choice, holding all the assets and liabilities except for bills. Other sectors have more restricted choice, industrial and commercial companies for example selecting from among only nine of the assets and liabilities. Over parts of the estimation period, loan rationing and exchange controls temporarily restricted the available choice of assets for some sectors.

Domestic private non-bank sectors and the overseas sector

There are three domestic private non-bank sectors: industrial and commercial companies; the personal sector (which was aggregated with unit and investment trusts during estimation); and the pension funds plus insurance companies. Each is assumed to make, separately, a portfolio choice among financial assets, subject to a budget constraint. These portfolio choices, the specification of which is described in section 3 and the estimation in section 4, depend on the expected rate of return on all assets. For domestic sectors, the budget constraint equals the sectors' current period income net of expenditure, plus last period's asset and liability holdings, revalued to take account of the current period's market prices. For the overseas sector, the budget constraint equals the previous period's revalued asset holdings minus the balance of payments current account surplus.

Income and expenditure for each sector, and the current account, are determined by the equations in the LBS macro-econometric model. These are described fully in Budd et al. (1984) and are not discussed further in this paper. The current market prices of financial assets are required not only to revalue last period's holdings, but also, together with one-period ahead expectations, to determine the expected rate of return on assets. These prices are determined endogenously within the financial model, as described in section 5.

There are several minor exceptions to the use of the formal portfolio choice model. Holdings of items such as accruals adjustments and trade credit are assumed to remain constant in real terms. A more important exception is the assumption that new issues of equities by industrial and commercial companies can be treated as exogenous. Relaxation of this assumption is the subject of further research. The company sector's budget constraint is adjusted to allow for new issues.

The return on equities is computed by dividing dividend payments, determined elsewhere in the LBS model (see Budd et al. (1984)), by the outstanding value of equities. This does not imply that equity prices in the model are related to earnings per share rather than income. Provided that retained earnings are paid out later (or are invested resulting in improved dividends later), this will be reflected in the current share price when the model is solved under the assumption of rational expectations.

Government policy

There is considerable flexibility in the choice of government policy instruments in the model. Bond, bill and high powered money supply, foreign currency intervention and equity sales are all potential instruments. The government can be assumed to adjust supply of one or more of these assets in order to fix short term interest rates at some target level, and by use of optimal control methods, the exchange rate or bond or equity prices can be targeted. Quantitative control over bank lending, exchange controls, and the effect of income and capital gains tax rates on investments in financial assets can all be examined. In addition, the financial model is linked to the full LBS macroeconometric model, allowing use of fiscal policy instruments.

This paper covers the effect of only a subset of these instruments: bond, bill and high powered money supply, and their use in fixing short term interest rates. The possibility of using the other instruments in the model is not considered here. Corker (1985) discusses the impact of foreign currency intervention in the model; Keating (1985a) examines the effect of issues of equities by the government; and Corker and Holly (1984) show how the exchange rate can be held constant during a temporary rise in UK short term interest rates by use of foreign currency intervention.

The government budget constraint is taken as given from its income and expenditure decisions. This means that three potential monetary instruments (bond, bill and high powered money supply) are reduced to two, because choice of any two determines the third by identity. As an alternative to fixing two quantities, the government can fix one quantity and one interest rate (or even no quantity and two interest rates, although this might lead to problems of price level indeterminacy). The simulation results shown in section 5 consider two cases. In the first case, short term interest rates and bond supply are fixed; in the second, short term interest rates and the bill supply are fixed.

The banks and building societies

The banks raise sterling deposits from, and lend to, persons and companies. (They also operate in foreign currency markets but although their gross transactions in this area are large, they are small in net terms.[4]) The banks are assumed to receive some non-interest-bearing sight deposits and to set the interest rates paid on other deposits, and charged on loans, at given mark-ups above or below the bill market rate. The bill market short-term interest rate is a market-clearing rate, although as noted above it is possible to assume that the government sets this short-term rate by supplying whatever finance the markets demand.

The mark-ups used to determine the deposit and loan rates are set in line with the banks' observed practice over the estimation period. The imposition of mark-ups is not necessarily inconsistent with rational behaviour by the banks. The mark-ups can be interpreted as an approximation to optimal monopolistic price-setting by the banks, on the assumption that they maximise profits subject to the interest rate set by the market-clearing short-term bill market. The banks are assumed to be price-takers in that market, while acting as a monopolist in the markets for other bank deposits and loans.

There is a significant objection to assuming that mark-ups based on past behaviour are consistent with current optimal behaviour. Reserve ratios and quantitative or qualitative controls on bank lending were imposed by government over much of the estimation period. Mark-ups that were optimal in those periods may not be optimal under the current derestricted regime. Without a fully specified model of optimal bank behaviour, it is difficult to respond to this objection, except by using mark-ups based only on the very recent past when deregulation was in operation. Even this would not allow for the effect of other factors that shift the deposit supply and loan demand curves faced by the banks.

The building societies are treated in a similar way to the banks, in that conventional mark-up rules are applied to reflect their past behaviour. This behaviour was presumably optimal, although the objective functions of the societies may include the aim of keeping lending rates down as well as or instead of maximising profits. As for the banks, the usefulness of the past interest rate setting behaviour as a guide to the future is limited by regime changes. The societies appear to have voluntarily imposed loan rationing during much of the estimation period, presumably to hold down mortgage interest rates. This has not occurred since 1981 when the removal of controls on bank lending has led to the entry of the banks into the mortgage market, preventing the societies from imposing mortgage rationing.

3. DERIVATION OF THE ASSET DEMAND EQUATIONS

Brainard and Tobin (1968) noted that when specifying a complete set of all the asset and liability demand equations for an agent, the expected yield of every asset must in general appear in every equation (although some coefficients can be zero), and for each rate of return the coefficients must sum to zero across the asset demands. In addition, the agent's wealth must appear in all asset demands and its coefficient must sum to unity. These requirements are needed to ensure that the budget constraint is always satisfied, and they have been incorporated into all subsequent empirical work. See for example Green (1984), and Backus et al. (1980). Often, this is achieved simply by omitting one equation and deriving it from the others using these restrictions.

Apart from the need to satisfy the accounting identity, no explicit model is used to justify the inclusion of all the returns, and wealth, in the papers referred to above. By contrast Parkin (1970), developing the portfolio choice model of Markowitz (1958), proposed an explicit theoretical justification for the inclusion of all returns, and wealth, in every asset demand equation. The Parkin model imposes all the restrictions suggested by Brainard and Tobin, plus symmetry and zero sum of coefficients on all the yields in each equation.

The asset (and liability) demand equations derived below are based on a modified form of Parkin's model. I impose further restrictions and extend the model to allow for adjustment costs. These changes are explained below.

Parkin assumes that agents have an exponential utility function, whose argument is the return on their portfolio. Assuming also that the return is normally distributed, the objective function of agents who maximise expected utility can be shown to be:

$$\text{Max} \quad Y'_t X_t - \beta_{/2} X'_t \Sigma X_t \qquad (3.1)$$

subject to $i' X_t = W_t$

Y_t is an n x 1 vector of expected asset yields (coupon plus anticipated capital gain or loss); X_t an n x 1 vector of asset and liability holdings at real market value (i.e. at current realisable value divided by some general price index such as the GDP deflator); β is a scalar coefficient of risk aversion; Σ is an n x n covariance matrix for the asset returns; i is a conformable unit vector and W_t, a scalar, is the agent's real wealth. Note that liabilities enter X_t with a negative sign.

The papers cited at the start of this section contain estimated equations for several non-risky assets, as part of a single agent's portfolio decision. Such equations cannot be derived directly from the Parkin mean-variance model, which implies that all non-risky assets are regarded as perfect substitutes and must all have the same yield. The model must be adapted to explain choice among several non-risky assets. This is done by re-interpreting Σ as the sum of two matrices. The first is a covariance matrix in which some rows and columns contain only zeros. The second matrix has entries representing the effect of other factors causing declining marginal utility from asset holdings. The matrix Σ is assumed to be positive definite, for domestic agents. A different assumption, explained at the end of this section, is made for overseas agents.

On this interpretation of Σ, the objective function (3.1) cannot be derived from an exponential utility function with only total portfolio return as its argument. Instead it must be derived from an extended utility function that also includes explicit allowance for utility from asset holding. This derivation is not shown here.

In addition to modifying the Parkin model by re-interpreting Σ, I also extend the objective function (3.1) to allow for costs of adjustment, implying a further modification to the underlying utility function. I assume that each period's decision can be treated separately. The implications of allowing instead for full intertemporal optimisation are discussed in section 4 below. This gives:

$$\underset{X_t}{\text{Max}} \; Y'_t X_t - \beta_{/2} X' \Sigma X_t - [X_t - P_t P_{t-1}^{-1} X_{t-1}]' \, \omega_{/2} [X_t - P_t P_{t-1}^{-1} X_{t-1}] \quad (3.2)$$

subject to $i'X_t = W_t$

where P_t is an n x n matrix with real asset prices (i.e. the asset prices divided by a general price index) on its diagonal and zeros elsewhere, and ω is an n x n matrix measuring costs of adjustment. Elements of ω are assumed to be non-negative. The term

$$[X_t - P_t P_{t-1}^{-1} X_{t-1}]$$

is thus an n x 1 vector of net purchases or net sales of assets, at current real market values. For the moment, I assume that there is no rationing of asset demands.

To find the optimum solution to (3.2), form the Lagrangian

$$L = Y_t X_t - \beta_{/2} X'_t \Sigma X_t -$$

$$[X_t - P_t P_{t-1}^{-1} X_{t-1}]' \omega_{/2} [X_t - P_t P_{t-1}^{-1} X_{t-1}] - \lambda(W_t - i'X_t) \quad (3.3)$$

where λ is a Lagrange multiplier. The matrix $\beta\Sigma + \omega$ is positive definite, given the assumptions that, for all domestic agents, Σ is positive definite and that all elements of ω are non-negative. It follows that the first order conditions are necessary and sufficient for an optimum solution to (3.3). This applies to domestic sectors. The case of overseas agents is discussed at the end of this section. The first order conditions, for domestic agents, are:

$$\frac{\partial L}{\partial X_t} = Y_t - \beta\Sigma X_t - \omega [X_t - P_t P_{t-1}^{-1} X_{t-1}] + \lambda i = 0 \quad (3.4)$$

$$\frac{\partial L}{\partial \lambda} = i' X_t - W_t = 0$$

These can be written:

$$\begin{bmatrix} \beta\Sigma+\omega & i \\ i' & 0 \end{bmatrix} \begin{bmatrix} X_t \\ -\lambda \end{bmatrix} = \begin{bmatrix} I & 0 & \omega P_t P_{t-1}^{-1} \\ 0 & 1 & 0 \end{bmatrix} \begin{bmatrix} Y_t \\ W_t \\ X_{t-1} \end{bmatrix} \quad (3.5)$$

The inverse of the left hand side matrix is

$$\begin{bmatrix} A & b \\ b' & d \end{bmatrix}$$

where $\quad \Omega = \beta\Sigma + \omega$

$$\mu = i'\Omega^{-1}i$$

$$b = \Omega^{-1}i/\mu$$

$$d = -1/\mu$$

$$A = \Omega^{-1}(I - ib')$$

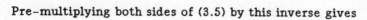

Pre-multiplying both sides of (3.5) by this inverse gives

$$X_t = AY_t + bW_t + A\omega P_t P_{t-1}^{-1} X_{t-1} \tag{3.6}$$

This is the form of the asset demand equations obtained by Parkin, augmented by the term in X_{t-1}. The matrix A gives the coefficients on the rates of return Y_t. It satisfies the Brainard-Tobin constraints, having a zero sum across assets for the coefficients on any rate of return. It also has the additional restrictions, noted by Parkin, of symmetry and zero sum across its rows.

Because of the constraints, A is singular. Hence it is not possible to use (3.6) to obtain an expression for rates of return Y_t in terms of asset demands X_t, by pre-multiplying by the inverse of A. Instead it is necessary to partition A to obtain a non-singular submatrix. See Green and Keating (1985).

The asset demand equations estimated in this paper are derived from (3.6) by assuming that Σ and ω are diagonal. This assumption means that agents regard asset return covariances (plus off-diagonal terms representing declining marginal utility) as negligible, and also that costs of adjustment are independent among assets. This is an extreme assumption, and it was adopted in order to achieve several important objectives:

(i) Parsimony during estimation. Without these extra restrictions (but assuming that ω is symmetric), there would be almost 160 structural parameters for the personal sector[5] and also large numbers for the other sectors;

(ii) Parsimony when the model is used for forecasting. Since the estimates from all sectors are to be combined in a complete market-clearing model of the financial system, which is in turn embedded in a complete macro-model of the UK economy, it was important that the system be kept relatively simple. Even with the assumption of diagonal Σ and ω, the market-clearing asset price equations take up several hundred lines of computer coding;

(iii) Allowance for rationing and resulting spillover effects explicitly in terms of the underlying structural parameters of the model. Rationing was caused by institutional controls, both on investment abroad and on bank and building society lending over much of the estimation period. The financial models of Backus et al. (1980) and Green (1984) also allow for rationing by imposing the constraint that spillover effects sum to zero, but in the model presented here the sum of the spillovers is set to zero automatically by the structure of the system, as described below.

Using the assumption that Σ and ω are diagonal, it is possible to obtain a very simple form for the asset demand equations. Continuing to assume that there is no rationing, (3.6) can be re-arranged as:

$$X_t = \begin{bmatrix} L_1 & & 0 \\ & L_2 & \\ & & \ddots \\ 0 & & \end{bmatrix} (Y_t - i\underline{y}_t + \omega P_t P_{t-1}^{-1} X_{t-1} - \underline{x}_{t-1}$$

$$+ \begin{bmatrix} L_1 \\ L_2 \\ \vdots \\ \vdots \end{bmatrix} W_t/\mu \qquad (3.7)$$

where using j as an index across assets, L_j is a scalar and is the jth diagonal element of the inverse of Ω (i.e. of the inverse of $\beta\Sigma + \omega$). Under the assumption of diagonal Σ and ω, this gives:

$$\mu = \sum_j L_j$$

The item $\underline{y}_t$ is a weighted average of the rates of return:

$$\underline{y}_t = \sum_j L_j y_{jt}/\mu$$

where y_{jt} is the return on the jth asset.

Analogously, $\underline{x}_{t-1}$ is a weighted average of last period's asset holdings:

$$\underline{x}_{t-1} = \sum_j [L_j \omega_j x_{jt-1} p_{jt}/p_{jt-1}]/\mu$$

where ω_j and p_{jt} refer to the jth diagonal element of the matrices ω and P_t respectively, and x_{jt-1} refers to the jth element of X_{t-1}. From expression 3.7, the demand for the jth asset x_{jt} can be written:

$$x_{jt} = L_j [y_{jt} - \underline{y}_t + (\omega_j p_{jt}/p_{jt-1})x_{jt-1} - \underline{x}_{t-1} + W_t/\mu] \qquad (3.8)$$

Hence the demand for each asset depends on the difference between the return on that asset and the weighted average return; on the difference, allowing for adjustment costs, between the previous period's holding of that asset and the weighted average asset holding last period; and on the budget constraint.

Rationing

During the estimation period, exchange controls were in force up to 1979, preventing domestic agents from freely buying overseas assets. In addition, institutional controls on bank and building society lending restricted personal, and in some cases company, borrowing. The periods covered by exchange control are known, but the periods in which lending was rationed are not known with certainty. I obtained information about length of mortgage queues from a major building society. Combining this with the known periods of Bank of England restrictions on bank lending and changes in hire purchase restrictions, I was able to construct time series for periods of loan rationing. Mortgages, hire purchase and other bank loans were treated separately and were not necessarily all subject to rationing at the same time. These series were taken as exogenous and no attempt was made to determine during estimation which periods were subject to rationing.

On the assumption that periods of rationing are known, and that rationing is either 'on' or 'off', it is possible to write the agents' decision during periods of rationing as a maximisation subject to equality, rather than inequality, constraints, and to treat their decision in other periods as completely unconstrained (apart from the need to satisfy the budget constraint). Thus in non-rationed periods, demands are obtained by differentiating (3.3), while under rationing the following Lagrangian is used:

$$L^* =$$

$$Y'_t X_t - \beta_{/2} X'_t \Sigma X_t - [X_t - P_t P_{t-1}^{-1} X_{t-1}]' \omega_{/2} [X_t - P_t P_{t-1}^{-1} X_{t-1}]$$

$$- \lambda(W_t - i'X_t) - \Delta(X_{1t} - X_1)$$

where the first m assets are assumed to be rationed; X_{1t} is an m x 1 vector representing the first m elements of X_t; X_1 is an m x 1 vector giving the levels at which the rationed assets are to be held, and is assumed to be exogenously imposed on the agents; and Δ is an m x 1 vector of Lagrange multipliers.

Analogous to the non-rationed case, the first order conditions are obtained and can be arranged as follows (the conditions derived by differentiating with respect to X_{1t} define optimal values of Δ and are not required):

$$\begin{bmatrix} \beta\Sigma_{22} + \omega_{22} & i \\ i' & 0 \end{bmatrix} \begin{bmatrix} X_{2t} \\ -\lambda \end{bmatrix} =$$

$$\begin{bmatrix} I & 0 & \omega_{22}P_{2t}P_{2t-1}^{-1} \\ & & \\ 0 & 1 & 0 \end{bmatrix} \begin{bmatrix} Y_{2t} - X'_1(\beta\Sigma_{12} + \omega_{12}) \\ + P_{1t}P_{1t-1}^{-1}X'_{1t-1}\omega_{12} \\ W_t - i'X_1 \\ X_{2t-1} \end{bmatrix} \qquad (3.9)$$

where X_{2t} is an (n-m) x 1 vector of the last n-m elements of X_t; Σ_{22}, ω_{22} are the bottom right submatrices of Σ and ω respectively, partitioned conformably with X_{2t}; conformable unit vectors are represented by i; P_{1t} and P_{2t}, and Y_{2t}, are the conformable partitions of P_t and Y_t respectively; and Σ_{12} and ω_{12} are conformable off diagonal submatrices of Σ and ω respectively. The inverse of the left-hand matrix in (3.9) can easily be obtained in an analogous way to the inverse obtained for (3.5) above. The resulting expression for the asset demands X_{2t} is:

$$X_{2t} = A_{22}[Y_{2t} - X'_1(\beta\Sigma_{12} + \omega_{12}) + P_{1t}P_{1t-1}^{-1}X'_{1t-1}\omega_{12}]$$

$$+ b_2(W_t - i'X_1) + A_{22}\omega_{22}P_{2t}P_{2t-1}^{-1}X_{2t-1} \qquad (3.10)$$

where
$$\Omega_{22} = \beta\Sigma_{22} + \omega_{22}$$

$$\mu_{22} = i'\Omega_{22}^{-1}i$$

$$b_2 = \Omega_{22}^{-1}i/\mu_{22}$$

$$A_{22} = \Omega_{22}^{-1}(I - ib'_2)$$

This expression is valid for periods when rationing is in operation. However, during some periods foreign assets and all loans were rationed, whereas during others only some loans were rationed or only foreign assets were rationed, and for a few periods there was no rationing at all. Thus the two blocks into which X_t must be partitioned vary from one period to another. To take account of this during estimation would be extremely difficult if ω and Ω were not diagonal. This is because (3.6), or different versions of (3.10), would have to be used in different periods, depending on which assets were rationed and all parameter restrictions would have to be carried from one form of equation to another. This was not attempted, and instead, as noted above, it was assumed that Σ and ω were diagonal. This simplifies the problem considerably. Using steps analogous to (3.7) and (3.8) above, these assumptions imply that the individual asset demands corresponding to (3.10) are:

$$x_{jt} = L_j[y_{jt} - \underline{y}^*_t + (\omega_j p_{jt}/p_{jt-1})x_{jt-1} - \underline{x}^*_{t-1} + W^*_t/\mu^*] \qquad (3.11)$$

where $\underline{y}^*_t$ and $\underline{x}^*_{t-1}$ are weighted averages of returns and lagged asset holdings respectively, computed in the same was as $\underline{y}_t$ and $\underline{x}_{t-1}$ except that only non-rationed assets are included. If s_j takes the value unity for non-rationed assets and zero for rationed assets:

$$\underline{y}^*_t = \sum_j s_j L_j y_j/\mu^*$$

$$\underline{x}^*_{t-1} = \sum_j s_j L_j x_{jt-1}/\mu^*$$

μ^* is the sum of the L_j's that correspond to non-rationed assets:

$$\mu^* = \sum_j s_j L_j$$

and W^*_t is the budget constraint W_t, minus the exogenously-imposed holdings of rationed assets:

$$W^*_t = W_t - \sum_j (1 - s_j) X_{jt}$$

where X_{jt} are the imposed holdings.

The expression (3.11) incorporates spillover effects. By construction, the sum of the spillovers on to non-rationed assets (i.e. the difference between 3.8 and 3.11) plus the sum of the difference between unconstrained and imposed holdings of rationed assets (3.8 minus the X_{jt}) is zero. To see this, notice that (3.8) was constructed to give asset demands that sum to the budget constraint W_t, while (3.11) is constructed to give demands that add up to the budget constraint net of the imposed holdings of rationed assets.

The expression (3.11) is valid for all periods, whatever the combination of rationed and non-rationed assets, and it also covers periods when no rationing occurs. This was the form of the equations used for estimation for all the domestic private non-bank sectors. Since parameter restrictions across the demand equations are implied by (3.11), some form of systems estimator must be used. See section 4.

The overseas sector

Overseas agents, like domestic agents, are assumed to have an objective function of the form (3.2), and the matrices Σ and ω are again assumed to be diagonal. In contrast to domestic agents, the overseas sector is assumed not to be subject to rationing. It is also assumed to regard foreign currency short term assets as riskless, with no decline in marginal utility as holdings rise and no transactions costs. Hence the corresponding row and column in ω and Σ contain only zeros although the remaining $n - 1 \times n - 1$ submatrix of Σ is assumed to be non-singular. The first order conditions obtained from (3.2) are therefore different from those shown earlier in this section. They are set out in Parkin (1970), under the heading 'no borrowing uncertainty', and I do not reproduce them here. Allowing for costs of adjustment, and using the assumption that Σ and ω are diagonal, gives:

$$x_{jt} = L_j^{**} \, (y_{jt} - y_{nt} + (\omega_j \, p_{jt}/p_{jt-1}) x_{jt-1}) \quad j = 1, 2, \ldots n - 1$$

$$x_{nt} = W_t - \sum_{j=1}^{n-1} x_{jt} \tag{3.12}$$

where foreign currency short term assets are the nth asset; and L_j^{**} is the jth diagonal element of the inverse of the top $n - 1 \times n - 1$ non-singular submatrix of $\beta\Sigma + \omega$. Other notation is as before, but the returns are all denominated in foreign currency so an expected depreciation of sterling depresses the overseas agents' perceived yield on sterling assets. The overseas sector demand equations were estimated in the form (3.12). Note that in contrast to (3.11), no cross equation parameter restrictions are implied, so single equation estimators can be used.

The asset yields

The above discussion has treated the expected yield or rate of return on each asset as a single item, y_{jt}. For estimation and model simulation, this was treated as three separate components: a coupon; an expected capital gain or loss; and a constant term representing utility from asset holdings. Both coupon and capital gain were multiplied by the appropriate tax rate:

$$y_{jt} = (1-t_{Ijt})r_{jt}/p_{jt} + (1-t_{Gjt})[(_t p_{jt+1}/p_{jt}) - 1] + C_j \tag{3.13}$$

where t_{Ijt} is the tax rate on income for this asset; t_{Gjt} is the tax rate on capital gains; r_{jt} is the real coupon or real interest received as a percentage, at a quarterly rate, of the nominal (not market) value of a unit holding of the asset; $_t p_{jt+1}$ is a one-period ahead price expectation and C_j is a constant measuring utility per unit of real asset holding. The tax rates vary from one sector to another.

4. ESTIMATION METHOD AND RESULTS

This section describes the estimation of the asset demand equations derived in the previous section. These are given by (3.11) for domestic sectors and (3.12) for the overseas sector. For estimation I assume that agents have rational expectations.[6]

The form of equation (3.11) requires cross-equation restrictions between the various asset and liability demands for each sector. Fully efficient estimation would involve use of a non-linear system method which was not possible on the available software.[7] Instead an iterative method was used, making use of the available single-equation estimators.

To start the iterative procedure some initial, statistically consistent parameter estimates were needed. These were found by estimating the following expression, which is obtained by subtracting the equation for x_{kt}, multiplied by L_j/L_k, from the equation for x_{jt}:[8]

$$x_{jt} = L_j[y_{jt} - y_{kt} + \omega_j(p_{jt}/p_{jt-1})x_{jt-1} - \omega_k(p_{kt}/p_{kt-1})x_{kt-1} + x_{kt}/L_k] \quad (4.1)$$

If there are n asset equations for a sector, then there are $n(n-1)$ expressions of this type for that sector. This means that for each parameter (except the constants) there are $2(n-1)$ different initial estimates. These initial estimates are statistically consistent, provided they are estimated using instrumental variables, but do not conform to the cross-equation restrictions.

Having obtained these initial estimates, each equation of the form (3.11) was estimated using instrumental variables for $j = 1 \ldots n$, holding all parameters at the initial estimates except for those subscripted j. The results were used to replace the initial estimates and the equations were re-estimated. This iterative procedure continued until convergence, defined by the residual sum of squares changing at a low rate between one iteration and the next. The estimates in any iteration are statistically consistent but the cross-equation restrictions are satisfied only when the estimation procedure has converged. Equations for assets subject to rationing were estimated using weighted least squares, with zero weights during periods of rationing and unit weights at other times. The adjusted budget constraint W^*_t, the average return $\underline{y}^*_t$, the average lagged asset holding $\underline{x}^*_{t-1}$ and the parameter sum μ^* are all affected by the presence or lack of rationing. This gives the spillover effects on to non-rationed assets noted in section 3. The assets subject to rationing are house purchase loans, bank loans, hire purchase loans and foreign currency assets.

For the model as a whole, interest rates and asset prices are assumed to be determined endogenously; also, outturn capital gains have to be used in place of unobservable expected. This means that all the interest rates, asset prices and expected capital gains included in the Y_t are corrrelated with the errors on all the asset

demand equations in the system and must be instrumented. Predetermined variables include previous period's interest rates, foreign
rates, and lagged asset holdings (not adjusted for price changes).

We now describe the estimation results for each of the domestic
sectors and for the overseas sector. In each table the estimates in
the first column are of the L_j of equation (3.11) or (3.12), the second
column contains estimates of the ω_j times L_j, while the third column
(headed 'constant') gives estimates of the C_j times the L_j.

Personal Sector

The results for this sector are shown in Table 1. After 10 iterations
the rate of decline of the residual sum of squares had fallen to about
6 per cent between iterations, compared to almost 50 per cent
between the first two iterations. In addition, the largest change
between iterations for any of the parameter estimates had fallen to
about half of one measured standard error and most of the estimates
were changing by rather less, and so it was assumed that the
estimates had converged. Certain parameters were set to zero at the
start of the estimation process. These were the coefficients on the
previous period's notes and coin and sight deposit holdings (on the
assumption that costs of adjustment for these are negligible) and the
constant terms for savings certificates and for risky assets (on the
assumption that no utility is received from transactions benefits for
these assets). These restrictions were not tested. Seven other
parameters were imposed during the estimation process, because the
estimates had started to converge on values outside the ranges
suggested by theory. The validity of these restrictions was tested by
an LR test conditional on the previous iteration's values being at the
restricted figures. The LR statistic (Tlog (restricted residual sum of
squares/unrestricted residual sum of squares)) was 5.99; with seven
degrees of freedom this implies that the restrictions are not rejected
at a 5 per cent confidence level. However, the power of this test is
reduced by its conditioning on the previous period's restricted values.

The standard errors reported in Table 1 are also conditioned on
the parameter estimates from the previous iterations.

The parameter estimates were not subjected to forecast tests.
However, the dynamic properties of the whole LBS model, including
the parameters described here, were studied by simulation. Some of
these simulations are described in the following section.

Industrial and commercial companies' (ICC) sector

In contrast to the personal sector estimates, the ICC sector
estimates converged after only four iterations. The rate of change in
the residual sum of squares had then fallen to just over 1 per cent
between iterations. The results are shown in Table 2.

There were nine assets in the ICC sector portfolio instead of
twelve for the personal sector and only three of those assets (bank
loans, foreign currency short term assets and foreign currency

Table 1. Personal sector (plus unit and investment trusts) – estimated results

	Relative return and budget constraint	Lagged dependent variable	Constant	Equation S.E.	Durbin–Watson or Durbin's h	Estimation period
	L_j	$L_j \omega_j$	$L_j C_j$			
Equities	4.07 (3.9)	0.97 (.03)	–	115.4	0.71 (h)	6903–8204
Gilts	2.28 (.41)	0.95 (imposed)	–	31.7	1.96 (w)	6903–8204
Bank loans	1.43 (.93)	0.96 (imposed)	-38.5 (8.2)	30.6*	1.04 (w)*	6903–8204 with zero weights on some periods
Time deposits	0.26 (.74)	0.95 (imposed)	40.3 (7.3)	20.4*	1.04 (w)*	6903–8204
Overseas 'shorts'	0.66 (.22)	0.84 (.09)	–	2.52	-1.89 (h)	7904–8204
Overseas securities	2.42 (.79)	0.94 (.05)	–	10.8	-1.33 (h)	7904–8204
Sight deposits	2.59 (1.87)	–	383.4 (15.5)	36.5	0.94 (w)	6903–8204
Notes and coin	3.53 (1.65)	–	182.0 (13.7)	32.2	1.68 (w)	6903–8204
Savings certificates	0.76 (.10)	0.95 (imposed)	–	7.74	1.38 (w)	6903–8204
Building Society shares	0.50 (imposed)	0.987 (.018)	16.94 (17.6)	16.3	4.32 (h)	6903–8204
Hire purchase	1.00 (imposed)	0.35 (.14)	-64.5 (11.8)	18.0*	2.26 (w)*	6903–8204 with zero weights on many periods
Mortgages	4.41 (1.34)	0.974 (.009)	-100 (imposed)	21.6*	0.36 (w)*	6903–8204 with zero weights on some periods

(standard errors in brackets)   * statistic based incorrectly on all observations including those with zero weight

Table 2. Company (ICC) sector-estimated results

| | Coefficient on: | | | | | |
	Relative return and budget constraint	Lagged dependent variable	Constant	Equation S.E.	Durbin-Watson or Durbin's h	Estimation period
	L_j	$L_j \omega_j$	$L_j C_j$			
Equities	0.870 (1.455)	0.989 (.041)	–	943.9	–1.347 (h)	7504–8204
Gilts	0.127 (.204)	0.977 (.081)	–	124.3	–2.668 (h)	7504–8204
Bank loans	1.549 (1.429)	0.977 (.087)	–2661.0 (3145)	1436	0.425 (h)	7504–8204 with zero weights on some periods
Wholesale deposits	1.783 (.603)	–	958.1 (250.3)	533.7	0.837 (w)	7504–8204
Time deposits	1.349 (.698)	0.774 (.089)	2024.2 (811.4)	529.5	0.979 (h)	7504–8204
Overseas 'shorts'	0.626 (1.100)	0.661 (.248)	–1407.9 (1030.9)	370.8	4.064 (h)	7904–8204
Overseas securities	2.817 (1.449)	0.935 (.127)	–	972.9	–0.990 (h)	7904–8204
Sight deposits	3.23 (0.926)	–	3967.3 (366.5)	549.8	1.372 (w)	7504–8204
Notes and coin	1.494 (.453)	–	1562.9 (179.3)	268.9	1.452 (w)	7504–8204

(standard errors in brackets)

Table 3. Pension funds and insurance companies – estimated results

	Coefficient on:					
	Relative return and budget constraint	Lagged dependent variable	Constant	Equation S.E.	Durbin-Watson or Durbin's h	Estimation period
	L_j	$L_j\omega_j$	L_jC_j			
Equities	7795.1 (885.5)	0.517 (.058)	–	293805	1.062 (h)	7503–8204
Gilts	3530.0 (105.9)	0.700 (imposed)	–	522190	1.472 (w)	7503–8204
Wholesale deposits	558.2 (45.8)	–	–	224094	0.139 (w)	7503–8204
Time deposits	257.2 (153.2)	0.531 (.139)	116958 (214956)	59394	3.110 (h)	7601–8204
Overseas 'shorts'	98.4 (6.80)	–	–	23083	0.925 (w)	7904–8204
Overseas securities	1349.2 (100.2)	0.650 (imposed)	–	341900	0.739 (w)	7904–8204

(standard errors in brackets)

Table 4. Overseas sector – estimated results

	Coefficient on: Relative return and budget constraint L^{**}_j	Lagged dependent variable $L^{**}\omega_j$	Constant $L^{**}_j C_j$	Equation S.E.	Durbin-Watson or Durbin's h	Estimation period
Equities	0.106 (.007)	0.969 (.036)	0.724 (.427)	.294	-0.172 (h)	6903-8204
Gilts	0.660 (.025)	0.725 (.152)	2.652 (1.34)	.616	0.597 (h)	7801-8204
Bank loans	0.390 (.317)	0.900 (imposed)	-3.211 (.477)	.964	1.62 (w)	7904-8204
Wholesale deposits	0.123 (.093)	–	1.267 (.062)	.228	1.99 (w)	7704-8204
Time deposits	0.144 (.290)	0.973 (.056)	2.03 (1.07)	.679	-0.537 (h)	7904-8204

(standard errors in brackets)

securities) were subject to rationing. As for the personal sector estimates, the constant terms on three of the risky assets (equities, gilts and overseas securities) were set to zero, as were the coefficients on lagged dependent variables for wholesale deposits, sight deposits and notes and coin. The constant term for foreign currency short term assets was not set to zero because holdings of this item are always negative. No further restrictions were imposed during estimation.

Pension funds and insurance companies

As for the other domestic sectors, the parameters for this sector were estimated using the iterative method described above. This method was assumed to have converged after seven iterations, when the residual sum of squares was falling by about 2 ½ per cent between iterations. In contrast to the company and personal sectors, the pension fund and insurance company sector was assumed to choose among only six assets and only two of these - foreign currency short-term assets and foreign currency securities - were subject to rationing during the estimation period.

The results are shown in Table 3. Constant terms for all assets except time deposits (which unlike the other assets yields transactions benefits) were set to zero before estimation began, as were the coefficients on lagged variables in the overseas short-term assets and wholesale deposit equations. Coefficients on two other lagged dependent variables - for gilts and overseas securities - were imposed during the estimation process. An LR test rejected these two restrictions marginally at the 1 per cent confidence level. The estimates for the equities equation have low measured standard errors and the Durbin's h statistic shows little evidence of misspecification. While the measured standard errors on the other equations are generally low, the Durbin-Watson and Durbin's h statistics suggest that some degree of misspecification may be present.

Overseas sector

As noted above, the form of the asset demand equations used for the overseas sector is (3.12) which differs from the form (3.11) used for the domestic sectors because it is assumed that foreign currency short-term assets have no non-zero entry in the covariance or cost of adjustment matrices for this sector. As a result the iterative estimation procedure used for the domestic sectors was unnecessary and straightforward 2SLS was used.

The results are shown in Table 4. One coefficient - on the laggged dependent variable for wholesale deposits - was set to zero before estimation on the assumption that there is no cost to changing holdings of this item. One other coefficient, on the lagged dependent variable in the equation for bank borrowing, was imposed because unrestricted estimates were above the range suggested by theory. This restriction was not rejected at a 1 per cent confidence level.

Unfortunately most of the estimation periods for this sector are short, due to data difficulties in the case of gilts and because exchange control prior to end-1979 restricted UK banks' business with the overseas sector. There is little evidence of misspecification from the Durbin-Watson and Durbin's h statistics and low standard errors for most coefficients.

Interpretation of results

The Durbin-Watson or Durbin's h statistics appear to provide evidence of misspecification for some of the domestic asset demands. An example is the very low Durbin-Watson statistic recorded for personal sector sight deposits. However, these statistics should in some cases be corrected to allow for the use of zero weights on periods subject to rationing. This was not possible on the available software and the results may therefore be biased towards indicating misspecification. A firm conclusion must await re-estimation on alternative software, but meanwhile it is useful to consider some of the more likely sources of misspecification.

The estimates are based on a model structure that imposes many restrictions and which were not tested. One example is the assumption that agents neglect off-diagonal elements in the Σ and ω matrices. This cannot be relaxed without extending the model to the full version proposed by Parkin, and the arguments against this were discussed in section 3. The assumption that agents treat each period separately appears to be easier to relax. Blanchard and Kahn (1980) have shown that full intertemporal optimisation can often be modelled with the introduction of only one extra parameter (a discount rate). However, I will demonstrate that the Blanchard and Kahn procedure cannot be applied in this case.

For full intertemporal optimisation, the single-period objective function (3.2) is replaced by:

$$\text{Max}_X \sum_{i=0}^{\infty} h^i \, [Y'_{t+i} X_{t+i} - \beta/2 \, X'_{t+i} \, \Sigma \, X_{t+i}$$

$$-(X_{t+i} - P_{t+i} P^{-1}_{t+i-1} X_{t+i-1})' \, \omega/2 \, (X_{t+i} - P^{-1}_{t+i} P_{t+i-1} X_{t+i-1})$$

subject to $W_{t+i} = i' \, X_{t+i}$ all i \hfill (4.2)

To solve this, form a Lagrangian and derive the first order conditions as for the single-period case. For the current period, these conditions can be written:

$$\begin{bmatrix} \beta\Sigma + \omega + hP_{t+1} P_t^{-1} \omega P_{t+1} P_t^{-1} & i \\ i' & 0 \end{bmatrix} \begin{bmatrix} X_t \\ -\lambda \end{bmatrix} =$$

$$\begin{bmatrix} I & 0 & \omega P_t P_{t-1}^{-1} & h P_{t+1} P_t^{-1} \omega \\ 0 & 1 & 0 & 0 \end{bmatrix} \begin{bmatrix} Y_t \\ W_t \\ X_{t-1} \\ X_{t+1} \end{bmatrix}$$

(4.3)

Pre-multiplying by the inverse of the left-hand side matrix and then imposing the assumption that Σ and ω are diagonal gives (analogous to (3.8)):

$$x_{jt} = \tilde{L}_{jt} \, [y_{jt} - \tilde{y}_t + (\omega_j \, p_{jt}/p_{jt-1})x_{jt-1} - \tilde{\underline{x}}_{t-1} +$$

$$h \, (p_{jt+1}/p_{jt})x_{jt+1} - h \, \tilde{\underline{x}}_{t+1} + W_t/\tilde{\mu}$$

(4.4)

where $\tilde{L}_{jt}$ is the jth diagonal element of the inverse of:

$$(\beta\Sigma + \omega + h P_{t+1} P_t^{-1} \omega \, P_{t+1} P_t^{-1})$$

and where $\tilde{\mu}$, $\tilde{y}_t$ and $\tilde{\underline{x}}_{t-1}$ are defined as μ, $\underline{y}_t$ and $\underline{x}_{t-1}$ respectively except that the $\tilde{L}_{jt}$ replace the $\tilde{L}_j$; and $\tilde{\underline{x}}_{t+1}$ is defined as $\tilde{\underline{x}}_{jt-1}$ with the x_{jt+1} replacing the x_{jt-1}.

The expression (4.4) differs from (3.8) in including the forward-looking decision variables x_{jt+1} and in its use of the $\tilde{L}_{jt}$ rather than L_j. This suggests that if agents do carry out full intertemporal optimisation, then the estimated results reported above will be misspecified due to the omission of the forward-looking terms, and also by use of the constant L_j rather than the time-varying $\tilde{L}_{jt}$. The inclusion of the forward-looking terms can in principle be dealt with by solving (4.4) forward recursively, to give x_{jt} as a function of expectations of all future exogenous variables. This procedure usually gives coefficients that follow a regular, geometrically declining pattern. See Blanchard and Kahn (1980). However, that result is not obtained in this case, because the derivation of the Blanchard and Kahn form requires that the matrix linking the forward-looking and current period variables be constant. In this case, the $\tilde{L}_{jt}$ are functions of the real asset prices and those prices also appear explicitly in (4.4), so the Blanchard and Kahn equations cannot be derived. Nor is it possible to use the result of Mishkin (1980) to argue that asset prices follow a random walk and that agents will expect them to be constant, because Begg (1984) has shown that this result is not in general valid.

An alternative approach would be to estimate the Euler equations (4.4) directly, replacing the forward-looking terms by their outturn values and using instrumental variables. Allowance would still have to be made for the inclusion of real asset prices in the $\widetilde{L}_{jt}$.

There are other possible causes of misspecification, which can be dealt with easily by simple extensions to the model. Seasonal dummies were excluded, on the grounds that all seasonal factors would be captured in the pattern of wealth. This was an extreme assumption and introduction of seasonal dummies might eliminate some of the observed autocorrelation. No allowance was made for the impact of technical change on the pattern of financial transactions, in particular the falling use of notes and coin. The demand for mortgage loans is likely to be related to expectations of house prices. This could be allowed for by introducing demand for housing as a further asset.

The seasonal dummies, a variable allowing for technical change, and other extra explanatory variables can be introduced into the model by adding a vector of exogenous variables (times a coefficient vector) to the expression for y_{jt} given at (3.13). The inclusion of an exogenous variable in any one asset demand equation will automatically affect all the others via the term y^*_t in (3.11).

5.   DERIVATION OF MARKET-CLEARING PRICES AND SIMULATION PROPERTIES OF THE MODEL

This section derives the market-clearing asset prices and then describes some simulation results from the financial model combined with the full LBS macro-econometric model of the UK.

The market-clearing asset prices are derived by summing the asset demands across all sectors and adding any exogenous asset supply such as government bond sales or foreign currency intervention. This sum is set to zero and re-arranged to give the asset prices. To derive the asset prices analytically, allowance must be made for the singularity of the matrix of coefficients in the asset demand functions (matrix A in equation (3.6), for example). This matrix, after aggregation across sectors, must be partitioned to give a non-singular submatrix. The resulting equations are quadratic in the current period's asset prices, which appear in the numerator for revaluing last period's holding and in the denominator for computing the expected capital gain and the yield from the coupon. It would not be practical to solve these equations analytically in a model of this size. See Keating (1985).

Because of the difficulty in obtaining full analytic solutions for the asset prices, I derive instead partially-solved expressions for the market-clearing asset prices. These equations give each price as a function of its own reciprocal and of all the other prices, and of the predetermined variables. Explicit solutions are then obtained numerically by a Gauss-Seidel solution algorithm. In practice, this method gives rapid convergence even when the asset price equations are solved simultaneously with several hundred other equations from the rest of the LBS model.

To derive these partially-solved expressions, substitute (3.13) into (3.11) to give:

$$x_{jt} = L_j[(1-t_{Ijt})r_{jt}/p_{jt} + C_j + (1-t_{Gjt})(1-L_j/\mu^*)(_tp_{jt+1} - p_{jt})/p_{jt}$$

$$-\underline{y}_t^+ + \omega_j x_{jt-1}(1-L_j/\mu^*)p_{jt}/p_{jt-1} - \underline{x}_{t-1}^+$$

$$+ x_{jt-1}p_{jt}/(p_{jt-1}\mu^*) + W_t^+/\mu^*]$$ (5.1)

where all symbols are defined above, except that $\underline{y}_t^+$, $\underline{x}_{t-1}^+$ and W_t^+ are defined analogously to $\underline{y}^*_t$, $\underline{x}^*_{t-1}$ and W^*_t respectively, with the terms in p_{jt} excluded. Write (5.1) as:

$$x_{jt} = p_{jt}E_{jt} + F_{jt}$$ (5.2)

where

$$E_{jt} = L_j[-(1-t_{Gjt})(1-L_j/\mu^*)/p_{jt} + \omega_j x_{jt-1}(1-L_j/\mu^*)$$

$$+ x_{jt-1}/(p_{jt-1}\mu^*)]$$

and

$$F_{jt} = L_j[(1-t_{Ijt})r_j/p_{jt} + C_j - \underline{y}_t^+ - \underline{x}_{t-1}^+ + W_t^+/\mu^*]$$

Notice that both E_{jt} and F_{jt} are functions of the reciprocal of the current period asset price p_{jt}.

The expression (5.2) is simply the re-arrangement of the demand for the jth asset by a single sector. To allow for the existence of many sectors, introduce a subscript g (across sectors) so the demand for the jth asset by the gth sector is:

$$x_{gjt} = p_{jt}E_{gjt} + F_{gjt}$$

(Note that the overseas sector demand (3.12) can be written in the same way, although the interpretation of E and F is different.) The government is assumed to choose as its exogenous policy instrument the _flow_ supply of the asset, not the stock, so supply is:

$$x_{jt}^s = S_{jt}/q_t + p_{jt}x_{jt-1}/p_{jt-1}$$

where x_{jt}^s is supply; and S_{jt} is the flow nominal supply and q_t a general price index. Aggregate demand plus supply must sum to zero to clear the market and so:

$$p_{jt} = \frac{\sum\limits_{g} F_{gjt} - S_{jt}/q_t}{x^s_{jt-1}/p_{jt-1} - \sum\limits_{g} E_{gjt}} \tag{5.3}$$

This is the expression used in the financial model to compute market-clearing asset prices. Note that the E's and F's are functions of all asset prices.

Simulations of the model properties

This section is intended to give only an introductory indication of the simulation properties of the financial model. Given the wide range of government instruments and exogenous variables in the model it is possible to give only a limited number of examples in this paper. For other examples, see Budd et al. (1984), Corker (1985) and Keating (1985).

The simulations are all made under the assumption of rational expectations, which is taken to mean that agents' expectations of asset prices are consistent with the model's forecasts. Two types of algorithm were used to achieve this consistency. The first was the penalty function method in which the sum of the squared differences between expectations and model forecasts is minimised, using a Newton method, with the expectations as instruments. See Holly and Zarrop (1983). The second method was a modified version of the Hall algorithm. In this method, the expectations are modified in each successive iteration by a fraction of the difference between expectation and outturn recorded in the previous iteration. See Hall (1984) and Fisher, Holly and Hughes-Hallett (1985). The second method generally converges more rapidly.

The simulations described here cover both a policy change and an exogenous shock. The policy change is an increase in government procurement spending. I consider the effect of this policy change both under bond finance and under bill finance, in each case assuming the change to be unanticipated. I also consider the effect of a bill-financed increase in government spending anticipated four quarters in advance. For the simulation of changing world interest rates, I assume that any change in public borrowing is financed by bills, and I examine both unanticipated and anticipated cases. In all simulations, the government is assumed to hold short-term interest rates at the base run levels. As for all simulations, it must be stressed that the results depend on this and other assumptions about the government policy response and about other variables that are assumed to be exogenous.

Simulation 1: Increase in government expenditure

In this group of simulations, government procurement spending is increased by £300m per quarter at 1980 prices. This is a rise of about 2 per cent, equivalent to about £1¾ bn per annum at 1985 prices.

Charts 1 to 7 show the model response under both bill and bond finance, and in the unanticipated and anticipated cases. I consider first the effects of bill finance, with the change being unanticipated.

Bill finance

Under bill finance the initial effect on output is large though it declines after five years (Chart 1). The main reason for the large fiscal multiplier is in the behaviour of the exchange rate, which drops immediately by over 9 per cent as the market discounts the future effects of the fiscal expansion (Chart 2). Initially domestic prices and wages change very little and so there is a large improvement in competitiveness. This raises exports and reduces imports. By contrast both consumption and investment are lower. As domestic prices rise, the gain in competitiveness is eroded and by the fifth year competitiveness is almost back to its base run level (Chart 3). The lagged effect on trade has still to work itself out, but it seems reasonable to suppose that eventually the increase in output from more government expenditure will be crowded out as the effect on imports and exports falls back to zero. After five years consumer prices are over 9 per cent higher and the money supply is raised by almost 7 per cent (Chart 4). The higher prices reduce consumption even though nominal wealth is increased at least for the first few years.

Because nominal bond sales, by assumption, are held at base run levels, the rise in goods prices means that the real supply of bonds is substantially reduced, and by an increasing amount. Reflecting this cut in supply, the bond price rises and continues to increase (Chart 5). The equity price also rises, with a jump increase of about 4 per cent and thereafter a rise of about 2 per cent per annum. This is broadly in line with goods prices so real equity prices are approximately stable after the initial jump.

Table 5 shows that a large part of the demand for bonds comes from the pension and insurance funds. These institutions initially sell overseas securities (about £¾ bn worth) and use the proceeds to buy an almost equal number of bonds. They also buy a substantial amount of equities in the first year. In the following years their purchases of bonds continue but at a slower rate. In real terms their bond holdings are raised by about 2 per cent by the end of the simulation. Bond purchases in the later years are financed by equity sales, but even so real equity holdings are about 1 per cent above the base run figure at the end of the simulation.

This initial swap out of overseas assets into UK bonds and equities illustrates one of the main properties of the portfolio model. When the price of one asset rises relative to another, the existing holdings are revalued and the portfolio moves away from equilibrium. Hence a flow is needed to offset this effect. This is what happens to the pension fund and insurance company sector. When asset prices jump at the start of the simulation, this sector's holdings of overseas assets are revalued by more than its UK bond and equity holdings. This is because the exchange rate falls by almost 10 per cent (i.e.

Chart 1: Increase in government spending – effect on GDP per unit change in government spending

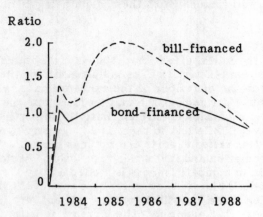

Chart 2: Increase in government spending – effect on the exchange rate

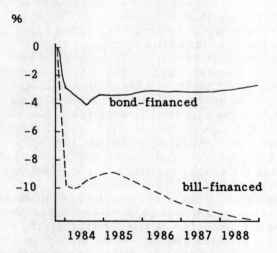

Chart shows percentage difference between base and simulations

Chart 3: **Increase in government spending - effect on the real exchange rate**

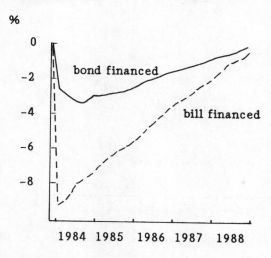

Chart shows percentage difference between base and simulations

Chart 4: **Increase in government spending - effect on consumer prices and money stock, assuming bill finance**

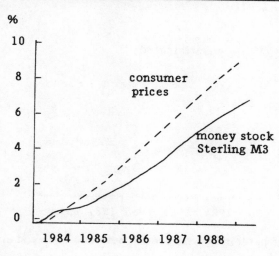

Chart shows percentage differences between base and simulation

Chart 5: <u>Increase in government spending – effect on bond prices,</u>
<u>assuming bill finance</u>

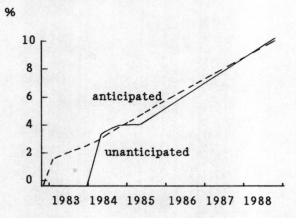

Chart shows percentage difference between base and simulations

Chart 6: <u>Increase in government spending – effect on the exchange</u>
<u>rate, assuming bill finance</u>

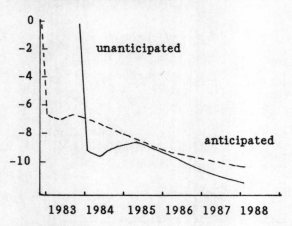

Chart shows percentage difference between base and simulations

114

Chart 7: <u>Increase in government spending – effect on GDP per unit change in spending</u>

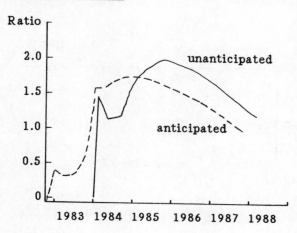

Chart 8: <u>1% increase in world interest rates – effect on the exchange rate</u>

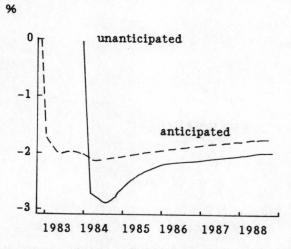

Chart shows percentage difference between base and simulations

Chart 9: <u>1% increase in world interest rates - effect on the real exchange rate</u>

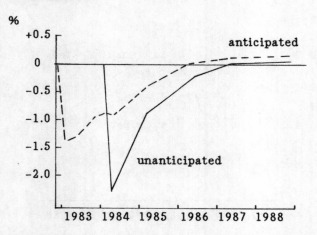

Chart shows percentage difference between base and simulations

Chart 10: <u>Increase in government spending - effect on UK bond prices</u>

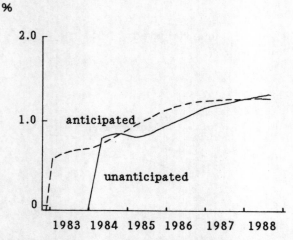

Chart shows percentage difference between base and simulation

Chart 11: <u>1% increase in world interest rates – effect on UK equity prices</u>

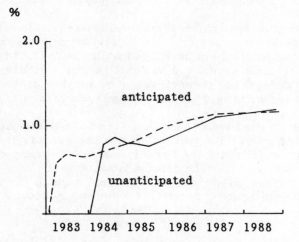

Chart shows percentage difference between base and simulations

Chart 12: <u>1% increase in world interest rates – effect on pension fund and insurance company investment flows</u>

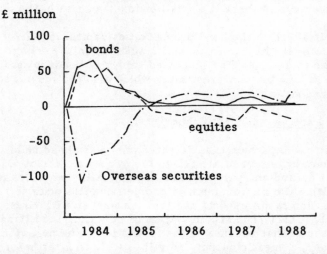

Chart shows absolute change between base and simulation, assuming the increase in interest rates was unanticipated

overseas asset prices rise by nearly 10 per cent) while bond and
equity prices jump up by only 2 and 4 per cent respectively. The
sector reacts by selling overseas assets and buying UK bonds and
equities.

Personal sector demand for short term assets falls in real terms
over the forecast period (see Table 6). In real terms, notes and coin
and sight deposit holdings are unchanged while the demand for time
and building society deposits, and National Savings certificates, falls
sharply. This reflects the assumption that nominal short-term
interest rates are unchanged from base run levels despite higher
inflation.

The funds diverted from these short-term assets are used to buy
longer-term securities. The personal sector has a steady demand for
bonds in the years following the fiscal injection (the supply comes
from the overseas sector). The demand is accompanied by a strong
demand for equities. After four years the real value of the personal
sector's holdings of long-term assets is increased by about 4 per cent.

Bond finance

Under bond finance the budget constraint of the government is
satisfied by issuing bonds rather than by issuing bills. The fiscal
multiplier in this case is lower (Chart 1), mainly because exports do
not rise as much. The central reason for this is that the exchange
rate falls on the impact of the fiscal expansion by less than 4 per
cent (Chart 2), compared to 10 per cent under bill finance. Hence
competitiveness does not improve by as much though it does come
back to equilibrium by the fifth year (Chart 3). Although bond
finance is being used there is a small endogenous rise in the money
stock.

The initial fall in the bond prices causes capital losses for the
personal sector so that nominal wealth actually falls causing
consumption to decline. The increased supply of bonds is associated
with a rise in long term interest rates which also crowds out some
forms of expenditure.

Anticipated and unanticipated shocks

When the fiscal expansion is anticipated one year ahead under bill
finance, there is an immediate fall in the exchange rate of 6.5 per
cent (Chart 6), and an appreciation of equity and bond prices which
raises wealth. The improvement in competitiveness prior to the
fiscal expansion raises exports and imports so that GDP rises
immediately (Chart 7). This simulation of an anticipated fiscal
expansion shows that because of the forward-looking behaviour of
asset markets, domestic output and prices start to alter before the
increase in government expenditure. When the fiscal expansion
actually occurs, prices are already 1.4 per cent higher. There is still
a large rise in output but again after five years the expansionary
effect is falling off rapidly.

Simulation 2: An increase in world interest rates

This group of simulations shows the effect of raising world interest rates (the model uses a weighted average of major currency 3-month rates) by 1 per cent, with the change unanticipated in one simulation and correctly predicted four quarters in advance in the other simulation. The response of the world economy is analysed by the LBS model, which suggests that the world price level falls by about ⅓ per cent over two years and after that starts to rise only marginally back to the base run figure.

In the UK, the nominal exchange rate falls initially by nearly 3 per cent in the case where the change is unanticipated; when it is anticipated there is a depreciation of just under 2 per cent at the date the news is received, followed by a marginal further depreciation to just over 2 per cent during the year up to the time when the foreign interest rate rises (see Chart 8). Thereafter, in both cases the nominal exchange rate appreciates slowly, settling down to a steady rise of about 0.1 to 0.2 per cent per annum by the end of the five-year simulation period. The real exchange rate jumps down initially, by slightly less than the nominal exchange rate because wages and prices have a small, immediate response to nominal shocks. In contrast to the nominal exchange rate this real depreciation is entirely eliminated within about three years of the interest rate increase (see Chart 9), reflecting the tendency of the wage, price and output equations rapidly to restore purchasing power parity. By the end of the forecast period, both output and employment have returned to base run levels and the level of UK prices and money supply (sterling M3) have risen by about 1 per cent. The UK inflation rate has returned almost precisely to the base run figure by the end of the simulation period.

The magnitudes of the differences between simulation and base run rates of change are very small by the end of the forecast period. Because of this, it is possible to make two different interpretations of the effect of the simulation on the steady state towards which the system is tending. On one view, the steady state levels of the real and nominal exchange rates, and of UK and foreign inflation, are all unchanged. This implies that there will be a 1 percentage point change in the steady-state risk premium in favour of sterling. Alternatively, the results can be interpreted as implying a steady state in which the excess of UK over world inflation is smaller in the simulations than in the base run, allowing some sustained appreciation of the UK nominal exchange rate to be consistent with an unchanging real exchange rate. On this second interpretation there has also been a movement in the risk premium in favour of sterling, but this shift is rather less than one percentage point. In either case, this move in the steady-state risk premium occurs because the initial jump fall in the nominal exchange rate raises the value of foreign currency assets held by UK residents and lowers the foreign currency value of sterling assets held by overseas residents.

Charts 10 and 11 show the effect of an increase in world interest rates on the remaining two asset prices, UK bonds and equities. Both

Table 5: **Changes in asset demands following an unanticipated increase in government procurement spending**

£ m i l l i o n

	After:	1 year	2 years	3 years	4 years
Pension and Insurance Funds					
Gilts	stock	2489	3904	5896	8461
	flow	670	340	368	434
Equities	stock	3772	5681	8498	12077
	flow	247	-154	-310	-348
Overseas securities	stock	1152	1372	2077	2961
	flow	-732	-5	90	76
Other assets	stock	193	290	440	829
	flow	193	97	150	389
Personal Sector					
Notes and coin; bank, building society and other deposits	stock	471	1704	3580	6014
	flow	471	1233	1876	2434
Bank, HP and other loans*	stock	-275	-791	-1510	-2790
	flow	-275	-516	-719	-1280
Gilts and equities	stock	4057	6485	10156	14618
	flow	55	184	455	474
Overseas securities	stock	1446	1648	2456	3533
	flow	-115	18	305	397

* A negative change implies an increase in the amount of loans.

For gilts, equities and overseas securities the flow is net of any asset price change. Often an increase in price, which increases the value of the stock, causes an outflow of the asset from portfolios.

Table 6:   Real changes to personal sector portfolios following an
           unanticipated increase in government procurement spending

Change to asset stock after 4 years

	Nominal change £ m	Real change in £m at constant 1980 goods prices†
Notes, coins and liquid deposits	6014 (2.9)	−5291 (−4.3)
Loans‡ (from banks, building societies and finance houses)	−2790 (1.4)	6640 (−5.7)
Gilts and equities	14618 (12.2)	3101 (4.3)
Overseas securities	3533 (13.1)	839 (5.2)

(percentage changes in brackets)

† Goods prices rose by just over 7 per cent between base and
simulation and so a positive percentage change of less than 7 per cent
in the nominal stock outstanding will be accompanied by a negative
percentage change in the real stock.

‡ Because the stock of borrowing is measured as a negative number,
an increase in loans outstanding is indicated by a negative figure for
the stock and a positive figure for the percentage change.

Table 7:   Changes in asset demands following an unanticipated 1%
increase in world interest rates

£ million

After:		1 year	2 years	3 years	4 years
Pension and Insurance Funds					
Gilts	stock	539	703	886	1054
	flow	178	28	27	22
Equities	stock	783	993	1332	1476
	flow	171	−10	−51	−40
Overseas securities	stock	264	214	268	324
	flow	−273	28	72	64
Other assets	stock	41	52	66	79
	flow	41	11	14	13
Personal Sector					
Notes and coin; bank, building society and other deposits	stock	177	498	867	1230
	flow	177	321	369	363
Bank, HP and other loans*	stock	−91	−213	−339	−561
	flow	−91	−122	−217	−222
Gilts and equities	stock	658	975	1433	1841
	flow	−31	77	153	121
Overseas securities	stock	394	338	425	518
	flow	−57	0	77	70

* A negative change implies an increase in the amount of loans.

For gilts, equities and overseas securities the flow is net of any
asset price change. Often an increase in price, which increases the
value of the stock, causes an outflow of the asset from portfolios.

Table 8: Real changes to personal sector portfolios following an unanticipated 1% increase in world interest rates

	Change to asset stock after 4 years	
	Nominal change £ m	Real change in £m at constant 1980 goods prices†
Notes, coins and liquid deposits	+ 1231 (0.6)	−976 (−0.8)
Loans‡ (from banks, building societies and finance houses)	− 561 (0.3)	1283 (−1.1)
Gilts and equities	+ 1841 (1.5)	+ 96 (0.1)
Overseas securities	+ 517 (1.9)	+ 83 (0.5)

(percentage changes in brackets)

† Goods prices rose by about 1 per cent between base and simulation, and so a positive percentage change of less than about 1 per cent in the nominal stock outstanding will be accompanied by a negative percentage change in the real stock.

‡ Because the stock of borrowing is measured as a negative number, an increase in loans outstanding is indicated by a negative figure for the stock and a positive figure for the percentage change.

of these prices exhibit the same jump-property as the exchange rate. When the change is unanticipated (solid line) the bond price immediately rises by about ¾ per cent. Thereafter the price rises further, to leave bond prices about 1 per cent above their base run level, about the same as the rise in consumer prices. The dashed line shows that anticipation of the change causes bond prices to rise before the world interest rates are altered. Both lines reach approximately the same long-run level. A similar pattern is followed by the price of equities. The supply of both bonds and equities is held constant in nominal terms so in real terms the supply falls, forcing up their price.

Pension and insurance fund portfolios are dominated by long-term assets and the interest rate change causes an immediate switch in their holdings. There is an immediate sale of overseas securities. The counterparts to this sale are purchases of almost equal quantities of bonds and of equities. This adjustment continues strongly for only two to three quarters (see Chart 12 and Table 7). Notice that even after some sales of overseas assets, the value of the sector's remaining overseas assets is still larger than in the base run because of the increase in the sterling price of foreign currency.

The personal sector behaves differently. When the interest rate change occurs, the leap in asset prices means that the personal sector is wealthier (as are the pension and insurance funds). However, adjustments to personal sector portfolios are much more gradual. There is little immediate trading of overseas securities which are only held in small quantities. By the later years of the simulation, the sector's real holdings of overseas assets are increased by about ½ per cent, while real holdings of bonds and equities have hardly changed (see Table 8). Real liquid assets fall by just under 1 per cent and borrowing declines by slightly over 1 per cent.

All the simulations exhibit irregular movements in the early periods, in addition to the initial jump. While these movements must reflect the dynamic structure of the model as a whole, Wickens (1984) has suggested a particular effect which may account for much of the irregularity. He notes that in discrete time rational expectations models, there will be effects due to expectational errors in the early periods after new information has been received. These effects die away in later periods, when all expectations are, by assumption, fulfilled.

CONCLUSION

The problems of constructing large-scale financial models are well-known. The work reported in this paper has attempted to reconcile the need for a strong basis in theory with the demands of practical modelling. The resulting compromise can be criticised from both sides; strong restrictions are applied by assuming diagonal covariance matrices and by assuming single period optimising; while the exchange rate equation is far more complex than usual in forecasting models and is difficult for users to understand. Nevertheless, the model produces simulation results that are broadly consistent both with theory and with modellers' intuition.

There are many possible areas in which the system presented here could be modified, extended or improved. An attempt could be made to estimate the Euler equations to allow for full intertemporal optimising; I have shown that because of price revaluations it would not be possible to use the reduced form suggested by Blanchard and Kahn. Extra explanatory variables could be introduced. Either or both of these changes might help to remove the autocorrelation, for which there is some, not conclusive, evidence. The system was estimated by repeated use of single equation estimators, and the use of proper systems estimation software should allow the testing of some of the restrictions imposed by the theory. In addition, the simulation properties of the model in response to some policy instruments have yet to be tested.

ACKNOWLEDGEMENT

I am grateful to my colleagues in the London Business School Centre for Economic Forecasting and to participants in seminars at the Money Study Group Conference and the Centre for Economic Policy Research for advice and assistance.

NOTES

1.   During estimation, data for unit and investment trusts were aggregated with the personal sector to reduce the number of asset demands during estimation.
2.   These three assets, collectively referred to as 'bills', are treated as perfect substitutes.
3.   For forecasting and simulation, the difference between the returns on foreign currency, short term assets and on foreign currency securities is imposed, although these two assets are treated as separate in agents' objective functions.
4.   Coefficients in the equations for the banks' very limited net holdings of foreign currency assets, and for the banks' and building society gilts holdings, are currently imposed.
5.   For the personal sector, which is assumed to choose among twelve assets, there would be 144 coefficients in both the A and the $A\omega$ matrices, plus 12 in the b vector. Assuming that ω was symmetrical, there are 66 symmetry restrictions and 5 zero column sum restrictions on each of A and $A\omega$, and a unit-sum restriction on b. Hence there would be 300 parameters, less 143 restrictions, implying 157 structural coefficients to be estimated.
6.   The problems of rational expectations estimation are well known - see for example Begg (1981, chapter 5) and Wallis (1980). We use outturn capital gains in place of expected, treating them as

endogenous variables using the instruments listed in the text.

7.   Note that the mean-variance model with covariance matrix not restricted to be diagonal implies both adding-up restrictions and symmetry restrictions on the coefficients on the rate of return. The former are automatically imposed by OLS estimation but the latter require a systems estimator.

8.   I am grateful to David Begg for suggesting this equation for determining initial, statistically consistent estimates.

9.   I am grateful to David Currie for suggesting a version of this intertemporal optimisation problem.

PORTFOLIO SELECTION AND INTEREST RATE SETTING BY THE DUTCH BANKING SYSTEM

Peter D. van Loo

1. INTRODUCTION

In a recent study on the Dutch financial system (van Loo (1983)) we explain the financial behaviour of eight sectors of the Dutch economy: the central bank, banks, institutional investors, mortgage banks, corporations, households, the government and foreigners. Crucial characteristics of the analysis are the use of cross-equation restrictions implied by the imposition of balance sheet constraints, the attention paid to the institutional details and the incorporation of flow effects in a general stock adjustment model. The present paper is based on the analysis of the behaviour of the banks, carried out as part of this system-wide study.[1] Section 2 describes the main characteristics of the Dutch banking system. The behaviour of the banks is modelled as a mixture of portfolio selection and interest rate setting. The portfolio selection (section 3) involves eight balance sheet items which are currently endogenous for the banks. Six balance sheet items are predetermined for the banks in the short run. Banks may affect the quantities of these assets and liabilities by adjusting the corresponding interest rate (section 4).

2. CHARACTERISTICS OF THE DUTCH BANKING SYSTEM

The banking system consists of the following four types of money-creating institutions: commercial banks, agricultural credit institutions, giro institutions and security credit institutions.[2] The commercial banks constitute by far the largest part of the banking system. Their share in the aggregate balance sheet total of the system was 72 per cent at the end of 1978 (see table 1).

Commercial banks are also the most diversified financial institutions. They are intermediaries which attract all types of deposits and, especially during the last years of the sample period, borrowed in the capital market. Their domestic investments include short-term business and consumer loans, short-term government securities, mortgage loans, private placements and bonds. Moreover,

Table 1: Balance sheet totals of the banking system at the end of
       1978

	Amount	%
Commercial banks	203232	72
Agricultural credit institutions	61679	22
Giro institutions	16394	6
Security credit institutions	308	0
Aggregate banking system	281613	100

NOTES: Amounts are in millions of guilders and in percentages of
         the sum. Commercial banks include non-member
         agricultural credit institutions. Agricultural credit
         institutions are exclusive of the mortgage bank section of
         the central cooperative bank ("Rabohypotheekbank").

SOURCES: De Nederlandsche Bank (1979, table 2.1),
         Rabohypotheekbank (1978), and internal data of the
         Netherlands Bank.

they are the most active banks in the international markets. At the
end of 1978, the share of claims on non-residents (including foreign
bonds and shares) in their balance sheet total was 42 per cent and
that of liabilities to non-residents 40 per cent.
       Nearly all agricultural credit institutions are members of the
cooperative organisation headed by the central cooperative bank,
Rabobank Nederland. They are gradually developing into diversified
financial institutions. Compared with commercial banks they invest
relatively more in the domestic capital market and gather more funds
in the form of savings deposits. Although the volume of their foreign
activities has risen considerably since 1973, it is still very modest.
The two giro institutions merged on January 1, 1979. Demand
deposits constitute the bulk of their liabilities, which also include
deposits held by the central government. Their main assets are
domestic capital market investments and balances required by
regulation. They do not extend short-term loans to the private
sector.
       Table 2 shows the balance sheet of the aggregate banking system
at the end of 1978 and the symbols of the balance sheet items.
Foreign assets are net of similar foreign liabilities because separate
quarterly data of short-term and long-term foreign assets and
liabilities are only available on a net basis. Net foreign assets are
defined as net claims on non-residents. They include assets and
liabilities that are denominated both in foreign currencies and in
domestic currency. Several balance sheet items are aggregated in
the following analysis. Long-term net foreign assets ($NFAL^b$) include
both foreign bonds and other long-term net foreign assets.
Short-term time and savings deposits (TS) include short-term time
deposits, foreign currency deposits and liquid savings deposits;

Table 2: The balance sheet of the banking system (at the end of 1978)

Assets	Symbol	Amount
Bank reserves (notes and coins with banks and balances with the Netherlands Bank)	R	909
Short-term (and medium term) government debt	SS^b	17342
Short-term net foreign assets (claims on non-residents)	$NFAS^b$	-10391
Short-term bank loans, extended to the private sector	LS	62884
Foreign bonds	$NFAL1^b$	1671
Foreign shares	–	135
Other long-term net foreign assets (claims on non-residents)	$NFAL2^b$	12003
Domestic bonds	LB^b	5980
Private placements	LP^b	38338
Mortgage loans	LM^b	50210
Domestic shares	–	117
Participations	–	538
Investments in real estate	–	291
Total assets		180027

Liabilities

	Symbol	Amount
Demand deposits	D	43399
Short-term time deposits	TS1	26649
Foreign currency deposits	TS2	3845
Liquid savings deposits	TS3	1891
Genuine savings deposits	TLB1	61248
Savings certificates to bearer	TLB2	7278
Long-term deposits	TLB3	5718
Deposits held by the central government	DG^b	978
Bonds	LBL^b	5357
Private placements	LPL^b	6687
Discounts and advances from the central bank including special loans	RL	5430
Capital and reserves	–	9543
Other liabilities	–	2004
Total liabilities		180027

NOTE: Amounts are in millions of guilders.

SOURCES: See van Loo (1983, p. 89).

Table 3: The growth of the bank assets

Year	Bank reserves		Short-term government debt		Short-term net foreign assets		Short-term bank loans		Long-term net foreign assets	
	Amount	%	Amount	%	Amount	%	Amount	%	Amount	%
1967	-15	-0	999	22	-693	-15	2064	46	223	5
1968	52	1	624	10	349	6	2090	35	61	1
1969	10	0	775	14	240	4	1154	21	52	1
1970	277	5	1021	17	-673	-11	1297	21	451	7
1971	-190	-2	204	3	1397	17	1583	20	466	6
1972	100	1	-715	-8	-551	-6	2435	26	651	7
1973	93	1	-57	-0	-972	-7	6362	49	892	7
1974	40	0	1415	10	-740	-5	6660	47	505	4
1975	27	0	1710	13	-338	-3	2093	17	1714	14
1976	73	0	1299	7	-4198	-24	5960	34	2942	17
1977	-8	-0	1235	7	-3665	-20	8553	47	1857	10
1978	119	0	3844	15	-5791	-23	10493	42	3920	16
Average	48	0	1029	9	-1303	-11	4229	36	1144	10

NOTES: Amounts are in millions of guilders and in percentages of the total. Detail may not add to total because of rounding.

Table 3: continued

Year	Bonds		Private placements		Mortgage loans		Total
	Amount	%	Amount	%	Amount	%	Amount
1967	165	4	1063	24	698	15	4504
1968	341	6	1160	19	1324	22	6002
1969	143	3	1494	27	1622	30	5490
1970	-54	-1	1532	25	2205	36	6056
1971	543	7	2633	33	1378	17	8015
1972	833	9	4375	47	2269	24	9397
1973	281	2	3616	28	2783	21	12998
1974	-26	-0	3353	24	2879	20	14086
1975	931	7	3151	25	3384	27	12671
1976	614	3	3886	22	7032	40	17607
1977	267	1	2232	12	7677	42	18146
1978	494	2	4593	18	7530	30	25202
Average	378	3	2757	24	3398	29	11681

long-term time and savings deposits with banks (TLB) consist of
genuine savings deposits, savings certificates to bearer and long-term
deposits. All items without a symbol in table 2 are summarised in the
variable "net other liabilities" (NOL^b), with capital and reserves as
the main component.

The substantial variations in the relative importance of the
assets, measured as annual net changes, are revealed in table 3.
Short-term bank loans, extended to the private sector, mortgage
loans and private placements[3] constitute the most important uses of
funds. Remarkable upsurges in the volume of short-term bank loans
occurred in 1973 and 1974 and in 1977 and 1978. The net increases in
mortgage loans exceed those in private placements in the period
1968-1970 and in the years after 1974. The proportion of long-term
net foreign assets has been growing since 1975. In almost all years
the flow of short-term net foreign assets was negative. The balance
sheet shows also that genuine savings deposits, demand deposits and
short-term time deposits are the most important sources of funds.

3. THE PORTFOLIO SELECTION OF THE BANKS

The market clearing process of financial markets differs between
auction markets and customer markets. <u>Auction markets</u> such as the
bond market and the market for short-term government debt, are
cleared by the interaction of the demand and supply curves of the
sectors. The interest rate follows from this interaction. <u>Customer
markets</u> can be described by an interest rate setting function and one
or more demand equations. The quantities of assets or liabilities in
these markets are largely demand-determined in the short run.

Six balance sheet items of the banks represent the supply side of
a customer market: demand deposits (D), short-term time and savings
deposits (TS), long-term time and savings deposits (TLB), short-term
bank loans (LS), mortgage loans (LM^b) and investments in private
placements (LP^b). These items are endogenous in the model of the
complete financial system, but predetermined for the banks
themselves. The quantity of demand deposits is assumed to be
determined solely by depositors preferences, because the interest
rate on demand deposits is largely set by convention. Demand
deposits are thus treated as predetermined in the analysis of bank
behaviour. The quantities of short-term and long-term time and
savings deposits are determined by the interaction of banks and
depositors. In most cases banks publicly announce an interest rate,
and accept all deposits that are offered at that rate. For several
parts of time and savings deposits (time deposits and, recently,
savings certificates to bearer) banks pursue a policy of active
liability management, implying that the rate setting function depends
on current variables. Nevertheless, the quantities of time and
savings deposits are partly demand-determined in the short run.

This is also the premise for the amounts of short-term bank
loans, mortgage loans and private placements. Overdrafts permit

corporations to use credit facilities up to a certain limit. In the short run banks can try to curb demand by raising the loan rate or other requirements, while in the longer run the limits of the overdrafts can be adjusted. Similarly, banks do not have close control of the level of their mortgage loans, although the interest rate and the level of approvals are used as instruments. In both segments of the credit market the transaction costs of changing interest rates and other requirements are higher than on auction markets such as the market for bonds. Furthermore, there is no secondary market for these credit instruments. To some extent, this also holds for private placements, but the interest rate on this type of loan reacts faster to new information than that on mortgage loans. Nevertheless, we treat the bank investments in private placements as predetermined relative to bank portfolio behaviour. The borrowings of banks in the market for private placements (LPL^b) on the contrary do constitute part of bank portfolio behaviour.

Two balance sheet items of the banks are also exogenous in the complete model. Deposits of the central government (DG^b) are held to be exogenous for the sake of convenience, because their amount is relatively small. Net other liabilities (NOL^b) include all other bank assets and liabilities, the fluctuations of which are not explained. The amounts of the predetermined balance sheet items determine the magnitude of the disposable funds (wealth) which the banks must allocate to the remaining endogenous assets and liabilities. The banks' wealth (W^b) is thus defined as the sum of the predetermined bank liabilities (demand deposits, short-term time and savings deposits, long-term time and savings deposits, deposits of the central government and net other liabilities), reduced by the predetermined assets (short-term banks loans, private placements and mortgage loans):

$$W^b = D + TS + TLB + DG^b + NOL^b - LS - LP^b - LM^b$$

The eight balance sheet items that are currently endogenous for the banks are: bank reserves (R), short-term government debt (SS^b), short-term net foreign assets ($NFAS^b$), long-term net foreign assets ($NFAL^b$), investments in domestic bonds (LB^b), borrowing by way of bonds (LBL^b) and private placements (LPL^b), and discounts and advances from the central bank including special loans (RL).

The portfolio adjustment model which will be used to describe the portfolio selection of these eight balance sheet items is an extended version of the so-called "general partial adjustment model". The adjustment of a particular asset to its equilibrium value not only depends on the deviation of the desired level of that asset at time t from its actual level at time t - 1, but because of the balance sheet constraints also on the deviation of the desired levels of other assets at time t from their actual values at time t - 1. The levels of the assets at time t - 1, scaled by lagged wealth, are therefore

Table 4: Hypotheses of bank portfolio selection

Explanatory variables:

Balance sheet items:	$\dfrac{W^b}{W^b_{-1}}$	$i_{SS}^{-1}T_{S*}\!\cdot\! f_p$ (x)	$i_{LB}^{-1}LB*$ (x)	$\hat{p}^e-p^*$ (x)	$i_{LB}^{-1}LP$ (x)	$i_{SS}^{-1}CB$ (x)	$\left[\dfrac{R}{W^b}\right]_{-1}$	$\left[\dfrac{SS^b}{W^b}\right]_{-1}$	$\left[\dfrac{RL}{W^b}\right]_{-1}$	$\left[\dfrac{NFAS^b}{W^b}\right]_{-1}$	$\left[\dfrac{NFAL^b}{W^b}\right]_{-1}$
$\Delta R/W^b_{-1}$	?	0	0	0	0	0	⊕	−	+	−	−
$\Delta SS^b/W^b_{-1}$	?	+	0	0	0	+	−	⊕	+	−	−
$-\Delta RL/W^b_{-1}$	?	0	0	0	0	−	−	−	⊕	−	−
$\Delta NFAS^b/W^b_{-1}$	?	−	0	0	0	0	−	−	+	⊕	−
$\Delta NFAL^b/W^b_{-1}$	?	0	−	+	+	0	−	−	+	−	0
$\Delta LB^b/W^b_{-1}$	?	0	+	−	+	0	0	0	+	0	0
$-\Delta LBL^b/W^b_{-1}$	?	0	+	−	+	0	0	0	0	0	0
$-\Delta LPL^b/W^b_{-1}$	?	0	+	−	−	0	0	0	0	0	0
Total of coefficients	1	0	0	0	0	0	−1	−1	1	−1	−1

Explanatory variables:

Balance sheet items:	$\left[\dfrac{LB^b}{W^b}\right]_{-1}$	$\left[\dfrac{LBL^b}{W^b}\right]_{-1}$	$\left[\dfrac{LPL^b}{W^b}\right]_{-1}$	$\dfrac{\Delta D}{W^b_{-1}}$	$\dfrac{\Delta TLB}{W^b_{-1}}$	$\dfrac{\Delta\Delta W^b}{W^b_{-1}}$	ncc^x	$\dfrac{\Delta(SS-SS^{cb})}{W^b_{-1}}^x$	$\dfrac{\Delta RR}{W^b_{-1}}$	$i_p^{\,x}$	bc^x	$\dfrac{\Delta SW}{W^b_{-1}}^x$	$\dfrac{\Delta SPL}{W^b_{-1}}$	reg^x	$\dfrac{CAB}{W^b_{-1}}$
$\Delta R/W^b_{-1}$	−	+	+	+	−	+	0	−	⊕	−	+	+	+	+	−
$\Delta SS^b/W^b_{-1}$	−	+	+	+	+	+	0	⊕	−	+	+	?	+	+	−
$-\Delta RL/W^b_{-1}$	−	+	+	+	−	+	0	−	−	⊕	⊕	?	⊕	+	−
$\Delta NFAS^b/W^b_{-1}$	−	+	+	?	?	?	0	−	−	−	+	−	+	⊕	⊕
$\Delta NFAL^b/W^b_{-1}$	−	+	+	?	?	?	0	−	−	−	+	?	+	+	−
$\Delta LB^b/W^b_{-1}$	−	0	0	−	+	−	⊕	−	−	−	+	?	+	+	−
$-\Delta LBL^b/W^b_{-1}$	0	+	0	−	+	−	−	−	−	−	+	?	+	+	−
$-\Delta LPL^b/W^b_{-1}$	0	0	+	−	+	−	−	−	−	−	+	?	+	+	−
Total of coefficients	−1	1	1	0	0	0	0	0	0	0	0	0	0	0	0

NOTES: The coefficients expected to be the largest in any column are circled. Explanatory variables with "x" as superscript are multiplied by W^b/W^b_{-1}.

135

determinants of the changes in asset holdings. Moreover, <u>flow effects</u> are incorporated in the stock adjustment model.

The general formulation of the portfolio adjustment model is:

$$
\frac{\Delta A_i}{W_{-1}^b} = \left(\sum_{j=1}^{n} \theta_{ij} \alpha_j \right) \frac{W^b}{W_{-1}^b} + \left[\sum_{k=1}^{n} \left(\sum_{j=1}^{n} \theta_{ij} \beta_{jk} \right) i_k \right.
$$

$$
\left. + \sum_{h=1}^{m} \left(\sum_{j=1}^{n} \theta_{ij} \eta_{jh} \right) Z_h \right] \frac{W^b}{W_{-1}^b} - \sum_{j=1}^{n} \theta_{ij} \frac{A_{j,-1}}{W_{-1}^b}
$$

$$
+ \sum_{\substack{j=1 \\ j \neq p}}^{n} \zeta_{ij} \frac{\Delta W_j^b}{W_{-1}^b} + \pi_i \frac{\Delta \Delta W^b}{W_{-1}^b} + \kappa_i \frac{\Delta X}{W_{-1}^b} \qquad i = 1, \ldots, n
$$

where A_i = actual holdings of asset A_i (i = 1, ..., n)

W^b = the banks' wealth (disposable funds), which must be allocated to eight assets

W_j^b = a predetermined item of the banks' balance sheet
with $\sum_{j=1}^{n} W_j^b = W^b$

i_k = the interest rate on asset A_k (k = 1, ..., n)

Z_h = all other determinants of the desired holdings of assets A_j (j = 1, ..., n; h = 1, ..., m)

X = explanatory variable summarising the exogenous disturbances that affect portfolio behaviour directly.

The specification involves five groups of explanatory variables:

- current wealth divided by lagged wealth (W^b/W_{-1}^b);
- determinants of the desired proportions of asset holdings, multiplied by W^b/W_{-1}^b;
- lagged values of the assets, expressed as a proportion of lagged wealth;
- flows of wealth components and changes in flows of wealth or its components, expressed as a proportion of lagged wealth;
- variables summarised by the last term at the right hand side of the equation ($\Delta X/W_{-1}^b$).

Table 4 shows the detailed <u>specification</u> and the hypothesised signs of the regression coefficients. The signs of the coefficients which, according to economic theory, may be either positive or negative are indicated by a question mark. Several parameters are set a priori at zero. The coefficients expected to be the largest in any column are circled. Liabilities are considered assets with a negative sign.

The coefficients of current wealth divided by lagged wealth (W^b/W^b_{-1}) are an average of constant terms of the desired asset proportions weighted by the partial adjustment coefficients Θ_{ij}. They describe the fixed allocation of total wealth (both existing and new wealth), independent of interest rates or other factors. The expected signs of these coefficients are uncertain but their sum should be equal to unity (see van Loo (1983), section 2.5, equation (24)). The desired proportions of asset holdings also depend on the (expected) rates of return of the assets involved. Assets are assumed to be substitutes. When an interest rate rises, other things being equal, holding more of the corresponding asset and less of the alternative assets becomes attractive. Together with the balance sheet restriction, this implies that the own asset effects of interest rates numerically exceed their cross effects on other assets. Interest rate differentials are used to reduce the multicollinearity among explanatory variables. In the following we explain the influences of these differentials in more detail.

<u>Differences between domestic and foreign interest rates</u> and also expected currency appreciations or depreciations can be major incentives for desired short-term and long-term international capital flows. In this model the interest rate on short-term government debt is compared with the covered foreign rate on short-term time deposits ($i_{SS} - i_{TS*} - fp$), where the forward premium (fp) represents the depreciation of the domestic currency against the foreign currencies expected during the term to maturity of the assets. A rise in this interest rate differential implies a desired reduction of short-term net foreign asset holdings and a growing attraction of short-term government debt. A larger positive difference between the yields on domestic and foreign bonds ($i_{LB} - i_{LB*}$) leads to substitution of long-term net foreign assets by domestic capital market instruments. Long-term net foreign assets are more attractive the higher the expected depreciation of the domestic currency against the foreign currencies. We employ the difference between the expected inflation in the home country and abroad ($\hat{p}^e - \hat{p}^{*e}$) as a proxy for the nominal depreciation expected in the long run. The (short-term) forward premium can function as an alternative proxy for the long-run expectation, provided that the direction of the expected exchange rate change is equal in the short and in the long run. The capital gain on bonds denominated in foreign currencies expected from anticipated exchange rate changes is uncertain as the remaining term to maturity of these foreign currency bonds exceeds the contract period of the forward exchange market.[4] Risk aversion implies that the weight of these uncertain exchange rate developments is smaller than that of observed

bond yield differentials. Consequently, the coefficients of the proxies for the long-run expected exchange rate movements will be numerically smaller than those of the long-term yield differential.

All these effects are based on the substitution hypothesis and the observation that the bulk of bank foreign assets and foreign liabilities is denominated in foreign currencies, especially in dollars.[5] Remember that the asset choice of foreign residents, who determine the demand for bank foreign liabilities, depends on foreign variables of the same kind as the domestic variables affecting the banks' demand for foreign assets. The list of determinants consists of foreign currency deposit rates with domestic banks, other domestic interest rates, a broad spectrum of asset yields abroad, foreign wealth and so on.[6] Because several of these factors are already included explicitly in the specification and representative foreign variables are difficult to measure, we shall not add more of these foreign variables to the specification.

We proceed by focusing upon the choice between various domestic earning assets. The difference between the bond rate and the interest rate on private placements ($i_{LB} - i_{LP}$) is included to describe the substitution between long-term net domestic assets; the difference between the interest rate on short-term government debt and the discount rate ($i_{SS} - i_{CB}$) should capture the substitution between short-term net domestic assets. The discount rate is an instrument of monetary policy. Other instruments which affect the desired proportions of bank asset holdings are discussed below.

The next eight independent variables are the lagged values of the endogenous assets expressed as a proportion of lagged wealth. The absolute value of the coefficient of the scaled lagged value of, for instance, bank reserves ($(R/W^b)_{-1}$) in the first row of the table shows that part of the gap between desired and lagged actual holdings of bank reserves bridged by banks during the current period. The remainder of the gap must be bridged by way of other short-term assets. Several of the coefficients of lagged endogenous variables are set a priori at zero in the equations of the long-term net domestic assets, because transaction costs make it forbiddingly expensive to use these assets as buffer variables.

Next, changes in several predetermined balance sheet items are introduced as <u>corrections to the fixed allocation of flows of new wealth</u> as described by the first explanatory variable (see van Loo (1983), section 2.5, equation (20)). For instance, we suppose that demand deposits (ΔD) will be invested to a greater extent in short-term assets than bank wealth as a whole. For long-term time and savings deposits (ΔTLB) the opposite case will hold. For simplicity, we shall not include any other changes in predetermined balance sheet items in the table. In any case, at least one of these changes should be excluded from the specification so as to avoid linear dependency between the explanatory variables. An acceleration in the flow of wealth ($\Delta\Delta W^b$) will lead to a temporary rise in the bank holdings of short-term securities at the cost of capital market investments, because immediate adjustment of these long-term investments is not always possible. In the empirical part this wealth variable will be disaggregated.

Because banks are money-creating institutions, their behaviour is constrained by measures of the monetary authorities which are imposed in order to achieve certain targets of monetary policy. A major intermediate target of Dutch monetary policy during our sample period was the national liquidity ratio, defined as the ratio between a broadly measured money supply and nominal national income. Given the expectations concerning the growth of real income and the rate of inflation, a target for the national liquidity ratio implies a desired increase in the supply of money. Banks create money by extending credit to domestic residents in excess of the increase in those bank liabilities which are no part of the money stock.

In the Netherlands the central bank has tried to curb excessive credit both by indirect credit control and by credit ceilings.[7] From 1961 to 1972 gross credit ceilings were in use in the form of a maximum permissible growth percentage for short-term bank loans granted to the private sector. During the period 1973-1977 the direct method of credit control was replaced by an indirect one. Banks were forced to hold a minimum percentage of their deposits in the form of short-term domestic assets. From 1977 to 1981 the central bank again attempted to restrain monetary expansion by means of credit ceilings, but now in the form of a limit on credit expansion net of increases in long-term bank liabilities.

An important complementary instrument is the quota scheme for bank borrowing from the central bank, which entered into force in September 1973. Until then, banks could obtain unlimited discounts and advances from the central bank at the official discount rates. Under the quota scheme, individual banks have to pay surcharges on the official rates as soon as they exceed their quotas. The hypothesis is that higher costs of the recourse to the central bank lead to higher interest rates on domestic credit and consequently to a dampening of the demand for credit. The quota scheme and the discount rate policy belong to the group of instruments that are primarily directed at the short-term financial markets. The aims of these intervention-type policies are to maintain orderly conditions in the markets for short-term credit and between these markets and the capital market, and to prevent undesired effects on the foreign exchange rate.[8] The scope for an independent monetary policy in a small, open economy largely depends on the central bank's capability to neutralise undesired inflows or outflows of liquidity through the balance of payments. The central bank has repeatedly taken measures to stimulate capital outflows during periods of current account surpluses and to stimulate capital inflows in the opposite case. Evidently, capital flows affect the supply of money so that conflicts may arise between the targets of fixed exchange rates and money stock control.

We now proceed to list major tools of monetary policy, most of which enter our specification of bank portfolio selection. Instruments that compel the banks to instant reallocation of their portfolio belong to the explanatory variables summarised by the term $\Delta X/W^b_{-1}$. All other instruments affect the desired proportions of asset holdings.

1. Net credit ceilings (ncc) stimulate banks to acquire long-term liabilities among which are bonds and private placements. The reason is that such purchases enlarge the possibility for the banks to extend loans to domestic residents.
2. From 1965 the gross credit ceiling on short-term credit expansion was supplemented by an informal net credit ceiling on long-term credit expansion. This instrument is not explicitly included in the table.
3. During the period of indirect credit control banks preferred to meet liquidity requirements by holding interest-bearing short-term government debt rather than non-interest-bearing reserves. Partly because several individual banks were holding only a small amount of short-term government debt at the start of the new policy regime, the stock of short-term government debt was simultaneously increased. Voluntary holdings of this type of secondary liquidity were occasionally restricted by insufficient supply. To stress that the stock of short-term government debt is mainly determined by the government's demand for funds, we add the flow of non-central bank holdings, scaled by lagged wealth $((\Delta SS - \Delta SS^{cb})/W^b_{-1})$ to the list of independent variables. The effectiveness of liquidity requirements cannot be captured by this variable.
4. The change in the holdings of required reserves, scaled by lagged wealth $(\Delta RR/W^b_{-1})$, results from two policy measures. During the years 1972-1973 and 1975-1976 ad hoc reserve requirements to be held by the banks as a percentage of their short-term deposits were imposed by the central bank. Moreover, compulsory reserves were to be held if the stock of short-term loans exceeded the gross credit ceiling.
5. The effects of the quota scheme for bank borrowing from the central bank[9] are described by two variables. From 1974, two types of surcharges were to be paid as soon as individual banks exceeded their quota: a fixed surcharge on bank borrowing up to a certain percentage in excess of the quota, and a variable surcharge excess borrowing. If this variable penalty rate (i_p) is boosted, the desired levels of bank borrowing from the central bank and bank holdings of short-term assets come down. If the borrowing ceiling or the quota expressed as a proportion of lagged wealth (bc) is lifted, the opposite reactions are to be expected.
6. The discount rate on promissory notes (i_{CB}) that was introduced above represents the official rates of the central bank. This interest rate serves as the basis for the rate on short-term bank loans.

7. Dollarswaps are temporary purchases of dollars by the central bank from the banking system for a specified period. The net flow of swaps is divided by lagged wealth ($\Delta SW/W^b_{-1}$). We hypothesise that the main effects are on short-term net foreign assets and on bank reserves.

8. Since the end of 1975 the item "discounts and advances from the central bank" has also included special loans granted at market rates ($\Delta SPL/W^b_{-1}$). These special loans do not belong to the borrowings of the quota scheme.

9. In van Loo (1983), section 3.8, we listed the most important regulations affecting long-term international capital flows so as to neutralise part of the exchange rate implications of surpluses or deficits on the current account. The regulation concerning the ceiling on the banks' net external liabilities was not important during our sample period, because the banks were holding net foreign assets. One of the regulations affecting short-term international capital flows was the prohibition for banks to pay interest on short-term guilder deposits held by non-residents from March 9, 1972 until the end of 1975. The franchise was raised several times. Moreover, these deposits had a negative interest rate of ¼ per cent per week from March 26, 1973 until May 17, 1973. We have attempted to capture the impact of this regulation by using a dummy variable (reg).

Besides all these tools of monetary policy, the Dutch authorities impose solvency requirements to reduce the risk of insolvency of the banks. These requirements involve a minimum amount of capital, reserves and subordinated debt, expressed as a proportion of the different types of credit granted to the private sector. Capital and reserves are part of our "net other liabilities", subordinated debt is included in the bank liabilities bonds and private placements.[10] The issuance of these liabilities is therefore stimulated by the solvency requirements. However, it depends more on the rapid expansion of credit extended to the private sector than on changes in the solvency requirements. We shall not attempt to include this phenomenon explicitly in our model of bank behaviour.

A positive current account of the balance of payments (CAB) means that there is net inflow of currencies from abroad. These short-term claims on non-residents are initially accumulated in the portfolio of the banks.

The balance sheet restrictions are included in table 4. The coefficients of W^b/W^b_{-1} and of the scaled lagged values of the liabilities should add up to unity, while the coefficients of the scaled lagged values of the assets should add up to minus unity. All other effects are reallocations of the portfolio, so that the sum of the coefficients is zero. The aggregation restrictions and several zero constraints on parameters are imposed in the estimation procedure.

The structural paremeters of the eight behavioural equations are estimated on a quarterly basis for the period 1967:I - 1978:IV by the method of <u>multivariate regression with cross-equation linear a priori restrictions</u> on parameters. Balance sheet restrictions make it necessary to estimate all structural parameters contemporaneously. We perform a stepwise estimation procedure to reduce the costs of computing these parameters. In the first step we analyse the following four endogenous parts of bank assets, restricted by the balance sheet constraints:

- short-term net domestic assets ($NDAS^b$) defined as the sum of bank reserves (R) and short-term government debt (SS^b) diminished by borrowing from the central bank (RL)
- short-term net foreign assets ($NFAS^b$)
- long-term net foreign assets ($NFAL^b$)
- long-term net domestic assets ($NDAL^b$), defined as net investments in domestic bonds ($LB^b - LBL^b$) reduced by bank borrowing by way of private placements (LPL^b).

The empirical results of the first step are shown in table 5. Next, we explain the composition of the short-term net domestic assets and the long-term net domestic assets, respectively, coefficients resulting from the first step being used as constraints in the second. The empirical results are listed in tables 6 and 7. The totals of the columns in table 6 are equal to the coefficients in the first row of table 5, and the totals of the columns in table 7 are equal to the coefficients in the fourth row of table 5. The equations describing the behaviour of the eight endogenous variables are thus shown in the three rows of table 6, the second and third row of table 5 and the three rows of table 7. We refer to the data appendix of van Loo (1983) for details of the definition and measurement of the variables.

The principal empirical findings of tables 5, 6 and 7 can be summarised as follows. One of the more interesting substantive outcomes is the existence of various substitution relationships amoung financial assets. A broad spectrum of yield variables plays a significant role in asset management. A selection of short-run impact elasticities, calculated for 1978, is shown in table 8. A unit differential between the interest rate on three-month government debt and the covered three-month eurodollar deposit rate ($i_{SS} - i_{TS*}$ - fp) affects the uses of funds most. A positive spread between these interest rates of one percentage point would have induced the banks in 1978 to an average shift from short-term net foreign assets towards short-term government debt to the amount of almost 500 million guilders[11] during the first quarter (see the parameters in the first two rows of table 5 and the second row of table 6). Consequently, the banks appear to play a major role in the arbitrage process underlying the <u>international interest rate parity.</u>

During the third quarter of 1976 rumours about a possible revaluation of the Deutsche mark caused a weakening of the other snake currencies. The dummy variable (d_{76III}) reflects the

Table 5: Estimates of bank portfolio selection

Part 1

	Explanatory variables:											
	$\left[\dfrac{W^b}{W^b_{-1}}\right]$	$i_{SS^{-1}}i_{TS^*}fp$	d_{76III}^x	$i_{LB^{-1}LB^*}^x$	$\overset{\cdot}{e}-\overset{\cdot}{p}^{*e\,x}$	$\left[\dfrac{R}{W^b}\right]_{-1}$	$\left[\dfrac{SS^b}{W^b}\right]_{-1}$	$\left[\dfrac{RL}{W^b}\right]_{-1}$	$\left[\dfrac{NFAS^b}{W^b}\right]_{-1}$	$\left[\dfrac{NFAL^b}{W^b}\right]_{-1}$	$\left[\dfrac{LB^b}{W^b}\right]_{-1}$	$\left[\dfrac{LBL^b}{W^b}\right]_{-1}$
Balance sheet items:												
$\Delta NDAS^b/W^b_{-1}$	0.543 (12.27)	0.036 (3.18)	0.108 (3.41)			-0.865 (14.70)	-0.700 (8.86)	0.824 (20.74)	-0.262 (5.59)		-0.729 (14.42)	0.775 (16.95)
$\Delta NFAS^b/W^b_{-1}$	0.415 (9.03)	-0.036 (3.18)	-0.108 (3.41)				-0.241 (2.91)		-0.738 (15.76)	-1.000 (-)		
$\Delta NFAL^b/W^b_{-1}$	0.029 (2.30)			-0.0095 (3.85)	0.0023 (3.85)	-0.135 (2.29)	-0.059 (2.20)	0.176 (4.43)				0.225 (4.92)
$\Delta NDAL^b/W^b_{-1}$	0.013 (1.65)			0.0095 (3.85)	-0.0023 (3.85)						-0.271 (5.35)	
Total of coefficients	1	0	0	0	0	-1	-1	1	-1	-1	-1	1

Part 2

	Explanatory variables:												R^2	RMSE	DW
	$\left[\dfrac{LPL^b}{W^b}\right]_{-1}$	$\dfrac{\Delta D}{W^b_{-1}}$	$\dfrac{\Delta TS}{W^b_{-1}}$	$\dfrac{\Delta TLB}{W^b_{-1}}$	$\dfrac{\Delta LS}{W^b_{-1}}$	$\dfrac{\Delta LP^b}{W^b_{-1}}$	$\dfrac{\Delta ALM^b}{W^b_{-1}}$	$\dfrac{\Delta RR}{W^b_{-1}}$	$\dfrac{\Delta(SS-SS)^{cb}}{W^b_{-1}}$	$\dfrac{\Delta SW}{W^b_{-1}}$	$\dfrac{\Delta SPL}{W^b_{-1}}$	$\dfrac{CAB}{W^b_{-1}}$			
Balance sheet items:															
$\Delta NDAS^b/W^b_{-1}$	0.631 (3.82)	0.220 (2.68)	-0.134 (5.27)		0.434 (3.32)		-0.566 (4.58)	0.362 (2.95)	0.356 (2.88)	0.158 (1.47)	-0.214 (5.30)		0.86	0.0271	2.11
$\Delta NFAS^b/W^b_{-1}$	0.369 (2.24)	-0.220 (2.68)		-0.213 (4.29)	-0.287 (2.65)	-0.416 (6.16)		-0.279 (2.29)	-0.231 (2.19)	-0.158 (1.47)	0.071 (1.41)	0.124 (2.54)	0.89	0.0229	2.30
$\Delta NFAL^b/W^b_{-1}$			0.032 (2.67)					-0.084 (2.05)			0.143 (2.53)	-0.124 (2.54)	0.89	0.0078	1.87
$\Delta NDAL^b/W^b_{-1}$			0.102 (4.15)	0.213 (4.29)	-0.147 (2.72)	0.416 (6.16)	0.566 (4.58)		-0.126 (2.53)				0.74	0.0115	1.84
Total of coefficients	1	0	0	0	0	0	0	0	0	0	0	0			

NOTES: The t-statistics in absolute value (not corrected for degrees of freedom) are reported in parentheses beneath the parameters. R^2 is the coefficient of determination not corrected for degrees of freedom, RMSE is the root-mean-square error, DW is the Durbin-Watson statistic. Explanatory variables with "x" as superscript are multiplied by W^b/W^b_{-1}.

143

Table 6: Estimates of the banks' purchases of short-term net domestic assets

Explanatory variables:

	$\dfrac{W^b}{W^b_{-1}}$	$i_{SS^{-1}}TS*-fp$ (x)	d_{76III} (x)	$\left[\dfrac{R}{W^b}\right]_{-1}$	$\left[\dfrac{SS^b}{W^b}\right]_{-1}$	$\left[\dfrac{RL}{W^b}\right]_{-1}$	$\left[\dfrac{NFAS^b}{W^b}\right]_{-1}$	$\left[\dfrac{LB^b}{W^b}\right]_{-1}$	$\left[\dfrac{LPL^b}{W^b}\right]_{-1}$
Balance sheet items:									
$\Delta R/W^b_{-1}$	0.195 (5.62)			-0.764 (10.06)	-0.220 (4.94)		-0.088 (3.01)	-0.174 (2.24)	0.249 (2.95)
$\Delta SS^b/W^b_{-1}$	0.097 (3.75)	0.036 (-)	0.108 (-)	-0.101 (1.33)	-0.177 (3.72)			-0.197 (2.41)	0.381 (4.51)
$-\Delta RL/W^b_{-1}$	0.252 (8.22)				-0.303 (6.76)	0.824 (-)	-0.174 (5.93)	-0.358 (3.71)	
$\Delta NDAS^b/W^b_{-1}$	0.543	0.036	0.108	-0.865	-0.700	0.824	-0.262	-0.729	0.631

Explanatory variables:

	$\dfrac{\Delta D}{W^b_{-1}}$	$\dfrac{\Delta TS}{W^b_{-1}}$	$\dfrac{\Delta LS}{W^b_{-1}}$	$\dfrac{\Delta\Delta LM^b}{W^b_{-1}}$	$\dfrac{\Delta RR^b}{W^b_{-1}}$	$\dfrac{\Delta(SS-SS^{cb})}{W^b_{-1}}$	$\dfrac{\Delta SW}{W^b_{-1}}$	$\dfrac{\Delta SPL}{W^b_{-1}}$	R^2	RMSE	DW
Balance sheet items:											
$\Delta R/W^b_{-1}$		-0.032 (1.60)	0.142 (2.77)		0.606 (11.06)	-0.150 (2.54)	0.158 (-)	0.240 (2.96)	0.87	0.0124	2.46
$\Delta SS^b/W^b_{-1}$	0.220 (-)		0.292 (5.70)		-0.244 (4.45)	0.657 (7.75)		0.157 (1.67)	0.78	0.0189	2.10
$-\Delta RL/W^b_{-1}$		-0.101 (5.00)		-0.566 (-)		-0.151 (1.43)		-0.611 (4.78)	0.86	0.0192	2.25
$\Delta NDAS^b/W^b_{-1}$	0.220	-0.134	0.434	-0.566	0.362	0.356	0.158	-0.214			

NOTES: See table 5.

144

Table 7: Estimates of the banks' purchases of long-term net domestic assets

Explanatory variables:

	$\dfrac{W^b}{W^b_{-1}}$	$i_{LB}^x - i_{LB*}^x$	$\hat{p}^e - \hat{p}^{*e}$	$i_{LB}^x - i_{LP}^x$	ncc^x	$\left[\dfrac{LB^b}{W^b}\right]_{-1}$	$\dfrac{\Delta TS}{W^b_{-1}}$
Balance sheet items:							
$\Delta LB^b/W^b_{-1}$	0.029 (9.90)			0.0040 (1.05)	0.010 (2.98)	-0.271 (-)	0.049 (4.92)
$-\Delta LBL^b/W^b_{-1}$		0.0011 (0.94)		0.0064 (2.63)	-0.010 (2.98)		0.011 (1.64)
$-\Delta LPL^b/W^b_{-1}$	-0.016 (5.41)	0.0084 (7.35)	-0.0023 (-)	-0.0104 (2.33)			0.042 (3.61)
$\Delta NDAL^b/W^b_{-1}$	0.013	0.0095	-0.0023	0	0	-0.271	0.102

Explanatory variables:

	$\dfrac{\Delta TLB}{W^b_{-1}}$	$\dfrac{\Delta LS}{W^b_{-1}}$	$\dfrac{\Delta LP^b}{W^b_{-1}}$	$\dfrac{\Delta\Delta LM^b}{W^b_{-1}}$	$\dfrac{\Delta(SS-SS^{cb})}{W^b_{-1}}$	R^2	RMSE	DW
Balance sheet items:								
$\Delta LB^b/W^b_{-1}$	0.213 (-)	0.087 (3.27)	0.200 (4.05)	0.296 (3.52)	-0.050 (1.63)	0.17	0.0071	1.36
$-\Delta LBL^b/W^b_{-1}$		-0.052 (3.18)				0.61	0.0048	1.75
$-\Delta LPL^b/W^b_{-1}$		-0.182 (7.58)	0.216 (4.37)	0.270 (3.21)	-0.076 (2.51)	0.59	0.0099	1.86
$\Delta NDAL^b/W^b_{-1}$	0.213	-0.147	0.416	0.566	-0.126			

NOTES: See table 5.

Table 8: Short-run interest rate elasticities of bank portfolio behaviour

$\epsilon(SS^b, i_{SS}) = 0.209$; $\epsilon(LBL^b, i_{LB}) = -0.162$

$\epsilon(NFAL^b, i_{LB*}) = 0.093$: $\epsilon(LPL^p, i_{LP}) = -0.198$

NOTES: The elasticities have been calculated as an average for 1978. The elasticity $\epsilon(NFAS^b, i_{TS*})$ is not presented, because the stock of bank short-term net foreign assets was negative in 1978.

speculation against the guilder, which resulted in a sharp upward revision of the expected depreciation of the guilder against the dollar and thus in a high value of the covered eurodollar deposit rate. Our estimates imply that the purchases of short-term net foreign assets by banks in response to the negative spread between the interest rate on short-term government debt and the covered eurodollar deposit rate were 2100 million guilders less than could be expected in periods without speculation. Because the dummy variable can be regarded as a correction term on the spread between the short-term domestic and foreign interest rates the presence of both explanatory variables in the same equations has been enforced.

The arbitrage effects of a unit spread between the domestic and foreign yields in the capital market ($i_{LB} - i_{LB*}$) are smaller than those of a similar differential in the markets for short-term financial assets ($i_{SS} - i_{TS*} - fp$), but the magnitude of the spread in the capital market is generally larger. A positive yield differential weakens the demand for long-term net foreign assets and reduces the issue activity of banks in the bond market and the market for private placements.[12] The long-term expected depreciation of the guilder against the foreign currencies is approximated by the difference between the expected inflation in the Netherlands and in the United States ($\hat{p}^e - \hat{p}^{*e}$). Expected inflation is measured as a four-quarter moving average of the actual rate of inflation lagged one quarter. An expected depreciation of the guilder in the future encourages the banking system to make loans denominated in foreign currencies. The shift is matched by borrowing in the domestic capital market. This variable illustrates that a weak currency leads to less lending in domestic currency and thus to a higher capital market yield as compared with foreign yields.

A positive spread between the yield on private placements (i_{LP}) and the bond yield (i_{LB}) of one percentage point in 1978 would have implied a negative impact effect on bank borrowing in the market for private placements of 145 million guilders on the average (see table 7). The offsetting shifts in the portfolio are a rise in the issue volume of bonds and a decline in the holdings of domestic bonds. Finally, we have found no evidence that the difference between the interest rate on short-term government debt and the discount rate ($i_{SS} - i_{CB}$) affects the composition of the portfolio.

All these redistributions among assets occur if the holdings of certain assets are too large and those of other assets too small as compared with the desired composition of the portfolio. For a given stock of bank wealth, the sum of these allocations over the whole portfolio is zero. Increases in bank wealth must also be distributed across the portfolio. They widen the gap between the desired and the lagged actual asset holdings in such a way that the sum of the partial effects for each lagged endogenous asset is equal to unity. In other words, the sum of the coefficients of a specific lagged asset is equal to minus unity. The tables show that the actual holdings of five assets (bank reserves, short-term government debt, bank borrowing from the central bank, short-term net foreign assets and bonds

bonds (LB^b)) depend on their own lagged values. This indicates that the banks bridge part of the deviation between the desired and lagged actual holdings of these assets within a quarter. For bank reserves, bank borrowing from the central bank and short-term net foreign assets the adjustment to new equilibrium is between 74 and 82 per cent of the deviation, those for short-term government debt and bonds are 18 and 27 per cent, respectively. During the first period after a shock the speed of adjustment will be different due to temporary effects of initial allocations and of shocks that influence portfolio selection directly.

We expect the adjustment for capital market transactions to be slow. In our estimates we find no adjustment at all for long-term net foreign assets and for the issues of bonds and private placements. This should not be interpreted as the absence of an adjustment path to the establishment of a new long-run equilibrium, because several variables (changes in required reserves, non-central bank holdings of short-term government debt, dollarswaps, special loans and the current account of the balance of payments) affect the composition of the portfolio immediately. The remaining part of the discrepancies is mainly allocated to the short-term assets. For instance, 26 per cent of the gap between desired and lagged actual holdings of short-term net foreign assets is bridged by temporary accumulations or decumulations of short-term net domestic assets. The greater importance of the own and cross discrepancies for short-term assets than for capital market investments may be explained by the relatively low transaction costs of reallocating existing stocks of short-term assets. This means that short-term domestic and foreign assets perform a buffer function in the short-term adjustment process. We emphasise that multicollinearity among several lagged proportions hampers the interpretation of the long-run parameters.

The coefficients of current wealth divided by lagged wealth (W^b/W^b_{-1}) describe the fixed allocations of total wealth, while the coefficients of scaled changes in the predetermined balance sheet items indicate correction terms to the fixed distribution of flows of new wealth. For instance, according to table 5, banks initially invest 76 per cent (0.543 + 0.220) of their new deposits (ΔD) in short-term net domestic assets, 20 per cent (0.415 - 0.220) in short-term net foreign assets and 4 per cent (0.029 + 0.013) in long-term foreign and domestic assets. New long-term deposits (ΔTLB) are invested for 54 per cent (0.543) in short-term net domestic assets, 20 per cent (0.415 - 0.213) in short-term net foreign assets, 3 per cent (0.029) in long-term net foreign assets, and 23 per cent (0.013 + 0.213) in long-term net domestic assets. It should be stressed that these allocation patterns are exclusive of the influence of the other explanatory variables. The hypothesis that long-term deposits are invested in the capital market to a greater extent than demand deposits is thus not rejected. A remarkable outcome is that investments in bonds and private placements appear to be complementary. Probably, these capital market investments depend on similar determinants, which do not appear explicitly in our specification.

The effects of flows of mortgage loans at the end of the initial period and thereafter are different if their size is not constant. Accelerated extension of mortgage loans ($\Delta\Delta LM^b$) leads to temporary additional borrowing from the central bank, because the crowding out of other capital market instruments partly occurs in the following period. Eventually, borrowing from the central bank is necessary for 25 per cent (0.252) of the extensions of mortgage loans, (table 6, column 1),[13] but at the end of the first quarter the percentage is 82 (0.252 + 0.566). Our estimates imply that accelerated extension of mortgage loans during the fourth quarter of 1975 to the (seasonally adjusted) amount of 379 million guilders led to a recourse to the central bank of about 310 million guilders in that quarter.

A major proportion of the variation in the stocks of bank reserves and short-term government debt can be explained by the changes in the required reserves (ΔRR) and the non-central bank holdings of short-term government debt ($\Delta SS - \Delta SS^{cb}$). An increase in the holdings of required reserves does not coincide with an equiproportional rise in total reserves, which implies that bank holdings of excess reserves become lower. The positive effect on bank reserves is compensated by a decline in short-term government debt and net foreign assets. Bank holdings of short-term government debt increase, both directly and indirectly, when the volume of this type of debt grows. Directly, banks accumulate 66 per cent of new issues, which is financed by reductions in bank reserves and short-term net foreign asset investments and by a rise in borrowing from the central bank, but also by diminishing net domestic capital market investments. Indirectly, banks accumulate a fraction of the new issues in response to higher interest rates on short-term government debt (i_{SS}).

Contrary to our expectations, we could not find any evidence of the restrictive influence of the quota scheme for bank borrowing from the central bank. Neither the variable penalty rate (i_p) nor the borrowing ceiling (bc) enter our empirical equations. Dollarswaps (ΔSW) cause a decrease in bank holdings of short-term net foreign assets and an increase in holdings of bank reserves of only 16 per cent. Special loans (ΔSPL) raise the amount of the discounts and advances including special loans. In theory, the absolute value of this coefficient should equal unity. Finally, the regulation affecting short-term international capital flows (reg) is not included because of multicollinearity with the current account position.

Since the second quarter of 1977 net credit ceilings (ncc) have stimulated banks to issue bonds and private placements to create more room for the extension of credit to domestic residents. Although there are but few observations for this instrument of monetary policy, our tentative conclusion is that especially the issuance of bonds has risen as a consequence of its use, and that bonds are also the outlet for additional funds. In van Loo (1983, chapter 6) we investigate the effect on the supply of mortgage loans and private placements by sector and on the corresponding interest rates. The overall interest rate effects of this instrument follow from the simulations with the complete model of the financial system.

A positive current account balance (CAB) induces a shift from long-term to short-term net foreign assets. Experiments with a proxy for the surplus or deficit of the non-monetary sectors instead of the current account balance were not successful. Usually, the deficit of the non-monetary sectors is assumed to have been the cause of the substantial decrease in short-term net foreign assets (see table 3) during the period 1976-1978. In our specification, this effect of monetary tightness is captured as follows. A deficit of the non-monetary sectors implies a decline in bank deposits held by international traders. From 1976 until 1978 the amount of new bank deposits was not always sufficient to finance the extension of short-term bank loans, mortgage loans and private placements, so that the flow of bank wealth (net disposable funds), as defined in our model, was sometimes negative. According to the estimates of table 5 (see column 1), a negative flow of wealth induces a decrease in short-term net foreign assets, because these assets perform an important buffer function.

The tables showing the bank portfolio selection model indicate that most of the estimated parameters are in agreement with our hypotheses. The portfolio choice appears to depend on a broad spectrum of domestic and foreign interest rates. The interest sensitivity of the short-term and long-term net foreign assets is remarkable because these assets also include net claims on non-residents denominated in guilders. Short-term net domestic and foreign assets perform a buffer function in the short-term adjustment process. Four tools of monetary policy explicitly restrict the portfolio decisions of the banking system: the net credit ceiling, reserve requirements, dollarswaps and special loans. The equations fail to capture the impact of the quota scheme of bank borrowing from the central bank. The degree of explanation of the equations is quite respectable in all cases with the exception of the equation for domestic bond holdings.

The flows of new bank wealth and the change in required reserves are examples of impact variables which affect the actual composition of the bank portfolio immediately and are independent of interest rates or other factors. [14] The impact variable include both important sources of funds (demand deposits, short-term and long-term time and savings deposits) and major types of bank investments (short-term bank loans, mortgage loans and private placements). These balance sheet items are relatively predetermined for the banks themselves. This makes banks fairly vulnerable to unexpected developments in these items, so that they are forced to hold more relatively liquid, short-term assets than institutional investors.

4. THE INTEREST RATE SETTING BEHAVIOUR OF THE BANKS

Banks may affect the demand for deposits and for several types of loans by adjusting the corresponding interest rate. This section investigates the interest rate setting behaviour of those balance sheet items of which the banks are the only supplying sector. These items are short-term time and savings deposits (TS), long-term time and savings deposits with banks (TLB) and short-term bank loans granted to the private sector (LS). The interest rate on demand deposits (D) is postulated to be constant. The movements in the yields on private placements and mortgage loans, items which are also supplied by other financial institutions, are explained in van Loo (1983, section 6.1).

Deposit interest rate setting is a major decision in the liability management of banks. It is a key factor in determining the size of a bank, measured by total assets or total liabilities. The theoretical interest rate setting functions, developed in van Loo (1983, section 2.4), are based on the traditional assumption of profit-maximising banks.

The deposit rate setting functions of profit-maximising banks include four categories of variables. For the <u>interest rate on short-term time and savings deposits</u> (i_{TS}), we specify:

$$i_{TS} = f(i_{SS}^{+}, \Delta TS / LIA_{-1}^{b}, reg, i_{TS_{-1}}^{+})$$

Similarly, we postulate:

$$i_{TLB} = f(i_{SS}^{+}, \Delta TLB / LIA_{-1}^{b}, reg, i_{TLB_{-1}}^{+})$$

First, the interest rate on short-term government debt (i_{SS}) functions as the link between foreign short-term interest rates and the discount rate on the one hand, and the domestic deposit rates on the other hand. Consequently, foreign variables and the discount rate do not enter the specification of the deposit rates explicitly, but exert their influence through the interest rate on short-term government debt. Second, banks offer a lower deposit rate when the demand for deposits grows. The current flow of new deposits (ΔTS or ΔTLB) can be used as a proxy for all demand effects. It is scaled by total bank liabilities lagged one quarter (LIA_{-1}^{b}). A rise in demand may affect the deposit rate positively, if banks maximise the volume of their deposits. Third, regulations affecting bank behaviour (reg) may also cause a discrepancy between the deposit rate and the interest rate on short-term government debt. Finally, the lagged deposit rate is included to account for lags in the adjustment of the deposit rate to its desired level. The adjustment coefficient is equal to one minus the coefficient of the lagged deposit rate.

The ordinary least-squares estimates for the interest rates on short-term time and savings deposits (i_{TS}) and long-term time and savings deposits (i_{TLB}) for the sample period 1967:I – 1978: IV, with a linear specification, are shown in table 9. The empirical equation for the short-term deposit rate includes the four categories of variables mentioned above:

1. The coefficient of the interest rate on short-term government debt is not significantly different from unity, so that movements in that rate lead to identical variations in the short-term deposit rate.

2. An increase in the demand for short-term deposits exerts a downward pressure on the deposit rate which is consistent with the hypothesis of profit maximisation. According to that estimate, the greatest effect amounts to 0.16 percentage points in the third quarter of 1973.

3. An important change in the regulation affecting deposit rate setting occurred in 1977. The Netherlands Bank monitors the liquidity of the banks under its supervision and imposes relatively fixed liquidity requirements.[15] In 1977 the liquidity requirement on short-term interbank deposits was tightened which made time deposits obtained from the private non-financial sector more attractive. The banks offered higher deposit rates to the private sector (i_{TS}) in response to that policy action. The liquidity requirement variable (liq) is unity in 1978 and zero elsewhere. The regression coefficient shows that the upward pressure on the deposit rate was more than one per cent.

   During the summer of 1976 rumours about a possible revaluation of the Deutsche Mark weakened the other snake currencies. The Netherlands Bank intervened in the exchange market and restricted the recourse of the banks to its facilities in order to strengthen the position of the guilder within the snake. The result was an extremely tight market for short-term funds. In turn, the banks tried to obtain more resources from the private sector by raising the deposit rate. The dummy variable $d_{76II,III}$ captures this effect.

4. The market for short-term time and savings deposits is rather efficient: almost the whole adjustment to new information occurs within a quarter.

The empirical equation for the <u>long-term deposit rate</u>, approximated by the savings deposit rate, is rather simple. The short-term response to a unit increase in the interest rate on short-term government debt is 0.05 percentage points. The quarterly adjustment of the deposit rate is only 21 per cent of the discrepancy between the equilibrium and the actual rate. The ultimate effect of the short-term rate is about 0.25 percentage points. Experiments regarding the possible effect of the bond yield have not been successful. The hypothesis that the imposition of a net credit ceiling by the Netherlands Bank has lifted the savings deposit rate has been rejected.

Table 9: Estimates of the banks' interest rate setting behaviour

---

The interest rate on short-term time and savings deposits:

$$i_{TS} = \underset{(1.00)}{-0.106} + \underset{(37.37)}{0.978i_{SS}} - \underset{(1.13)}{2.819} \frac{\Delta TS}{LIA_{-1}^b} + \underset{(9.70)}{1.231liq}$$

$$+ \underset{(4.43)}{0.887d_{76II,III}} + \underset{(1.79)}{0.044i_{TS_{-1}}}$$

$$\bar{R}^2 = 0.99, \quad RMSE = 0.23, \quad DW = 1.60$$

The interest rate on long-term time and savings deposits:

$$i_{TLB} = \underset{(3.49)}{0.649} + \underset{(7.96)}{0.053i_{SS}} + \underset{(18.66)}{0.785i_{TLB_{-1}}}$$

$$\bar{R}^2 = 0.91, \quad RMSE = 0.11, \quad DW = 1.74$$

The interest rate on short-term bank loans granted to the private sector:

1967:I - 1973:II

$$i_{LS} = \underset{(13.29)}{1.488} + \underset{(50.93)}{1.003i_{CB}}$$

$$\bar{R}^2 = 0.99, \quad RMSE = 0.09, \quad DW = 2.60$$

1973:III - 1978:IV

$$i_{LS} = \underset{(13.86)}{0.958i_{CB}} + \underset{(4.37)}{0.286i_{CB_{-1}}} + \underset{(8.25)}{0.587}\max(i_{TS} - i_{CB} - 1.5, 0)$$

$$+ \underset{(5.44)}{0.384}\max\{(i_{TS} - i_{CB} - 1.5)_{-1}, 0\} + \underset{(2.28)}{0.241ncc}$$

$$\bar{R}^2 = 0.99, \quad RMSE = 0.20, \quad DW = 1.80$$

NOTES: The t-statistics in absolute value (corrected for degrees of freedom) are reported in parentheses beneath the parameters, $\bar{R}^2$ is coefficient of determination corrected for degrees of freedom, RMSE is the root-mean-square error, DW is the Durbin-Watson statistic.

Until August 1973, the <u>overdraft rate</u> (i_{LS}) for prime borrowers, including commission, was equal to the discount rate on promissory notes of the central bank (i_{CB}) plus a mark-up of about 1.5 percentage points. The simple equation in table 9, estimated for the period 1967:1 – 1973:II, reflects the tie. For the banks the discount rate was the peg with which marginal returns on assets and marginal costs on sources of funds were equated at the optimum.[16] The rationale for the tie was that until September 1973 the Netherlands Bank was willing to provide unlimited discounts and advances to the banking system at a fixed discount rate.

The specification of the overdraft rate setting function since the third quarter of 1973 is not completely similar to that of the deposit rate setting functions:

$$i_{LS} = f(i_{CB}^+, \ \max(i_{TS}^+ - i_{CB}^+ - 1.5, 0), \ \Delta LS/LIA_{-1}^b, \ reg, \ i_{LS_{-1}}^+)$$

Since September 1973 a quota scheme for bank borrowing from the central bank has been in force (see also the previous section). The Netherlands Bank imposes a limit on the average recourse of an individual bank at the lombard rate. A surcharge must be paid as soon as a bank exceeds its quota, so that the coefficient of the discount rate in the rate setting function may exceed unity. Since October 1973, the banks have imposed an additional flexible mark-up on the loan rate, depending on the tightness of the market for short-term ("money market") investments and the discount policy. The hypothesis is that this mark-up will be used as soon as the interest rate on short-term time and savings deposits (i_{TS}) exceeds the basic overdraft rate for prime borrowers (i_{CB} + 1.5%).

Three other explanatory variables should be mentioned. Banks raise the loan rate when the demand for loans is boosting. Again, the current flow (ΔLS) is used as a proxy for all demand effects and it is scaled by total bank liabilities lagged one quarter (LIA_{-1}^b). Regulations affecting bank behaviour (reg) may also affect loan pricing. Finally, the lagged loan rate is included to allow for lags in the adjustment process.

The ordinary least-squares estimate for the linear version of this equation during the sample period 1973:III – 1979:IV is the equation at the bottom of table 9. Introduction of lagged independent variables gives slightly better results than a specification with the lagged dependent variable ($i_{LS_{-1}}$). During several quarters the banks have exceeded their quota. The surcharge to be paid is reflected by the more than proportional total effect of the discount rate on the loan rate. Any positive difference between the "money market" rate and the discount rate is fully accounted for in the loan rate setting after two quarters. Demand effects exert no influence. Finally, since the third quarter of 1977 the net credit ceiling (ncc) has raised the loan rate by about 0.24 percentage points.

The evidence presented in this section shows that both the

deposit rates and the loan rate depend either directly or indirectly on the interest rate on short-term government debt. In our model the latter rate is the crucial variable in the transmission mechanism between foreign and domestic financial markets for short-term funds. Fluctuations in short-term foreign interest rates thus have an impact on the deposit rates and the loan rate through the rate on short-term government debt.

5. SUMMARY

This study provides the results of an empirical analysis of bank behaviour in the Netherlands. Commercial banks constitute the largest part of the banking system and are also the most diversified financial institutions. Genuine savings deposits, demand deposits and short-term time deposits are the most important sources of funds, while short-term bank loans, mortgage loans and private placements are the major outlets.

Bank portfolio behaviour involves eight balance sheet items which are currently endogenous for the banks: bank reserves, short-term government debt, short-term and long-term net foreign assets, investments in domestic bonds, borrowing in the capital market by way of bonds and private placements and borrowing from the central bank. The portfolio choice appears to depend on a broad spectrum of domestic and foreign interest rates. For instance, banks play a major role in the arbitrage process underlying the international interest rate parity. Flows of deposits and several types of loans are examples of impact variables which affect the bank portfolio independent of interest rates. These balance sheet items are relatively predetermined for the banks themselves. This makes banks fairly vulnerable to unexpected shocks in the demand for deposits and the demand for loans, so that they are forced to accumulate more liquid assets than institutional investors.

Four tools of monetary policy explicitly restrict the portfolio decisions of the banking system. Net credit ceilings compel banks to borrow in the capital market in order to enlarge the possibility to extend loans to domestic residents. Required reserves imply more holdings of bank reserves and less holdings of short-term government debt and net foreign assets. Dollarswaps cause a decrease in short-term net foreign assets and an increase in bank reserves. Special loans raise the amount of bank borrowing from the central bank. Moreover, monetary tightness or ease caused by flows of funds between the Netherlands and abroad affects bank behaviour mainly through the size of the deposits. The equations fail to capture the impact of the quota scheme of bank borrowing from the central bank.

Interest rate setting involves balance sheet items which are outside the short-run control of banks: demand deposits, short-term and long-term time and savings deposits, short-term bank loans, mortgage loans and private placements. The interest rate on demand deposits is postulated to be constant. The interest rates on time and savings deposits are linked to the rate on short-term government debt, which in turn interacts with the corresponding foreign rates. The discount rate set by the central bank serves as the basis for the interest rate on short-term bank loans. Since 1973, any positive difference between the short-term time deposit rate and the discount rate is fully accounted for in the loan rate setting after two quarters. The net credit ceiling has also raised the loan rate to some extent. Mortgage loans and private placements are assets which are also supplied by other financial institutions. These yields are not explained in this paper.[17] In a model of the complete financial system they are linked to foreign long-term interest rates via the yield on domestic bonds.

APPENDIX: LIST OF SYMBOLS AND DESCRIPTION OF THE DATA

Unless otherwise stated, the variables have the following characteristics. Guilder magnitudes are measured in millions of guilders at current prices. Stock variables are end-of-quarter data. The corresponding flows are net increases or decreases in the stock variables. These and other flow variables are measured on a quarterly basis. Interest rates and forward premiums are quarterly averages, measured in percentage points on an annual basis.

As far as possible, the seasonally unadjusted financial stock data have been constructed by decrementing backward from the end-of-year stocks for 1978 using the quarterly flows. This procedure guarantees that the flows are indeed equal to the net increases or decreases in the stocks, and avoids inconsistencies from breaks in time series. Data of the real side of the economy provided by the Central Planning Bureau have been seasonally corrected by the CPB method. Data of financial stocks and of other real variables have been seasonally adjusted by the multiplicative moving method, in most cases for the period 1961:I - 1978:IV. Several variables have not been seasonally corrected either because the stocks were both positive and negative during the sample period or because the time series is very erratic. These variables are: CAB, LPL^b, $NFAL2^b$, $NFAS^b$, R, RL and SS^{cb}. Interest rates and forward premiums have not been seasonally adjusted either.

The Quarterly Statistics of The Netherlands Bank are the main source of the financial flow and stock data. This data set has been extended and adjusted in several ways by using both other sources and our own estimates. We refer to van Loo (1983) for more details.

LIST OF VARIABLES

bc	Borrowing ceiling for bank borrowing from the central bank, expressed as a proportion of lagged bank wealth. The ceiling concerns the quota available without surcharges.
d_1	Dummy variable reflecting the period that the bank loan rate was dependent only on the discount rate. Equals unity in the period 1967:I - 1973:II and zero elsewhere.

d_2 Dummy variable reflecting the period that the bank loan rate was also dependent on the situation in the market for short-term funds. Equals unity in the period 1973:III – 1978:IV and zero elsewhere.

$d_{76II,III}$ Dummy variable reflecting rumours about a possible revaluation of the Deutsche mark. Equals unity in 1976:II and 1976:III and zero elsewhere.

d_{76III} See $d_{76II,III}$. Equals unity in 1976:III and zero elsewhere.

fp   Forward premium of the guilder against foreign currencies (in the theoretical part) or against the US dollar (in the empirical part).

i_{CB} Discount rate on promissory notes.

i_{LB} Bond yield measured as the average yield on the latest three long-term central government bonds.

$i_{LB}{}^*$ Yield on long-term government bonds in the United States.

i_{LP} Interest rate on private placements, measured as the rate on private placements issued by public utilities.

i_{LS} Interest rate on short-term bank loans, measured as the overdraft rate including commission for prime borrowers.

i_P Penalty interest rate: variable surcharge on bank borrowing above the fixed surcharge excess borrowing.

i_{SS} Interest rate on short-term government debt, measured as the rate on three-month loans to local authorities.

i_{TLB} Interest rate on long-term deposits with banks, measured as the average of the rates on ordinary savings deposits and time savings deposits withdrawable three months after notice.

i_{TS} Interest rate on short-term time and savings deposits, measured as the rate on three-month time deposits in large amounts.

i_{TS*} Interest rate on foreign short-term time deposits, measured as the uncovered rate on three-month Eurodollar deposits.

liq   Liquidity requirement variable to capture the tightening of the liquidity requirement on short-term interbank deposits. Equals unity in 1978 and zero elsewhere.

ncc   Net credit ceiling: variable to capture the tightness of this ceiling. Equals unity since 1977:III and zero elsewhere.

$\hat{p}^e$ Expected rate of inflation, measured as a four-quarter moving average, lagged one quarter, of the rate of change of the price level of the gross national product.

$\hat{p}{*}^e$ Expected rate of foreign inflation, measured as a four-quarter moving average, lagged one quarter, of the rate of change of the price level of the gross national product in the United States.

reg   Regulation variable to capture the prohibition for banks to pay interest on short-term guilder deposits. Equals unity

	from 1972:II to 1973:II, 0.5 from 1973:III to 1974:I, 0.25 from 1974:II to 1975:IV and zero elsewhere. Source: Den Butter, Fase en Huijser (1979). The same symbol has been used in section 4 to indicate regulations affecting the interest rates on bank deposits and short-term bank loans.
CAB	Current account balance, measured as a two-quarter moving average.
D	Demand deposits.
DG^b	Deposits of the central government with giro institutions. These institutions belong to the sector "banks".
LB^b	Bonds held by banks.
LBL^b	Bonds issued by banks.
LIA^b	Total liabilities of banks.
LM^b	Mortgage loans supplied by banks.
LP^b	Private placements with banks (bank assets).
LPL^b	Private placements of banks (bank liabilities).
LS	Short-term bank loans (granted to the private sector).
$NDAL^b$	Long-term net domestic assets of banks.
$NDAS^b$	Short-term net domestic assets of banks.
$NFAL^b$	Long-term net foreign assets of banks (the sum of $NFAL1^b$ and $NFAL2^b$).
$NFAL1^b$	Foreign bonds held by banks.
$NFAL2^b$	Other long-term net foreign assets of banks.
$NFAS^b$	Short-term net foreign assets of banks.
NOL^b	Net other liabilities of banks.
R	Bank reserves.
RL	Bank demand for discounts and advances (including special loans) from the central bank.
SPL	Special loans of banks granted by the central bank.
SS	Short-term government debt.
SS^b	Short-term government debt held by banks.
SS^{cb}	Short-term government debt held by the central bank.
SW	Dollarswaps.
TLB	Long-term time and savings deposits with banks.
TLB1	Genuine savings deposits with banks.
TLB2	Savings certificates to bearer issued by banks.
TLB3	Long-term deposits with banks.
TS	Short-term time and savings deposits with banks.
TS1	Short-term time deposits with banks.
TS2	Foreign currency deposits with banks.
TS3	Liquid savings deposits with banks.
W^b	Wealth of banks.

NOTES

1.   This study is my PhD dissertation at Erasmus University, Rotterdam, 1983. The model of the Dutch financial system consists of 91 equations, of which 47 are behavioural equations. It has been estimated with quarterly data for the period 1967-1978 and has been used to analyse the dynamic response of the financial system to a variety of exogenous shocks. We started the study in 1980 with a data set available at that time. Updating of this data set has been neglected so far in view of the high effort needed to gather more recent data of so many variables.

2.   The revised Act on the Supervision of the Credit System, in force as from January 1, 1979, records commercial banks (including non-member agricultural credit institutions) as "universal banks" and agricultural credit institutions as "banks organized on a cooperative basis".

3.   Private or direct placements are capital market instruments which are negotiated between lender and borrower and have only a limited degree of marketability. The market for private placements is the largest segment in the Dutch capital market. This springs mainly from the important volume of contractual savings through institutional investors.

4.   See van Loo (1980-2, section 3.2).

5.   Den Butter, Fase en Huijser (1979, p. 165).

6.   We refer to Korteweg and van Loo (1977, p. 28) for more details.

7.   Den Dunnen (1973, 1979, 1981), Bosman (1980, 1984) and Korteweg (1980) provide surveys of recent monetary policy in the Netherlands. See also Zijlstra (1979) and Kessler (1981).

8.   See Timmerman (1977).

9.   See Timmerman (1977) and Wessels (1982).

10.   See Annual Report of the Netherlands Bank, table 7 of the Statistical Annex.

11.   This amount is the product of the estimated parameter (0.036) and the average value of bank wealth (W^b) over 1978 (13787 million guilders). During the sample period bank wealth varied between 10039 and 21462 million guilders.

12.   In the model of the complete financial system the domestic bond yield reacts somewhat less than proportionally on shocks in foreign bond yields.

13.   Note that mortgage loans reduce the amount of bank wealth.

14.   Compare Laidler (1984).

15.   These liquidity requirements differ from the more flexible liquidity requirements used as an instrument of monetary policy.

16.   Van Loo (1980-1, section 4.2).

17.   See van Loo (1983, section 6.1).

A MARKOWITZ APPROACH TO REGULATION: THE CASE OF FRENCH OPEN MUTUAL FUNDS

Georges Gallais-Hamonno

INTRODUCTION

The French Open Mutual Funds

As is well known, closed funds were first devised in Scotland, around 1870, but the first open fund was the Massachussets Investors Trust introduced in Boston in 1924. Although the "open" formula proved a success and was adopted over Europe in the 50's, it was only in 1964 that the first French open funds were created (Sociétés d'Investissement à Capital Variable - SICAV).[1] For the past 20 years, they have developed satisfactorily: at the end of 1983 there were 200 of them and they possessed some 7% of the total value of the French equity capital quoted on the Paris Stock Exchange.

Open funds offer to households a large choice either of managers (all banks and many insurance companies have several SICAV), or of portfolio objectives and/or portfolio specialization.

The objectives of this paper

As compared to their American counterparts, French funds present some originality as regards portfolio management: three legal guidelines have to be followed for portfolio composition and this limits their risk-return space.

The objective of this paper is to analyse empirically the effect of such legal constraints. Section I presents the regulations bearing on the composition of the portfolios. Section II deals with the method used. If the Markowitz efficient frontier is well-known as an analytical tool, the empirical implication of the theory of expected market equilibrium seems to be rather new. Section III presents the results.

I. THE REGULATIONS ON SICAV PORTFOLIOS

As regards their portfolios, the managers of French open funds have to satisfy three legal requirements.

1. "The bond of bonds": every fund should at any time have at least
30% of its total assets invested in French Bonds and/or in French
Francs liquidity.

The Lorain Committee unanimously advocated this constraint
when they recommended the creation of SICAV. The official reason
advanced for such a constraint is that of decreasing the risk of the
portfolio. Another less official reason was that the Treasury feared
it would be difficult to sell its Government bond issues if SICAV were
left free to buy only stocks. This requirement is compulsory for all
SICAV, whatever their financial objectives.

The other two are not legally compulsory: either the SICAV
chooses to elect them or not; but once chosen the SICAV has to
comply with it (or them) and cannot reverse its decision.

2. A first limit to international diversification: the SICAV should
have less than 50% of its portfolio invested in foreign equities (stocks
and bonds) in order to become eligible for the Firms-Profit-Sharing
Funds.

This requirement was instituted in 1969 by General de Gaulle,
who was then trying to promote the ownership of equities among
French salaried workers. Any firm employing more than 50 persons is
requested by law to have a profit-sharing plan, the funds for which
come from a withdrawal from profits after tax (with an equal
tax-credit). Thus the scheme is in effect paid for by all taxpayers.

This profit sharing plan is invested in a firm (or inter-firms)
Open Investment Fund,[2] which may either specialize in the firm's
stock (if the firm is quoted), or buy and manage a diversified
portfolio; this portfolio can be composed of individual equities or of
SICAV shares or of both.[3]

As this scheme is paid for by taxpayers, the international
diversification of the firms' open investment funds is limited to 5%
of their assets, whereas 95% of them are to be invested in French
equities. In order to become eligible, i.e. to be considered as a
French stock by the Firms-Funds, a SICAV should have less than 50%
of its portfolio invested in foreign equities.[4] Thus, about half of the
SICAV which have specialized in stocks (as distinct from those
specializing in bonds) have elected to comply with this rule, so as to
be sold to Firms-Funds.

3. A second limit to international diversification: this consists of
the "Monory" Guideline. In order to be eligible for the tax benefit of
the Monory fiscal deduction, the SICAV should have 60% of their
assets invested in French stocks. With the compulsory 30%
investment in bonds, this means 90% invested in French equities and
only 10% in international ones. This rule was instituted in July 1978,
when the finance minister, M. Monory, introduced the possibility for
taxpayers to deduct up to 5,000 FF from taxable income if the
equivalent amount is invested in French bonds or stocks and if the
investment lasts for at least 5 years. This measure has met with
great success and some thirty-five SICAV were created with such

specialization in French equities for tax avoidance purposes.

II.   THE METHOD USED: THE MARKOWITZ EFFICIENT FRONTIER

The Markowitz efficient frontier seems to be the pertinent analytical tool for coping with such a problem. Indeed, because of the regulation constraints, some existing securities become "ineligible" for the portfolio. Thus, the eligible efficient frontier is modified. It may be dominated (less efficient than) the efficient set which would have been obtained without legal requirements.

As the guidelines bear on international diversification, the 27 indices of the 22 Stock-Exchanges existing in 1950 (as in Table 1 overleaf) were used for individual securities.[5]

The method is to estimate the efficient sets[6] with and without constraints, by computing the efficient portfolios combining these indices (which is tantamount to assuming that Funds managers obtain their desired risk-return level by combining different national markets, while buying on each relevant Stock Exchange a one-beta-portfolio). The shifts in the efficient frontiers are used to measure the impact of the phenomenon studied.

The period under observation: 1951 – 1964

As was said, French Open Funds were created in 1964. We shall use data over the time-span before that date for a purely logical reason. The impact of legal guidelines should be studied before the imposition of a regulation, in order to prevent enforcements with perverse effects. Thus, when the Lorain Committee (who recommended the creation of SICAV) debated the adoption or otherwise of legal requirements, they should have analysed the potential effects using existing data, i.e. bearing on the period before 1964.

We now work on the assumption that the ex ante distributions of annual returns expected by Funds Managers for the period after 1964 are measured by the actual (ex post) ones for the period 1950 – 1964.

The data used

The distribution of yearly rates of return for each national index is computed using the two closing days (December 31 T and T – 1).

As French funds are not allowed to use hedging (no more than short sales or leverage), the annual rates of return are corrected for the rate of exchange variations between the country concerned and the French Franc. Thus, these adjusted rates of return measure the gains or losses accruing to a French holder of the fund.

Table 1 shows the two basic parameters of the analysis: the average rate of return and the standard error of the distributions, which measures, as usual, the risk. (In order to have one more year's data, we use the 1964 rates of return.) The last column shows the average returns estimated with the ISML regression (see below).

Table 1:   1951-1964 Risk and Return of International Indices

	ACTUAL*		ESTIMATED ON ISML
	Average Return % Ra	Risk (Standard Error) % RKa	Average Return 27 indices % Re**
1. French Bonds	9.25	4.4	7.0
2. French Stocks	18.7	20.5	13.2
3. USA	14.6	11.9	9.9
4. United Kingdom	11.2	13.8	10.6
5. Netherlands	19.3	27.7	15.9
6. Federal Germany	24.7	27.8	15.9
7. Italy	17.3	21.5	13.5
8. Belgium	9.3	9.3	8.9
9. Switzerland	10.9	17.6	12.0
10. Norway	5.0	9.6	9.0
11. Sweden	12.2	12.9	10.3
12. Canada Industrial	13.0	10.6	9.4
13. Canada Mining	10.6	16.3	11.6
14. Canada Paper	16.2	19.6	12.8
15. South Africa gold mines	1.2	15.1	11.1
16. Australia	8.4	13.9	10.6
17. Japan	28.9	35.3	18.8
18. Denmark Industrial	8.0	10.7	9.4
19. Denmark Mining	9.2	13.2	10.4
20. Israel	12.3	41.6	21.1
21. Venezuela	8.8	21.9	13.7
22. South Africa Industrial	11.5	20.3	13.0
23. Austria	22.8	22.8	14.0
24. Finland	12.2	21.0	13.3
25. Mexico	6.3	17.6	12.0
26. New Zealand	8.9	14.0	10.7
27. Spain	6.6	31.6	17.3

* Based on yearly rates of return adjusted for rate of exchange fluctuations relative to the FF.

** $Re = 5.41 + 0.378\ RKa$
T. Student: (2.99)† (2.077)†
$R^2 = .261$ F. Fischer: 8.838†
† - significant at 5% level.

Figure 1 International Security Market Line - (1951 - 1964)

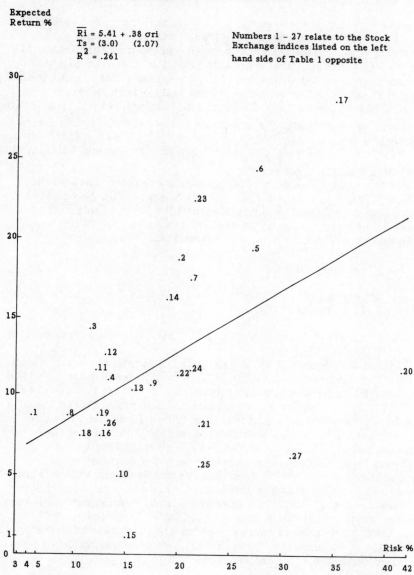

The estimate of an international security market line (ISML)

As Figure 1 shows, the ex post 1950-1964 risks (measured by the standard error) and returns are very much scattered in the risk-return space. This reflects the well-known fact that financial markets were (and still are) segmented and that the several economies were (and still are) not fully integrated. The result is that financial flows between countries do not fully offset differences in returns adjusted for risk and currency fluctuations. In our risk-return space, five securities clearly "dominate"[7] the others: French Bonds (1), USA (3), Austria (23), Federal Germany (6) and Japan (17). Thus, only these - and especially not the French Stocks - would be elected in the different efficient portfolios.[8]

But the logic of modern portfolio theory requests that markets should be in equilibrium and that managers expect this to be so: that is why the International Security Market Line facing the Funds Managers has been estimated in the risk return space. More precisely, the following model was estimated:

$$\overline{Ri} = a\,(\sigma\,Ri) + b + \epsilon$$

with $\overline{Ri}$ = average rate of return over 1950-1964 for security i [proxy for E (ri)]

σRi = standard error of security "i" rates of return distribution.

This model departs from the accepted theoretical one, in which the SML is stated in terms either of beta coefficients (Sharpe (1964)) or of covariance between security returns and market (Fama (1968)).

This "impure" model was chosen because it prevents the use of a variable representing a "world index" in which all of the 27 indices would appear. With such a world index, many (if not all) of the estimated beta coefficients would have been statistically not significant, which would have deprived of any significance the subsequent regression which uses them as the determinant variable.

We thus assume that the Funds managers do control the risk of the several national portfolios they are buying, and expect the return to be the adjusted rate of return on the ISML. Technically, this means that the estimated rates of return are substituted for the actual ones in the expected returns vector for the quadratic programming of the efficient frontiers.

Summary of the method

1.   Computation of annual rates of return of 27 national indexes, and adjustment for rates of exchange variations relative to the French Franc.
2.   Estimates of the ISML and the estimated returns are used for ex ante ones.
3.   Computation of efficient portfolios with a progressive inclusion of legal constraints.

III. THE RESULTS: THE COST OF REGULATION

Five efficient frontiers were estimated, using the 1951 – 1964 rates of return data of 27 national indices (corrected for exchange fluctuations). These frontiers are:

A   Frontier without constraints

B   Frontier with French Bonds $\geq$ 30%

B'   Frontier with French Bonds + French Stocks $\geq$ 50% (in order to analyse separately the impact of the Bond-Rule and that of the limited international diversification rule)

C   Frontier with the 1969 regulation, i.e. French Bonds $\geq$ 30% <u>and</u> French Bonds + French Stocks $\geq$ 50%

D   Rule 1969 – Frontier for a "growth-SICAV" i.e. French Bonds = 30% <u>and</u> French Stocks $\geq$ 20% (the idea is that a SICAV with a growth objective will try to have as many stocks as possible and will just comply with the minimum bond-requirement

E   "Monory Guideline", i.e. French Bonds = 30% <u>and</u> French Stocks $\geq$ 60%

Figure 2 shows the results.[9]

As we expected, <u>the basic result of each of these three legal requirements is to increase the risk for any given level of expected return</u>: all the "regulated" frontiers shift from left to right. Moreover, the "regulated" frontiers are truncated, thus preventing the managers from obtaining some level of risk-return; the Maximum Expected Return Portfolio drops from 21.16% without requirements to 16.93% with the 30% bond requirement, to 17.16% with the 50% maximum international diversification and to 15.33% with both these regulations.

Some remarks can be made:

1.   A look at the securities elected by the different portfolios of frontier A (without requirements) shows that French Stocks are never elected. The reason is that in the 13% expected-return range, three indices are doing better than the French Stock index, namely Venezuela, South African Industrial and Finland; they present a similar return but a negative covariance with the French Bonds and negative covariance between themselves.

From the French Government's point of view, this fact makes credible the necessity for legal limits on international diversification: without any legal requirements, there would be a potential danger of all savings being invested abroad, and nothing on the French Stock Exchanges.

2.   The requirements of a minimum 30% invested in bonds is useless or has a perverse effect (cf. frontier B). The managers of portfolios in a low risk return class (empirically below 12%) buy bonds. This is the rationale for the creation, on their own accord, of SICAV with a yield-objective and a portfolio combining only bonds with different maturities. For higher returns, this legal requirement – the

Figure 2 Efficient Frontiers (with and without constraints)

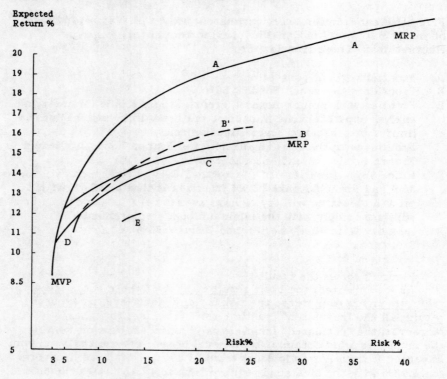

official reason for which, let us remember, was to decrease risk -
increases it. And this cost, in terms of increased risk, is
proportionate to the level of return, and increases very rapidly.
3.   The limit to international diversification (cf. B') is interesting,
because its effect is not the same for all risk-return classes. For low
classes, its perverse effect (i.e. risk increase) is greater than that of
the bond-requirement, because to have at least 50% invested in
French equities is more stringent than to have 30% invested in bonds
(and 70% of potential international diversification). But for a higher
risk-return class (empirically above 14.5%), this regulation seems to
be less perverse, because 50% in French Stocks makes it possible to
obtain a greater return (for the same risk) than a compulsory 30% in
French Bonds. This is why the Maximum Return Portfolio is 17.60%
versus 16.93%.
4.   Of course, the combination of both requirements leads the
frontier C to a more pronounced rightward shift.
5.   The growth objective, with the bond requirement at its minimum
30%, is inadequate for some low risk-return levels when bond
portfolios are more efficient. This is the meaning of the first three
portfolios on the D frontier: empirically, below a 12% expected
return, the manager would do better to hold more than 30% in bonds
and the remaining up to 50% in French Stocks.
6.   The Monory requirement frontier E (30% in bonds and 60% in
French Stocks) appears to be very strict. Empirically the efficient
set is composed of only two portfolios: the Minimum Variance
Portfolio holding only three foreign indices (Japan, Israel and South
African Industrial, which are negatively correlated between each
other), besides 90% in French equities, and the Maximum Return
Portfolio holding only the one with the greatest risk-return level
(Israel).

But the basic fact is the quadrupling of the level of risk of the
Minimum Variance Portfolio, which jumps from 3.1% (1-A, B, C) to
13.8%! This measures the cost, in terms of risk and return, of the
fiscal incentive. As the incentive is the deduction from taxable
income of the amount invested, the advantage is equal to the
marginal rate of taxation. In other words, as long as the potential
decrease in value (as measured by the security standard error of
returns) is less than the individual's marginal rate of taxation, the
tax-payer is losing nothing and his effective return remains positive.
This fiscal advantage might therefore be considered as offsetting the
increase in risk. Unfortunately, with the data on hand, this does not
seem to be the case. The household has a choice between either

i)   buying the 12% return portfolio on C with a risk equal to
4.69, which has a 5% chance (2 times the standard error) of
getting an annual return of 2.62%, or
ii)   buying the 12% return M.V.P. on E with a risk equal to
13.86%, thus having a 5% chance of getting an annual return of
-15.7% for 4 years (compulsory delay). An investment of 100F
thus becomes 50.45 F.

Everything depends upon the marginal rate of taxation. At 50%, a 100 F investment costs only 50% and the return is +0,22 per annum. Below this rate, the return will be negative. Thus the increase in risk seems to offset the fiscal incentive.

CONCLUSION

In this paper, we have examined the consequences of regulations for the French Open Funds, and have demonstrated that their effects are either negligible or perverse. In any event, we have argued that in considering the impact of regulations, it is necessary to go beyond the supposed reasons for their imposition to understand their true impact on the institutions subject to them.

ACKNOWLEDGEMENTS

I thank the participants of the Doctoral Workshop of the Graduate School of Business at the University of Chicago for their comments and especially Professors Hamada and Scholes. I thank Miss F. Barbot, MA student in Finance for her computational assistance.

NOTES

1.   For a full exposition, see G. Gallais-Hamonno (1970).
2.   "Fonds communs de placement". From a legal point of view, these FCP are equivalent to the American Open Funds. SICAV are different, because they have the legal status of Limited Company, and thus escape the "manager/trustee" duality.
3.   Almost all Firms-Funds have chosen the "portfolio" alternative. About half of them invest in individual stocks whereas the other half invest in SICAV.
4.   As the SICAV have some 5% of their assets in liquidity, 50% of the portfolio means some 47.5% of their assets.
5.   Sources of data: French Bonds - INSEE index; French Stocks - CAC Index; all others - IMF Financial Statistics (which gives no explanation on the index published).
6.   The computations were made on the Institute's WANG computer, thanks to a program written by M. J.J. Lacrampe, lecturer, who is to be thanked for his help and remarks.
7.   In the sense used by Francis (1976, p. 398): between two assets of the same risk, the one with higher expected return "dominates" the other.
8.   Except if some "dominated" securities have negative covariances with the "dominant" ones and if this negative-covariance effect offsets the direct return-variance effect.
9.   See Appendix 1 for the risk-return of each portfolio. MVP: Minimum Variance Portfolio. MRP: Maximum Return Portfolio. Appendix 2 shows the number of securities held in each portfolio: from a maximum of 11 to a single one.

<u>Appendix 1</u>: Risk (σRp) of Efficient Frontiers

E f f i c i e n t   F r o n t i e r

Expected Return:	A	B	B'	C	D	E
Minimum Variance Portfolio						
σRp =	3.12	3.12	3.12	3.12	5.54	13.86
Minimum Variance Portfolio Expected Return						
[E(Rp)] =	(8.52)	(8.52)	(8.52)	((8.52)	(10.58)	(12.0)]
E(Rp) = 9%	3.19	3.19	3.19	3.19		
10%	3.58	3.58	3.59	3.59		
11%	4.09	4.09	4.45	4.45	5.59	
12%	4.69	4.70	6.23	6.23	6.30	
13%	5.37	6.78	8.34	8.76	8.76	
14%	6.12	10.10	10.70	12.42	12.42	
15%	7.60	13.98	13.22	17.80	17.80	
16%	10.35	18.69	16.58			
17%	13.65		22.68			
18%	17.38					
19%	21.55					
20%	27.06					
21%	38.83					

Maximum Return Po: E(Rp)

      (21.16) (16.93) (17.16) (15.33) (15.33) (12.13)

Maximum Return Po: σ(Rp)

      41.66 29.56 25.06 22.55 22.55 14.48

A: without constraints

B:w(French Bonds) ≥ .30 B' = w(French Bonds + French Stocks) ≥ .50

C:w(French Bonds) ≥ .30 and w(French Bonds + French Stocks) ≥ .50

D:w(French Bonds) = .30 and w(French Stocks) ≥ .20

E:w(French Bonds) = .30 and w(French Stocks ≥ .60

Appendix 2: Diversification of Efficient Portfolios: number of securities held.

		Efficient Frontier					
		A	B	B'	C	D	E
Expected Return:							
Minimum Variance Portfolio		8	8	8	8	8	5
E(Rp) =	9%	11	11	11			
	10%	10	10	10	10		
	11%	8	8	8	8	8	
	12%	7	7	8	8	8	
	13%	7	9	7	7		
	14%	7	8	7	7		
	15%	6	7	5	4		
	16%	8	4	6			
	17%	7					
	18%	6					
	19%	5					
	20%	3					
	21%	3					
Maximum Return Po:		1	2	2	3	7	3

A: without constraints

B:w(French Bonds) $\geq$ .30 B' = w(French Bonds + French Stocks) $\geq$ .50

C:w(French Bonds) $\geq$ .30 and w(French Bonds + French Stocks) $\geq$ .50

D:w(French Bonds) = .30 and w(French Stocks) $\geq$ .20

E:w(French Bonds) = .30 and w(French Stocks $\geq$ .60

THE DEMAND FOR LONG-TERM GOVERNMENT SECURITIES IN THE UK BY THE NON-BANK PRIVATE SECTOR

Glenn Hoggarth and Paul Ormerod

INTRODUCTION

This paper examines the determination of sales of long-term government securities to the non-bank private sector (referred to as gilts below) in the UK over the period 1975-1983. The main motivation is to examine the performance of different mechanisms of expectation formation on capital gains on gilts and equities in the context of a demand for gilts equation. Previous work by Spencer (1981) for the 1967-77 period showed the importance of expected capital gains on gilts, but only examined one specification and did not take account of the potential impact of expected capital gains on equities. Strictly speaking, of course, the relevant expectation variable for gilts is the expected capital gain on gilts plus the rate of interest on gilts minus the rate of interest on a capital certain asset such as 3-month local authority deposits. This is in fact the variable which we use, although as Chart 1 shows, the series is dominated by expected capital gains. For this variable we examine three alternative methods of expectation formation. First, a simple autoregressive scheme. Second, a specification relating the variable to lagged values of the exchange rate, inflation, money supply change, interest rates, the public sector borrowing requirement and the outstanding stock of long term public sector debt. Third, a simple equation which relates expectations of capital gains on gilts just to the rate of interest prevailing on gilts at the end of the previous period. For the expected capital gains on equities, we relate movements to a series of lagged economic variables similar to those used for the gilts variable, but also including gross trading profits of companies.

We initially examined the series (L + CG - S) for weak efficiency using monthly data where L is the rate of interest on gilts, CG is the capital gain on gilts, and S is the rate of interest on 3-month local authority deposits. In other words, we investigated whether it is possible to construct autoregressive schemes which enabled systematic profits to be made. We find that weak efficiency holds, a result which carries over to the context of quarterly data to which we then move for purposes of comparison with earlier work.

It is possible, however, to reject the concept of strong efficiency both for the rate of return on gilts relative to a capital certain asset and for the capital gain on equities. Both this result and the findings of weak efficiency are the same as those obtained by Spencer. Our result is, however, more powerful because Spencer simply noted statistically significant variables in the context of a regression of (L + CG - S) on lagged economic variables over the full sample period, whereas we show predictive power by regressing (L + CG - S) and capital gains on equities on lagged values of economic variables, and carrying out sequential one-step-ahead forecasts. We find that the correlation between the actual values of the dependent variables and those fitted by this procedure is significantly different from zero.

The various expectation formation mechanisms are then examined in the context of a demand for gilts equation. A variety of estimation techniques are used:

(i)   ordinary least squares

(ii)   seemingly unrelated regression

(iii)   three stage least squares

(iv)   seemingly unrelated regression taking into account the cross-equation restrictions on parameters implied by the various hypotheses on expectations.

2. THE CONTEXT

A prior question to consider is whether the data of sales of long-term government securities to the non-bank private sector reveals a demand or supply schedule. Over the 1975-83 period successive governments have had monetary growth targets, which have mainly focussed on the broad definition of money, sterling M3. At the very start of this period, the targets were notionally secret, although they have been explicit over virtually the whole of the period. A feature of the targets for monetary growth in the UK is that the target rate of growth is more often than not exceeded, and there have been very few periods indeed when the authorities have been able to feel confident that monetary growth was both within the target range and likely to remain within it in the near future. In these circumstances, we can be confident that the observed data effectively reveals the demand for gilts rather than the supply schedule of the monetary authorities. Table 1 reinforces this view, by comparing the public sector borrowing requirement in each financial year from 1975/76 through 1982/83 and net sales of gilts to the non-bank private sector. Gilt sales to the non-bank private sector are the major instrument available to the authorities to neutralise the public sector deficit from the point of view of monetary creation. As can be seen, the deficit has been greater than net gilt sales. Further, there has been a substantial contribution to monetary growth over this

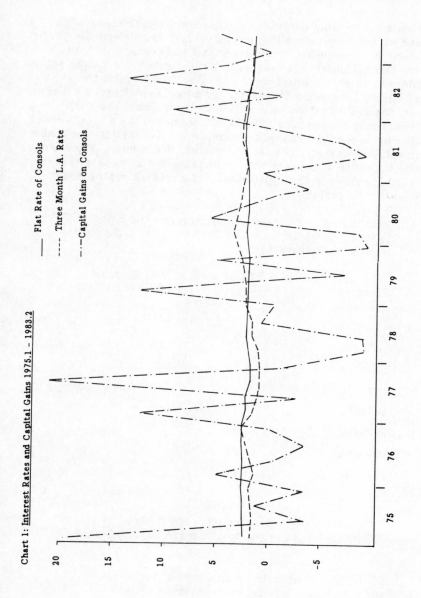

Chart 1: Interest Rates and Capital Gains 1975.1 – 1983.2

— Flat Rate of Consols

---- Three Month L.A. Rate

-·-·-Capital Gains on Consols

period from the lending activities of the commercial banks. The combined effect of bank lending to the private sector and the public sector deficit on potential monetary growth has meant that on occasions the authorities have in fact 'over-funded' the public sector deficit by gilt sales. In other words, they sold more gilts than was required simply to finance the deficit by non-money creating means. However, the ability of the authorities to 'over-fund' the public sector borrowing requirement should not be viewed as a supply shock, but rather as dependent on market demand conditions. In short, the government sold as many gilts as the market could bear. Moreover, given the authorities' concern over exceeding the monetary targets, there is little evidence that gilt sales to the private sector were rationed over the period.

Table 1: Public Sector Borrowing Requirement and Net Sales of Long-Term Public Sector Debt to the Non-Bank Private Sector

Financial Year	PSBR*	Net Sales of Long-Term Debt
	£ Billion	
1975/76	10.36	3.86
1976/77	8.83	5.79
1977/78	5.36	4.92
1978/79	9.62	6.18
1979/80	10.49	8.33
1980/81	13.58	8.89
1981/82	8.74	7.10
1982/83	8.92	4.46

* Since this paper was written, the definition of PSBR has been revised so these are not the latest estimates.

SOURCE: Economic Trends Annual Supplement 1984, & Financial Statistics (various issues)

A further illustration of the willingness of the authorities to meet the demands of the market is as follows. The present Conservative administration has been notionally committed since 1979 to the long run target of zero inflation, and in a very practical sense has made the control of inflation its main policy target. Yet throughout the early 1980s, the monetary authorities have continued to issue gilts maturing in the 21st century carrying double digit coupons. If inflation really were to approach zero, the real debt

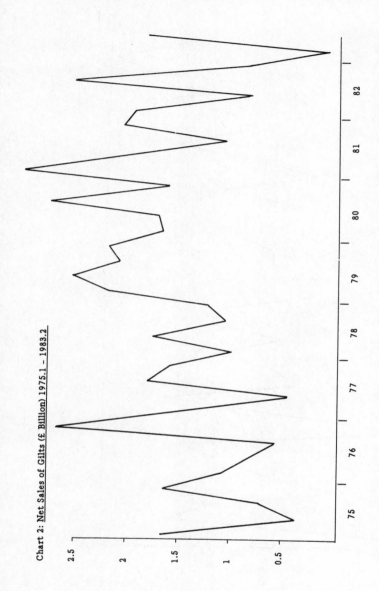

Chart 2: Net Sales of Gilts (£ Billion) 1975.1 – 1983.2

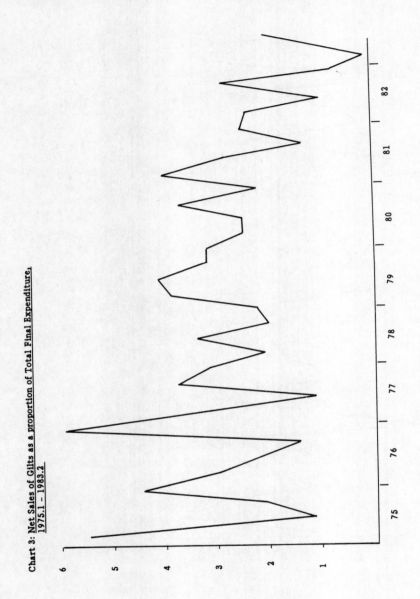

Chart 3: Net Sales of Gilts as a proportion of Total Final Expenditure, 1975.1 – 1983.2

burden of these issues would be very substantial.

A further question arises as to whether the equation should be specified in nominal or real terms. In other words, whether the dependent variable should be gilt sales in nominal terms or whether the nominal value of sales should be deflated by a variable such as total final expenditure. Theoretical arguments can be made to justify either approach, so in the empirical spirit of allowing the data to determine the more appropriate specifications, we estimated specifications in both real and nominal terms. Charts 2 and 3 respectively plot net gilt sales in billions of pounds and as a proportion of total final expenditure. To anticipate, we also investigated a 'mixed' specification in which the dependent variable was in real terms but explanatory variables such as personal wealth in nominal.

3. WEAK EFFICIENCY

We initially examined the series (L + CG - S) using monthly data for weak efficiency. This was done by carrying out Box-Jenkins screening procedures on the autocorrelation function of the series. The screening was carried out over a variety of sample periods. For example, we looked at the period January 1977 through October 1983, over which explicit monetary targets were in operation, as well as a longer series from March 1973 through October 1983. The possibility of a structural switch following the election of the Thatcher government, which some commentators regarded as giving greater credibility to monetary targets, was also examined. Table 2 presents a variety of results, but regardless of the sample period chosen, the concept of weak efficiency could not be rejected on these tests. In other words, the null hypothesis of a random autocorrelation function could not be rejected.

The results obtained on monthly data are also valid using quarterly data. To take just one example, over the period 1974:4 through 1983:2, the Box-Pierce Q-statistic for a random autocorrelation function of (L + CG - S) over eight lags was 6.47 compared to the critical value of 15.51. Even taking account of the fact that the Q-statistic is known to have a low power, the null hypothesis is clearly not rejected. We also attempted to see whether sequential one-step ahead forecasts could be made using an autoregressive process. In other words, we estimated an autoregressive process for (L + CG - S) over the period 1975:1 through 1979:3, and used it to predict 1979:4. The estimation period was then advanced to 1979:4 and a prediction for 1980:1 carried out, and so on through to 1983:3. Over the full sample period 1975:1 through 1983:3 the equation is

$$(L + CG - S) = 0.02 - 0.14 \; (L + CG - S)_{-1} + 0.11 \; (L + CG - S)_{-2} \qquad (1)$$
$$ (0.014) \quad (0.17) \qquad\qquad (0.17)$$

$$- 0.19 \; (L + CG - S)_{-3} - 0.25 \; (L + CG - S)_{-4}$$
$$ (0.17) \qquad\qquad (0.15)$$

Table 2: AUTOCORRELATION FUNCTIONS OF (L + CG - S)

PERIOD						LAG					
1	2	3	4	5	6	7	8	9	10	11	12

March 1973 - October 1983

Autocorrelation

-0.09	0.03	-0.09	0.10	0.04	0.13	-0.08	-0.05	0.03	0.03	-0.06	-0.03

Standard Error

0.09	0.09	0.09	0.09	0.09	0.09	0.09	0.09	0.09	0.09	0.09	0.09

Box-Pierce Q

1.22	1.37	2.48	3.82	4.06	6.27	7.18	7.52	7.64	7.82	8.31	8.46

January 1977 - October 1983

Autocorrelation

-0.10	-0.04	-0.01	0.00	0.02	0.11	-0.14	0.02	0.13	-0.04	-0.06	-0.12

Standard Error

0.11	0.11	0.11	0.11	0.11	0.11	0.11	0.11	0.11	0.12	0.12	0.12

Box-Pierce Q

0.82	0.99	1.01	1.02	1.08	2.21	3.86	3.93	5.52	5.72	6.13	7.4

July 1979 - October 1983

Autocorrelation

-0.15	0.12	-0.11	-0.02	0.02	0.17	-0.09	-0.00	0.13	-0.06	0.02	-0.16

Standard Error

0.14	0.14	0.14	0.14	0.14	0.14	0.15	0.15	0.15	0.15	0.15	0.15

Box-Pierce Q

1.32	2.11	2.80	28.4	2.89	4.55	5.03	5.08	6.12	6.40	6.50	8.20

$\bar{R}^2 = 0.034$; se = 0.079; DW = 1.87; $F(4,30) = 1.30$; LM(4) = 5.6

where the figures in brackets are standard errors and where LM(4) is the Lagrange Multiplier test for random residuals from one through four lags.

A comparison of the one-step ahead predictions using (1) (estimated over the appropriate periods) from 1979:4 through 1983:3 gave a correlation coefficient of -0.08, which is not significantly different from zero, with a value of Theil's inequality coefficient of 1.54. This procedure is a more precise way of testing for weak efficiency than simply examining whether significant values of the autocorrelation function exist over the entire sample, or sub-periods of it, under consideration. This latter test is widely used in the weak efficiency literature in financial and foreign exchange markets, but does not show whether it is possible to make systematic profits using autoregressive schemes constructed in advance of the investment decision.

The specification in (1) was in fact used as the autoregressive expectation scheme in the demand for gilts equation.

Strong Efficiency

Two equations were constructed to examine the property of strong efficiency. First, the variable (L + CG - S) was regressed on lagged values of the following economic variables:

- BOEE, the Bank of England effective exchange rate for sterling
- D4RPI, the annual rate of inflation as measured by the Retail Price Index
- DMS, the quarterly change in the money supply measured by sterling M3 in billions of pounds
- L, the end-period* quarterly rate of interest on long-dated gilts (to be precise, Consols)
- PSBR, the public sector borrowing requirement in billions of pounds
- LRGST, the log of the stock of public sector long term debt held by the private sector, deflated by the GDP deflator at market prices

* It is perhaps appropriate to note at this stage that (L + CG - S) refers to data at the end of the quarter, i.e. end-period data.

A general specification was initially estimated, containing all lags on the above variables from one through four. The idea of using lagged values is that these values are known at the end of each quarter and hence actual values of them can be used to forecast (L + CG - S) at the end of the next quarter. We therefore avoid the potential problem of having to construct forecasting schemes for explanatory variables which appear with current values, noted for example by Wallis (1980).

The choice of these variables was governed by the view that all of them would potentially be noted by financial markets and would potentially affect movements in $(L + CG - S)$.

In terms of the final specification of the equation, we adopted the approach of allowing the data to determine which variables should be excluded from the general specification and which should appear in the preferred, parsimonious equation.

The ordinary least squares estimate over the period 1975:1 through 1983:3 is as follows:

$$
\begin{aligned}
(L + CG - S) = & -0.42 - 0.0012\,DBOEE_{-3} + 0.008\,D4RPI_{-3} \quad\quad (2)\\
& \;\;(0.09)\;\;(0.003) \quad\quad\quad\quad (0.004)\\[6pt]
& -0.013\,D4RPI_{-4} - 0.0057\,DMS_{-2} + 36.6\,L_{-1}\\
& \;\;(0.004) \quad\quad\quad (0.0037) \quad\quad (6.7)\\[6pt]
& -0.018\,PSBR_{-3} - 0.026\,PSBR_{-4} + 0.72\,LRGST_{-1}\\
& \;\;(0.007) \quad\quad\quad (0.008) \quad\quad\;\; (0.18)
\end{aligned}
$$

$\bar{R}^2 = 0.655$; SE 0.047; DW = 2.00; LM(4) = 5.2; Chow F (9,17) = 0.4

The equation provides a powerful explanation of $(L + CG - S)$ and is econometrically well specified. However, the data-coherent approach which we adopted means that some aspects of the equation are not theoretically clear-cut in their interpretation. Spencer (op.cit) adopted a similar approach although there are a number of important differences between (2) and the equation reported by Spencer for the 1967:3 - 1977:4 period. Spencer, for example, could find no significant impact of the PSBR, and his point estimates on this variable were in fact positive. We obtained significant and negative coefficients, according well with the view held in financial markets that the higher the PSBR the higher will be interest rates and hence the lower will be gilt prices. The importance of monetary targets over this period is reflected in the change in money supply variable, although its statistical significance is not very strong. This suggests that the higher has been monetary growth, the higher are interest rates expected to be to attempt to bring this back within target, and hence the expectation of capital losses on gilts arises. The positive sign on the lagged value of the interest rate on gilts, L, supports the 'Grand Old Duke of York' strategy on gilt sales which the authorities are often thought to follow (see, for example, Artis and Lewis (1981)). In other words, in order to guarantee high gilt sales, the authorities raise domestic interest rates to the point where the market expects them to fall and hence expects to make capital gains on gilts. Equation (2) suggests that the higher the interest rate on gilts now, the lower it will be in the next period since the higher will be capital gains. Spencer found a similar result on the long rate of interest.

The remaining variables in (2) are in varying degrees less clear in their theoretical interpretation. In sum the coefficients on inflation are negative, which is what one would expect given the dislike of inflation which pervades financial markets. A similar result was noted by Spencer. The positive sign on inflation lagged three periods in (2) was indicated by the data. The sign on the outstanding stock of gilts is clearly positive, in contrast to the result obtained by Spencer, although he noted that the introduction of monetary targets towards the end of his estimation period changed the expectations formation process. Our interpretation is that this reflects such supply-side factors as are present in the market: the higher is the stock of gilts outstanding, the less the immediate need of the authorities to issue debt to fund the public sector deficit, and hence the more relaxed their attitude to domestic interest rates will be. The long lag on the exchange rate, which the data indicated should appear in first difference form, is the most puzzling aspect of equation (2), although it is statistically very well determined. It could be consistent with the view that the worse the current account, the higher domestic interest rates are expected to be in anticipation of a response from the authorities. The longer lag on the exchange rate means that, for example, a sharp appreciation of sterling three quarters previously will be accompanied by a worsening of the current account in the immediate future once the J-curve effect has worked through.

Equation (2) is by no means a statistical artifact. Carrying out the sequential one-step ahead forecasting procedure described for the autoregressive scheme, we obtain a correlation coefficient between the predicted and actual values of 0.687, which is significantly different from zero at the 5 per cent level. Table 3 sets out the predicted and actual values.

Equation (2) was used as the basis for the 'economic' expectations generating process in the demand for gilts. We also examine a much simpler version of expectations formation, which simply related to expected capital gains on gilts and ignored the differential between long and short interest rates. We regressed the end period price of Consols against the lagged value of the rate of interest on Consols, and obtained the following result over the 1975:1 through 1983:3 period:

$$PCNSLEND = 35.50 - 1.19 \, RCNSLEND_{-1} \qquad (3)$$
$$(2.80) \quad (0.16)$$

$\bar{R}^2 = 0.603$; SE = 1.58; DW = 1.77; LM(4) = 2.4; Chow (2,31) = 1.2; Arch (9) = 3.5; White (1) = 0.3

where Arch and White are tests of the null hypothesis of homoscedastic residuals, and have a chi-square distribution.

In some ways this is a perverse result, and is in contrast to the role of the lagged value of the long interest rate in (2). Equation (3) suggests that the higher are long rates at the end of the previous period, the lower are Consol prices at the end of the current period, and hence by implication the higher are long rates of interest. We

<u>Table 3:</u> Actual and Predicted Values of (L + CG − S) using
sequential one step ahead predictions

Period	Actual	Predicted
1979:4	−0.102	−0.020
1980:1	−0.092	−0.057
:2	0.052	0.021
:3	0.010	0.007
:4	−0.044	−0.046
1981:1	0.008	−0.024
:2	−0.089	−0.109
:3	−0.069	0.033
:4	0.007	0.050
1982:1	0.098	0.145
:2	0.011	0.048
:3	0.146	0.088
:4	0.050	0.059
1983:1	0.003	0.011
:2	0.053	−0.057
:3	−0.015	−0.053

Root Mean Square Error	=	0.052
Mean Absolute Error	=	0.041
Mean Error	=	−0.004
Theil's Inequality Coefficient	=	0.583

used this extrapolative formulation as an expectations generating mechanism, and denote it subsequently by EPG. In terms of nomenclature, the expected values generated by (1) are referred to as ARTEST, and by (2) as TEST.

The sequential one step ahead forecasts produced by (3) give a correlation between predicted and actual of 0.607 over the period 1979:4–1983:3, with root mean square error of 1.98 and a Theil inequality coefficient of 0.08.

For the Financial Times All-Share Index, an approach similar to that used for (2) was adopted. The index (FT) was regressed on a variety of relevant economic variables, once again using only lagged values. The data determined the preferred, parsimonious specification which is as follows, estimated by OLS over the period 1975:1 through 1983:3:

$$FT = -121.8 - 1324S_{-1} + 1.86RPDI_{-3} + 0.70NW_{-1} - 1.49DBOEE_{-1} \quad (4)$$
$$(103) \quad (886) \quad (1.43) \quad (0.59) \quad (0.89)$$
$$+ 0.50FT_{-1} + 9.17PRO_{-1}$$
$$(0.23) \quad (4.16)$$

$\bar{R}^2 = 0.968$; SE = 16.69; DW = 1.621; LM(4) = 10.4; Chow(7,22) = 2.0; Arch (8) = 10.2; White (21) = 23.5

and where S is the interest rate on local authority 3-month deposits, RPDI is real personal disposable income, NW is financial wealth of the non-bank private sector, and PRO is gross trading profits of companies before depreciation and stock appreciation.

The equation has plausible properties, and is well specified except that the LM statistic indicates a certain amount of residual correlation since the critical value at 5 per cent is 9.49 (the Durbin h-statistic is not defined).

Table 4 sets out the sequential one step ahead forecasts and actual values of the FT index over the period 1979:4 through 1983:3.

4. THE RESULTS

We carried out initial Box-Jenkins screening procedures on both the sales of gilts in nominal terms (NSG) and gilts in real terms (GDTFE), in other words deflated by total final expenditure. The autocorrelation function for the latter variable was essentially flat, although there is evidence of some third-order autocorrelation in the series. With nominal gilt sales, the third-order autocorrelation is clear.

It would be tedious to go through the entire set of results under different expectations formation mechanisms and different estimation procedure in detail. Table 6 summarises the results on the different expectations procedures examined.

SURE and NLSURE and Zellner's Seemingly Unrelated Regression estimation, are seemingly unrelated taking account of the cross-equation restrictions implied by the expectations formation

Table 4: Actual and Predicted Values of FT all-share index using sequential one step ahead predictions

Period	Actual	Predicted
1979:4	230.8	255.8
1980:1	248.5	307.2
:2	261.2	261.8
:3	292.3	255.4
:4	292.7	260.0
1981:1	301.2	285.9
:2	317.0	316.2
:3	308.9	342.0
:4	310.0	318.2
1982:1	322.4	320.1
:2	330.3	310.9
:3	356.9	329.3
:4	379.4	357.9
1983:1	412.5	396.6
:2	448.2	431.2
:3	448.6	449.1

Correlation Coefficient	=	0.918
RMSE	=	25.3
Mean Error	=	4.16
Theil's Inequality Coefficient	=	0.583

Table 5: Autocorrelation Function of NSG 1974:4-1983-2

LAGS

	1	2	3	4	5	6	7	8
Autocorrelation	0.09	-0.05	0.40	0.02	0.09	0.18	-0.11	0.03
Standard Error	0.17	0.17	0.17	0.20	0.20	0.20	0.20	0.21
Box-Pierce Q	0.25	0.35	6.32	6.43	6.84	8.23	8.89	9.08

This information was used in the specification of the equations

Table 6: Summary of Results on Expectation Variables in demand for gilts equation

		O L S	SURE	3SLS	NLSURE
Nominal	EPG	+,0	+,0	+,0	+,0
	EFT	-,**	-,**	-,0	-,*
	TEST	+,0	-,0	+,0	+,**
	EFT	-,*	-,*	-,*	+,0
	ARTEST	+,0	+,0	+,0	+,0
	EFT	-,*	-,*	-,0	-,**
Real	EPG	+,0	+,0	-,0	+,0
	EFT	-,**	-,**	-,**	-,**
	TEST	-,0	-,0	-,0	-,0
	EFT	-,**	-,**	-,**	-,0
	ARTEST	+,0	+,0	-,0	-,0
	EFT	-,**	-,**	-,**	-,**
Mixed	EPG	+,**	+,**	+,*	+,**
	EFT	-,**	-,**	-,*	-,**
	TEST	-,0	-,0	+,0	+,0
	EFT	-,**	-,**	-,*	-.**
	ARTEST	+,0	-,0	+,0	-,*
	EFT	-,**	-,**	-,**	-,**

NOTE   Significance: 0 indicates not significantly different from zero at 10% on a one-tailed test

* significant at 10%

** significant at 5%

+ or - indicates the sign of the point estimate on the coefficient equation. In other words, for each of the systems estimated, the demand for gilts equation and the relevant expected gain on gilts equation plus the expected FT equation were estimated jointly. Under the non-linear procedure, however, the expectations generating mechanisms were substituted directly into the demand for gilts equation. In other words, in the system

$$Y = a_1 + b_1 X^e + \ldots + e_1 \tag{5}$$

$$X = a_2 + b_2 Z + \ldots + e_2$$

we estimate

$$Y = a_1 + b_1 (a_2 + b_2 + Z \ldots) + \ldots + e_1$$

$$X = a_2 + b_2 Z + \ldots + e_2$$

In fact, in terms of most of the coefficients in the system, the choice of estimation technique made little difference to the results. The main area of difference is on the significance of the expectation terms in the demand for gilts equation. As expected, the autoregressive scheme on (L + CG − S) gave insignificant results, except in the mixed case under NLSURE, where it is significant at the 10 per cent level but incorrectly signed. We expect in general the sign on EPG, TEST and ARTEST to be positive, and on EFT, the expected value of the FT index, to be negative.

Full details of the results are available on request from the authors, and here we simply give a flavour of the results obtained.

<u>Ordinary Least Squares</u>   Estimation period 1975:1–1983:2

<u>Nominal</u>

$$NSG = 0.44 - 41.5LSAV - 0.028EFT + 0.102EPG \tag{6}$$
$$ (1.39) \quad (16.7) \qquad (0.016) \qquad (0.089)$$

$$+ 0.029DNW + 0.479NSG_{-3} + 0.064NW_{-1}$$
$$ (0.026) \qquad (0.161) \qquad (0.040)$$

$\bar{R}^2 = 0.368$; SE = 0.554; DW = 2.37; LM (8) = 12.6; Chow (6,21) = 3.6

and where LSAV is the yield gap between Consols and 3-month local authority deposits, EFT is the expected capital gain on equities and EPG is the expectation of capital gain on Consols. NW is net financial wealth of the non-bank private sector, and DNW is its first-difference.

Real

$$\text{GDTFE} = \underset{(0.047)}{0.009} - \underset{(0.28)}{0.64\text{LSAV}} - \underset{(0.00003)}{0.00012\text{EFT}} + \underset{(0.0013)}{0.00046\text{EPG}} \qquad (7)$$

$$+ \underset{(0.023)}{0.048\text{DNWTFE}} + \underset{(0.131)}{0.259\text{GDTFE}}_{-3} + \underset{(0.025)}{0.036\text{NWTFE}}_{-3}$$

$\bar{R}^2 = 0.404$; SE = 0.0098; DW = 2.17; LM(8) = 22.8; Chow(6,21) = 0.5

and where NWTFE is net wealth deflated by total final expenditure.

Mixed

$$\text{GDTFE} = -\underset{(0.029)}{0.017} - \underset{(0.00029)}{0.00088\text{EFT}} + \underset{(0.0019)}{0.0047\text{EPG}} \qquad (8)$$

$$+ \underset{(0.0005)}{0.0011\text{DNW}} - \underset{(0.0006)}{0.0018\text{D2GST}}_{-1} + \underset{(0.0007)}{0.0020\text{NW}}_{-1}$$

$\bar{R}^2 = 0.372$; SE = 0.010; DW = 2.15; LM(8) = 11.9; Chow(6,22) = 1.2; Arch(8) = 6.8; White(16) = 9.9.

and where D2GST is the second difference of the outstanding stock of long-term public sector debt held by the non-bank private sector deflated by total final expenditure. As expected, this has a negative sign.

In the general specification of the equations, a variety of factors were included, such as interest rates, wealth, income, as well as the expectations variables. Although the OLS results are theoretically subject to bias, in practice as already noted the results are very similar across estimation results. They are reported here because of the comparative ease with which tests for white noise residuals and homoscedastic residuals can be carried out compared to the system estimators. In general, the preferred equations do pass a range of tests for validity of specification.

A strong result is that the expected capital gain on equities is almost invariably significant and correctly signed.

In terms of statistical significance on EPG, the results of the mixed equation, in which the dependent variable is in real terms but explanatory variables such as wealth are in nominal terms, are easily the best. In this specification, the coefficient is significant at the 5 per cent level and correctly signed under three out of the four estimation techniques used, and significant at the 10 per cent level in the other.

The results using the economic information contained in TEST from equation (2) are rather disappointing. The only time this variable is significant is in the NLSURE estimation of the nominal specification.

Equations (6) – (8) illustrate a number of points about the results in general:

(i)   The demand for gilts essentially depends upon the expected rate of return on gilts relative to capital certain assets, the expected capital gain on equities and the net wealth of the non-bank private sector.

(ii)   Interest rate and income terms play little or no role in the preferred equations.

(iii)   The data indicates that where interest rates are significant, the relevant specification is the differential between Consols and 3-month local authority deposits. The negative sign on this variable in (6) and (7), however, suggests that it is acting as an additional expectations term in an extrapolative fashion. In other words, the higher is the yield gap now, the higher it is expected to be in the immediate future, and hence the lower are gilt prices expected to be. This interpretation is reinforced by the fact that in the specifications where the data indicate that it should appear, the variable EPG which is based upon one of the two components of LSAV becomes insignificant.

(iv)   The evidence suggests that expectations on gilts over this period have in general been extrapolative, and hence have contributed to the volatility of the market. This is in contrast to the results for the 1967-77 period obtained by Spencer, whose specification of the generation of expectations suggested that speculative behaviour had the effect of stabilising the long-term interest rate. His specification is similar to expectations generated from (2) in our results in this respect. But as noted, this particular variable did not perform well in a statistical sense, and in fact was out-performed by a more naive model based upon extrapolative expectations, which Spencer did not investigate.

(v)   Again in contrast to Spencer's results, the constant term in the equations is almost always insignificant. Spencer interpreted the significant constant term as indicating hedging demand, following Merton (1973).

We also present results on the post-sample forecasting performance of the system. Tables 7 and 7A respectively set out the results for the mixed equation using EPG for the sample periods 1975:1-1983:2 and 1975:1-1980:4.

The forecasting performance over the period 1981-1:1983:2 is by no means bad, in what is a very rigorous test of the specification.

Excluding the observations 1982:4 and 1983:1, which were exceptional, the average error is only -£0.14 bn a quarter, compared to the mean of the dependent variable of £1.89 bn. The 1982:4 and 1983:1 periods coincide with both the run-up to the 1983 General Election and a policy statement by the economic spokesman of the main Opposition Party, Labour, that his party would, amongst other things, devalue sterling by 30 per cent. The statement led both to an actual sterling devaluation and the lowest gilt sales over a six month period since the financial crisis at the end of 1974.

Table 7: Seemingly unrelated regression - 1975:1 - 1983:2

Parameter	Estimate	Standard Error	T-Statistic
CONST	-0.185338E-01	0.2597E-01	-0.7136
EFT	-0.878582E-03	0.2516E-03	-3.492
EPG	0.486411E-02	0.1701E-02	2.859
DNW	0.760220E-03	0.4204E-03	1.808
D2GST(-1)	-0.187547E-02	0.5690E-03	-3.296
NW(-1)	0.203371E-02	0.6428E-03	3.164
CONST	34.5347	1.977	17.47
RCNSLEND(-1)	-1.11948	0.1551	-7.218
CONST	-203.077	65.24	-3.113
S(-1)	-1564.92	559.2	-2.798
FT(-1)	0.281677	0.1569	1.796
PRO(-1)	5.09768	2.701	1.887
RPDI(-3)	3.12459	0.9057	3.450
NW(-1)	1.2459	0.4106	3.128
DBOEE(-1)	-0.935895	0.5863	-1.596

Dependent Variable	= GDTFE
Sum of Squared Residuals	= 0.29062E-02
Regression Standard Error	= 0.92453E-02
Mean of Dependent Variable	= 0.27123E-01
Standard Deviation	= 0.12710E-01
R-Squared	= 0.4548 (with constant)
Adjusted R-Squared	= 0.4709 (with constant)
Durbin-Watson Statistic	= 2.1445

Dependent Variable	= PCNSLEND
Sum of Squared Residuals	= 80.821
Regression Standard Error	= 1.55418
Mean of Dependent Variable	= 20.394
Standard Deviation	= 2.4189
R-Squared	= 0.5814 (with constant)
Adjusted R-Squared	= 0.5937 (with constant)
Durbin-Watson Statistic	= 1.7084

Dependent Variable	= FT
Sum of Squared Residuals	= 7413.2
Regression Standard Error	= 14.766
Mean of Dependent Variable	= 247.26
Standard Deviation	= 83.000
R-Squared	= 0.9674 (with constant)
Adjusted R-Squared	= 0.9684 (with constant)
Durbin-Watson Statistic	= 1.7054

Table 7A: Seemingly unrelated regression - 1975:1 - 1980:4

Parameter	Estimate	Standard Error	T-Statistic
CONST	-0.42341E-01	0.5939E-01	-0.7124
EFT	-0.248857E-02	0.1621E-02	-1.535
CONST	30.6342	12.43	2.464
S(-1)	-351.628	260.1	-1.352
FT(-1)	-0.184878	0.1297	1.425
PRO(-1)	3.56267	2.391	1.490
NW(-1)	1.95027	0.5838	3.341
EPG	0.841247E-02	0.4213E-02	1.997
CONST	33.8163	2.329	14.52
RCNSLEND(-1)	-1.07175	0.1801	-5.950
DNW	0.248793E-02	0.9549E-03	2.605
D2GST(-1)	-0.763474E-01	0.3603E-01	-2.119
NW(-1)	0.615927E-02	0.4397E-02	1.401

Dependent Variable = GDTFE
Sum of Squared Residuals = 0.18108E-02
Regression Standard Error = 0.86858E-02
Mean of Dependent Variable = 0.30058E-01
Standard Deviation = 0.12369E-01
R-Squared = 0.4854 (with constant)
Adjusted R-squared = 0.5068 (with constant)
Durbin-Watson Statistic = 2.0700

Dependent Variable = PCNSLEND
Sum of Squared Residuals = 53.863
Regression Standard Error = 1.4995
Mean of Dependent Variable = 20.079
Standard Deviation = 2.2633
R-Squared = 0.5420 (with constant)
Adjusted R-Squared = 0.5611 (with constant)
Durbin-Watson Statistic = 2.0214

Dependent Variable = FT
Sum of Squared Residuals = 4293.1
Regression Standard Error = 14.132
Mean of Dependent Variable = 205.01
Standard Deviation = 50.767
R-Squared = 0.9191 (with constant)
Adjusted R-Squared = 0.9225 (with constant)
Durbin-Watson Statistic = 1.4914

Table 8:   Post Sample Forecasts of NSG, 1981:1-1983:2, £Bn

Period	Actual	Fitted
1981:1	2.911	2.903
:2	2.089	3.234
:3	1.066	0.079
:4	2.029	2.998
1982:1	1.914	0.0429
:2	0.865	0.859
:3	2.471	2.437
:4	0.867	4.564
1983:1	0.256	2.911
:2	1.804	2.587

CONCLUSION

In this paper we have examined the demand for long-term government securities in the UK by the non-bank private sector. The estimation period from 1975 to 1983 is one over which target rates of growth of the money stock have been set by successive governments. The results confirm the previous work by Spencer (1981) over the 1967-77 period, that expectations on the rate of return on gilts relative to the rate of interest on short-term capital certain assets are an important determinant of the demand for gilts. In addition, we have found that the expected capital gain on equities also exercises an important influence on gilt sales and hence indirectly on the rate of growth of the money supply.

Spencer noted, however, that the expectations-generating mechanism which he used was unstable towards the end of the estimation period following the adoption of monetary targets. This is confirmed, for our investigation of a similar approach to the expectations-generating process produced somewhat different results. For example, over the 1975 to 1983 period, the public sector borrowing requirement appears with significant and negative coefficients, whilst it is insignificant over the earlier period.

More importantly, however, an expectations-generating mechanism which is based on a simple extrapolative scheme of previous interest rates is statistically determined much more clearly than one which incorporates more explicit economic information. The result holds using a variety of estimation techniques. This suggests that during a period over which monetary targets were in operation, extrapolative expectations on capital gains on gilts introduced potential instability into the market.

INSURANCE REGULATION IN THE UNITED KINGDOM AND THE FEDERAL REPUBLIC OF GERMANY

Elizabeth Hammond and John Kay

Regulation of financial markets in the UK has been given topical importance by the recent publication of the Gower Report (1984) and of government proposals based on it (Financial Services in the United Kingdom, HMSO, Cmnd. 9432). The Gower Report applies the discipline of law to the subject matter of financial markets. This paper attempts to apply the discipline of economics to the subject matter of regulation. We argue that this difference of perspective leads to radical differences in conclusion. For Gower, it is almost taken for granted that all financial markets require a framework of regulation and that self-regulation is to be preferred to statutory regulation. We do not believe that either of these premises is well supported by economic analysis of the performance of regulated industries. We suggest that the legal approach leads to an excessive concern with particular instances of misbehaviour, and the measures required to prevent them, at the expense of a general concern for the impact of regulatory structures on the economic performance of industry. Our comparison of the lightly regulated UK industry with the highly regulated German regime suggests that in terms of impact on consumers the first of these issues – the incidence of losses from fraud, insolvency and other abuse – is of very little significance relative to the second – the levels of costs, prices and innovative capabilities which result.

It is particularly appropriate to undertake a comparative study of insurance markets because of the potential – as yet largely unrealised – for trade between member states of the EEC. There is a close association between the removal of barriers to trade and establishment and the harmonisation of regulatory structures. Moreover it is between Britain and Germany that the most potential for trade and integration exists. The British insurance industry may be prepared to accept tighter regulation in return for the possibility of readier access to the German market. The recent unwelcome (and ultimately unsuccessful) bid by the largest German insurer, Allianz, for a leading British insurance company indicates that the German industry is alive both to the dangers and the possibilities.

REASONS FOR REGULATION

Extensive regulation of the provision of financial services is common in most countries. Why do financial products attract, or require, a greater degree of regulation than most commodities? We can identify three main reasons. First, the imbalance of information between buyers and sellers, present in almost all markets, is particularly great when financial services are sold to private individuals. Second, financial markets are, for obvious reasons, particularly vulnerable to the entry of dishonest suppliers and credulous consumers. Third, while some financial transactions are as straightforward as the purchase and sale of everyday commodities, many involve a continuing and complicated relationship over time in which the details of the contract are largely implicit and often would not be made explicit. Thus the state's role in the regulation and enforcement of contracts is a particularly onerous one.

Asymmetry of information between buyers and sellers is a well known cause of market inefficiency and one which is likely to be present in most markets for financial services. A principal reason for using financial intermediaries is that they have better information than the consumer does. Moreover, information has the character of a public good. It is really not worth my while investigating in detail the solvency of an insurance company before I place my premiums with it and, if I do, the information that it is solvent (or indeed insolvent) is something that can be made available to other prospective customers at little cost.

In insurance markets, there is a reciprocal asymmetry; the insured typically has better information about the nature of the risk than the insurer. Thus there is the possibility of a 'market for lemons' (Akerlof (1970)), in which good and bad risks are distinguishable to the insurer only by the fact that it is mainly the bad risks which present themselves to him. This adverse selection is a possible source of market inefficiency and may promote excessive risk categorisation or the failure of some contracts to be provided at appropriate prices to low risk individuals.

Dishonesty may be seen as an extreme form of information asymmetry. While the criminal law exists to deal with it, bringing prosecutions for fraud is rarely easy and in any event with fraud, as with burglary, prevention is better than cure. In general, we override the apparent preferences of consumers who wish to buy products which are unsafe or hazardous to health. There are similar, but less compelling, arguments for protecting people from the consequences of their own cupidity.

The state is necessarily involved in contract enforcement and where these contracts are vague or implicit it may need to define their terms. Certainly these problems exist in the insurance market. UK law imposes obligations of disclosure on the insured so onerous that an insurance company could rarely be successfully sued for failure to meet a claim. With profits life policies offer rights to policyholders very much less than the expectations which induce customers to take them out. As these examples illustrate, it is the need to maintain a trading reputation rather than law or regulation which is the principal source of pressure to honour reasonable expectations. But this is not an infallible recourse and British insurers have given assurances to the Office of Fair Trading not to withhold payment unreasonably and legislation now protects the expectations of policyholders, as well as their rights.

FORMS OF REGULATION

These are reasons for regulation: we now consider its form. There are many possible levels of operation of direct government regulation on an insurance market. The following list gives a non-exhaustive range of different types of direct government regulation that could confront an institution in a market for insurance:

a) compulsory information disclosure to customers;

b) compulsory information disclosure to the public;

c) a government prescribed standardised form of information;

d) government solvency monitoring;

e) government prescribed solvency guarantees;

f) control of entry into the market – licensing and authorisation;

g) regulation of insurance contract terms and conditions;

h) investment regulation;

i) price regulation; and

j) profit regulation.

Each step in this list involves a greater degree of involvement in the activities of the insurer.

Requiring a company to disclose information to its own customers is of little true benefit. Few people have the necessary skills to decipher a mass of financial information and once one is already a customer it is too late to be receiving such information. Requiring a company to disclose information to the general public is slightly better as outsiders with relevant expertise can acquire the financial information and base recommendations upon it, and a journalist, for instance, could publicise certain aspects of the information.

Yet a lack of uniformity in the information disclosed is likely to hinder severely any attempt at comparison, particularly if the regulations do not specify exactly what is to be disclosed. A standard form of information – prescribed by government or otherwise – can alleviate many of these problems by providing a basis for uniform comparisons across a number of companies. None of these forms of regulation interfere with the decisions of companies; they simply impose obligations to provide information. Together they define the scope of 'freedom with disclosure', the principle governing insurance regulation in the UK for around a century. However, repeated experience in financial markets has shown that when a company actually experiences financial difficulty disclosure is quickly abandoned, usually with the enthusiastic support of a regulatory authority which sees this as a necessary means of averting collapse. Freedom with disclosure is therefore an ineffectual principle because as soon as any form of regulation is in place an orderly liquidation by the regulatory authority is universally preferred to a collapse induced by competition in the market place.

Thus the next stage of regulation is quickly reached; one in which the regulatory agency monitors solvency and shuts down organisations which fail to meet its criteria. The difficulty is that this activity is not always successful and when it fails the public tends, not unreasonably, to blame the regulatory authority. This leads to compensation, or solvency guarantees, which may be provided by the agency, by the government, or by companies collectively. The existence of guarantees inevitably raises the question of who is to qualify them.

Entry control, the next level of government regulation, much more directly affects the market than the foregoing forms of regulation. A variety of issues can be dealt with under this form, for instance, licensing and authorisation can have as pre-conditions: a minimum capital requirement, persons involved deemed to be fit and proper, business scope limited, structure of company prescribed, set solvency margins (see above), regular standard form information disclosure (see above), and many others. Such regulation may be detrimental to competitive processes particularly if it is so complex and wide-ranging as to constitute a significant barrier to entry for new would-be competitors.

Contract regulation and investment regulation take the process one step further as now the day to day running of insurance business is affected directly. When governments specify the terms and conditions of contracts and how and where a company may invest its money it becomes difficult for a market participant to adjust flexibly to changes in the market. Competition is stifled and allocation of funds is unlikely to bring the highest return. Comparison between companies is easier for consumers to undertake and investment should prove safer and more stable because of government control. Under price regulation, where premium levels are set or determined according to a government prescribed formula, the costs and benefits above are both intensified. Without price competition other forms, such as competition in quality of service, may become more evident. Price regulation also implies standardisation of the risk categories into which companies partition different forms of insurance. Such categories are likely to become ossified and oblivious to changes in the fluid market place. Profit regulation is the last level on the spectrum and represents a significant degree of government interference in the running of a business. Evasion tactics would be expected on behalf of some institutions in order to thwart the regulation. Furthermore it could be a disincentive to the efficient operation of institutions in the market.

In terms of the above spectrum of levels of direct regulation it is possible to identify particular points at which certain industries are located. The UK pension fund sector is approaching point (a) (disclosure to customers), while the UK life insurance sector has been between (c) and (d) (standardised form of information and solvency monitoring) and has recently moved to (e) and (f) (solvency guarantee and entry control). This is an odd contrast as life insurance is provided in the UK in a competitive market whereas pensions are not. Meanwhile German insurance is regulated with (g), (h), (i) and (j) (contract and investment regulation, price and profit regulation). Germany has no solvency guarantee regulations as such, because the higher levels of regulation are presumed to make it unnecessary. However, for automobile insurance a (voluntary) association of insurers exists which collects a small yearly premium from its members (now all automobile insurers) which would cover large liabilities of policyholders affected by a firm's insolvency. Both the UK and West Germany have controls on the entry of firms to their respective insurance markets, but the controls are lightly exercised in the UK and much more rigorously in Germany. Contract, investment, price and profit regulations do not exist in the UK (apart from the 1976 Valuation of Assets Regulations which stipulate that certain assets are to be taken into account only to a specified extent in determining the required margin of solvency) but are general in Germany.

Regulatory practice in the two countries

In the German automobile insurance industry premiums are basically calculated by means of a markup rule. First, the expected losses are calculated by the association of insurers. This projected industry-wide loss experience serves as net premium unless a firm had a higher loss experience during the previous year or unless a firm can show it had a lower loss experience during the preceding three years. This net premium is augmented by margins for administrative expenses and commissions for agents, which are calculated for each firm from its individual experience. Finally, a profit margin of a 3 per cent rate of return on premiums is conceded. Profit regulation takes the following form: surpluses in excess of the 3 per cent of premium volume allowed must be returned to policy-holders in the form of ex post dividends. Thus ex ante premium calculations and the ex post profit sharing allow a 3 per cent return on premiums. The combination of these two regulatory mechanisms is applied to the most important line of third party liability insurance. Recently, first party liability insurance has been partly deregulated.

The West German life insurance industry is also subject to premium and profit regulations. The long-term nature of mixed life insurance policies provides the justification for strict premium regulations. The regulatory agency argues that premium competition would lead to insolvencies which would hurt the consumer and should therefore be prevented. Consequently, the agency requires all firms to charge the same premiums based on life tables. Minor differences do exist, but they are negligible relative to the premiums, and relative to the substantial differences in the cash values of policies. This uniform premium level is extremely high and leads to excessively high surpluses, of the order of magnitude of 30 per cent and more of premium income. The profit regulations allow a firm to retain only 10 per cent of their surplus as profit, at least 90 per cent must be returned to the policyholders in the form of dividends. The yearly dividends are accumulated and paid to the policyholders with the death payment or with the savings capital at the end of the contract. In fact, most firms return a larger fraction than the required minimum of 90 per cent.

The history of insurance regulation in the UK is mainly a story of attempts to shut stable doors after particular horses have bolted. The collapse of the Albert, a proprietary life office, in 1869, led to the legislation which formed the basis of the regulation of insurance in Britain for the next century. The Albert, being undercapitalised, was brought down by a spate of surrenders and the Life Assurance Companies Act (1870) required any company providing life insurance to deposit £20,000 with the Accountant-General as security. This Act established the principle of 'freedom with disclosure', described above, whereby the legal restrictions on company operation were substantially confined to obligations to report information. By 1909 the main requirements which had been imposed on life insurance companies in 1870 were extended to all the principal forms of insurance, other than marine insurance.

Automobile insurance became an expanding part of the total insurance industry. In 1966, nine motor insurance companies failed in one year. It was subsequently demonstrated that in most cases the activities of these companies had been fraudulent. A particular characteristic of the automobile insurance market in both countries is that a minimum level of cover is compulsory. This is cited in Germany as necessitating the obligation to serve and premium regulation (since otherwise insurance companies would control access to the roads) but British experience, which makes insurance available at high prices from specialist companies to even the worst risks, provides little support for this argument. British experience does show, however, that compulsion in purchase requires monitoring of solvency. The reason is that there is likely to be a group of customers who are not concerned with the quality of the product they are compelled to buy - in this case, the probability that their insurer will actually be able to pay. Thus the rapid growth of motoring in the UK was accompanied by the rise, and eventual failure, of these mismanaged or fraudulent companies who sold policies to customers whose only concern was to obtain a piece of paper entitling them to drive.

These collapses precipitated the Companies Act of 1967, which radically tightened legislation governing the provision of insurance. This Act empowered the then Board of Trade to control insurance companies by refusing authorisation, imposing conditions of operation and refusing to allow a company to accept new business. The principle of 'freedom with disclosure' was dead, all insurance business in the UK was conducted at the discretion of the Board of Trade and, potentially, on such terms as that body might dictate.

The Board of Trade proved incapable of shouldering these responsibilities as shown by the collapse of the Vehicle and General Insurance Company in 1971. It had captured 10 per cent of the UK private motor insurance market in only ten years through a policy of low premiums, especially for low risk drivers, combined with generous commissions for brokers. Though warned of the precarious financial position of Vehicle and General, the Department of Trade took no action. In 1974 a number of life assurance companies ran into difficulties and though most were taken over by other companies, one, Nation Life, was not rescued and it was forced into liquidation. These incidents led to the 1975 Policyholders Protection Act. This Act, as its name implies, provides for the protection of policyholders in the event of an authorised insurance company being unable to meet its liabilities. The protection is financed by the imposition of a levy on the insurance industry and a Policyholders Protection Board was established to supervise this process. In the event of an insurance company insolvency, the liabilities will be met in full in the case of compulsory insurances and in other cases the Board will pay 90 per cent of the full value of the claims. Now, under the existing legislation affecting the insurance industry, the Department of Trade has unlimited discretion to determine who conducts insurance business and to a lesser extent how they conduct the business. However, this wide power is largely left unexercised and if companies are behaving reasonably there is no interference in their operations.

PERFORMANCE UNDER REGULATION

Our analysis of performance considers four principal indicators:

i)   industry price structures,

ii)   product variety,

iii)   industry cost structures, and

iv)   product quality - solvency

                        - service quality.

For all of the above measures the performance of automobile insurance companies and life insurance companies was studied.

Industry price structures

(a)   Life insurance

Two different aspects of the price of life insurance were examined. Firstly, the premiums charged for term (pure risk) insurance in both

countries were compared. Table 1 below shows the relevant
premiums charged.

Table 1: Net Premiums for 100.000 DM Worth of Pure Risk
Insurance for 1981

Contract period in years	Age of policy holder	Cheapest German firm	Immediate Rebate Policy Premiums of "Equity & Law"	Most expensive British firm	Cheapest British firm
3	30	256	256	156	104
3	45	464	442	334	223
3	55	1161	1053	800	637
5	30	261	261	160	104
5	45	503	476	372	300
5	55	1279	1154	967	794
10	30	280	279	163	105
10	45	634	588	499	381
10	55	1592	1426	1316	1129
15	30	374	357	186	126
15	45	878	797	649	524
15	55	1984	1763	1690	1467

As this table makes clear, all UK firms are substantially cheaper than
any German firm in providing term life insurance, e.g. for a
30-year-old policyholder with a 3 year contract the British premium
could have been as low as 40 per cent of the German premium. The
difference tends to decrease with the age of the policyholder and
generally to decrease with the length of the contract. The low
British premiums can partly, at least, be explained by a tax subsidy in
their favour. The taxation of UK life insurance companies is by a
method known as the 'Income minus Expenses' basis (I-E). Taxation
is based upon the investment income generated by the fund with
relief given for management expenses. Because term insurance
yields no significant investment income, the expenses of such
business can be offset against the income from savings type insurance
policies giving a tax subsidy to the term life premiums.

Pure risk life insurance is a more or less homogeneous product,
and direct price comparisons are therefore possible. The 'price' of an
endowment policy is less well defined. We therefore measured the
rate of return a policyholder with an endowment life insurance policy
could have obtained in the UK and West Germany. A mixed or
ordinary life insurance policy is a combination of a pure term life
insurance contract and a savings plan. Part of the premium paid is a
pure risk insurance premium and part represents a savings

component. The split between the two is not explicit in the
contract. However, a split between the two components can be
inferred and thus an estimate can be made of the rate of return
earned on life insurance saving. It is possible to ask at which interest
rate the savings component would have to accumulate to match the
cash values of the mixed whole life policy. Two methods were
employed to determine the appropriate apportionment of the total
premium to the pure term risk premium. Firstly, the 'Finsinger'
method (Finsinger (1982)) which uses the market price of term life
insurance in any year and secondly, the 'Kay' method (Kay 1982))
which uses the actuarially fair price (i.e. probability of death) in any
year. The rates of return calculated using the 'Kay' method are
uniformly lower than those calculated by the 'Finsinger' method
because the administrative costs of the insurance company are a high
proportion of the premium for comparatively small amounts of term
assurance. Netting out the explicitly administrative component of
the term-life quotes leads to estimated rates of return that are
considerably closer to those produced by the 'Kay' method.

In the UK a 25 year with-profits endowment policy carrying a
monthly premium of £10 and purchased by a 30-year-old male from
amongst the most successful UK companies was studied. The policy
was purchased on 1st February 1957, and ran to 1st February 1982. In
Germany the contract used was bought by a 35-year-old male in 1955
and ended in 1980 from a sample of 55 firms. Table 2 below, gives
the results of the comparison using the 'Kay' method.

Table 2: Average Rates of Return on Life Insurance Saving and
Other Forms of Saving

	Average yield on 25-year life insurance policy		Average yield on medium-dated Government securities in %	
Great Britain	Pre-tax	8.4	Pre-tax	9.1
	After-tax	9.5	After-tax	4.8 – 9.1
Germany	Pre-tax	5.5	Pre-tax	6.6 – 7.8
	After-tax	6.0 – 11.0	After-tax	3.2 – 7.8

The after-tax rate of return on life insurance saving includes the tax
subsidy given to policyholders via the reliefs available in each
country on the premiums paid in the course of the contract
(withdrawn in the UK in 1984). The second column provides a
comparison of returns available from other investments. It is
difficult ultimately to decide which country offered the best relative
return on savings. The German returns are lower than the British,
but so is the general level of German interest rates. A person's
individual tax position will greatly affect the end result and really
determines which is the most profitable investment.

(b)   Automobile insurance

It is very difficult to compare the premiums charged in each country for different types of motor vehicle insurance. Of prime importance is the fact that the insured risk in the two countries is vastly different. Germany has a very high death toll on the roads while Britain's is among the lowest in Europe. On measures including per number of inhabitants, per kms. driven and per number of cars, the British figure is approximately half the German one. It has been suggested (Adams (1984)) that some of the difference could be explained by the differences between the insurance markets. The British market, being largely unregulated, has developed a finely tuned system of risk classification. Thus, the premiums of different risks closely reflect their respective expected losses. In particular, traffic penalties are taken into account. Hence, there are stronger incentives to prevent losses than in Germany, where the regulatory agency set up a relatively crude system of risk classification. More work is to be completed in this area of automobile insurance.

Product variety

It is in product variety that the difference between the insurance industries of the two countries is most striking. In Germany contract terms are standardised and agreed collectively after negotiations with the regulatory agency. It follows that innovation is both difficult to introduce and generally ineffectual as a competitive weapon. Approval by the regulatory agency is generally obtained after years of arguments, discussion and lobbying and then is often introduced by all firms at the same time. There is no advantage in being the first for this reason. In Britain, by contrast, the consumer is faced with a blinding variety of products. The most important innovation in UK life insurance has been the development of unit-linked policies, by which the proceeds are linked to the performance of funds of property, equities or other investments. As with most major product introduction in UK life insurance, this has been pioneered by new entrants to the industry and subsequently adopted by established firms.

   Not all of these innovations are necessarily desirable. One group has been concerned to exploit the variety of anomalies which continue to characterise the tax treatment of insurance in the UK. A second group is designed to use the liberal regulatory regime of the insurance industry to avoid tighter regulation applied elsewhere: for example, authorised unit trusts cannot be sold at the door and may not invest in property, but both these restrictions can be evaded if the unit trust is disguised as a life insurance policy. However these are further illustrations of the flexibility of response to changing circumstances of the British industry, a flexibility both unknown and impossible in Germany.

   The difference in variety of contract extends to difference in variety of risk categories. In Germany there is a common risk

classification, negotiated between the industry and the regulatory
authority. For life insurance, this differentiates only by age: in
Britain, sex is automatically a criterion and, for substantial amounts
of term insurance, other personal characteristics will be relevant.
For German motor insurance, residence and profession (grouped into
three categories) are the main personal characteristics considered:
English companies base their risk assessment on an extensive list of
criteria. Thus it is clear that the German regulatory system reduces
the number of criteria applied in assessing risk and compresses their
range; moreover, it creates relatively little pressure, either for
individual companies or for the industry as a whole, to relate these
characteristics closely to individual risks.

Industry cost structures

(a) Life insurance

Descriptive cost functions for both the UK and West German life
insurance industry were constructed. It is apparent from the UK data
that there are significant economies of scale at the smaller end of
the market (as measured by net premium income) but the advantages
of size dwindle rapidly and then level off until small diseconomies set
in at the top end. The cost measure employed - the expense ratio
(ratio of management expenses and commission payments to premium
income) - was minimized at premium income of about £200 million
p.a. There proved to be a wide range of values within which the
expense ratio is extremely close to its minimum value. For premium
income in the band £165 - 250 million p.a. the expense ratio is very
close to its minimum value of 23 percentage points. This minimum
value is derived from an equation specified for companies who are
members of the various Life Offices' Associations. Such membership
was found to reduce the expense ratio by 7.6 percentage points.
However, it is important to note also that few companies actually
operate within this range - only 3 of the sample of 55. The UK data
was also analysed to establish the relevance, if any, of other factors
in determining cost, in particular the structure of ownership. The
type of ownership of a company proved not to be a significant
determinant of the level of costs of operation of a company.

The West German data for life insurance company costs was
analysed in a similar way but gave very different results. The
regression results for the average cost equation show very significant
ownership related cost differences. Economies of scale are present
in that average costs decline with the size of the company as
measured by premium income. No evidence of diseconomies at the
upper range of premium income was found, though. The results
indicate that public enterprises produce at lower average costs than
do private stock companies. Their average total costs are less than
three quarters of those of private firms. Mutual companies' costs
seem to fall between public enterprises and stock companies' costs.
However, the operating costs (total costs minus sales and

marketing costs) of public enterprises do not significantly differ from those of private firms. Hence, the substantial cost savings of public enterprises are mostly realised within the sales organisation. Given the generally held thesis that private firms tend to operate more efficiently than similar public firms, the reversal here indicates that the presence of regulation is affecting the operation of private firms. Private firms spend more on their marketing and sales in an attempt, it appears, to increase the premium income revenue they receive. Because the profit regulation is in the form of a certain percentage return allowed on premium income, the incentive is there for private firms to inflate their premium income.

(b) Automobile insurance

For the UK, Department of Trade returns for a 10 year period were analysed for the top 20 automobile insurance companies which represent 92 per cent of the non-Lloyd's market. The results are given in Table 3 below which shows commissions, expenses, claims, underwriting results and the residual as a percentage of premium income.

Table 3: Percentage of Premium Income as Allocated

Year	Commission	Expenses	Claims	Underwriting loss	Residual
1971	13.57	15.30	61.32	-3.23	14.13
1972	13.60	14.35	57.14	-1.08	18.28
1973	13.55	13.90	58.32	-0.64	16.74
1974	13.59	15.01	62.57	-3.65	15.82
1975	12.56	16.19	62.31	-4.74	13.85
1976	12.14	16.44	57.90	-0.33	13.68
1977	11.92	15.34	58.38	-1.46	12.48
1978	12.03	14.55	58.19	-1.51	14.87
1979	11.69	14.40	59.60	-3.97	15.99
1980*	11.25	15.73	63.39	-4.50	13.04
Average	12.06	15.10	59.90	-2.50	14.90

*Information only available for 16 companies (76% market) in 1980.

A further analysis of Department of Trade returns for the years 1981 and 1982 indicated that the expenses involved in settling claims amounted to an average 6.32 per cent of the claims paid. On the basis of this one would expect approximately 3.8 per cent of premium income to be used in expenses for settling claims. Table 4 below gives the final analysis expressed as a percentage of premium income.

Table 4:   %

	%
Claims	59.9
Commission	12.6
Settlement expenses	3.8
Other expenses	11.3
Underwriting	-2.5
Residual	14.9

Loss ratios and expense ratios for the German automobile insurance industry are given in Table 5 below.

Table 5:

Year	Loss ratio for the retained business %	Expense ratio for the retained business %	Technical surplus as % of retained premium volume
1976	77.43	15.64	2.30
1977	80.25	14.78	1.78
1978	84.59	13.72	-0.30
1979	79.56	13.04	3.37
1980	83.18	12.98	1.74
1981	82.81	12.89	1.69
1982	81.65	12.59	3.02
Average	81.35	13.66	1.94

Note that these German figures relate to the retained business only.

The expense ratio is for administrative cost excluding claims handling costs, that is, settlement expenses. Given the higher insured risk on the roads in Germany as compared to the UK, mentioned earlier, we would expect the German expense ratio to be lower as the premium income level is inflated and the costs of processing claims are excluded from the measure. In fact the UK has a lower expense ratio at 11.3 per cent as compared to Germany's ratio of 13.7 per cent for retained business only. A better German comparative figure would relate to the gross business as German insurers cede, on average, 34 per cent of their premiums to reinsurance. The data exclusively made available to Dr. J. Finsinger by the German regulatory agency on gross figures for 1980 only, show an average expense ratio of 16 per cent.

Product quality

(a) Solvency

In one respect at least, insurance regulation in West Germany has been successful. It has virtually eliminated insolvencies. Since the Law for Insurance Regulation took effect in 1901, only one insolvency and three bankruptcies have occurred. The insolvent firm was taken over by the Allianz and policyholders did not suffer any losses. The first bankruptcy concerned a Dutch transport insurance company whose German subsidiary did not sell any policies subject to regulatory supervision. The second bankruptcy involved an American company which exclusively sold insurance to American soldiers stationed in Germany. A third bankruptcy occurred in July 1984. The German insurers voluntarily agreed to relieve private policyholders. What is to happen to industrial policyholders, mostly transportation firms, is not yet known.

The history of insolvencies in the UK is not quite as good, as indicated previously in the discussion of the UK regulatory legislation this century. The majority of failures have been of automobile insurance companies, mostly fraudulent, although the largest, Vehicle and General, was the result of mismanagement. The one case of life insurance company insolvency - Nation Life - is in one sense misleading in that the company was not engaged in real insurance business to any substantial degree. Its principal activity, and the one which led to the collapse, was deposit taking; this took the technical form of insurance principally in order to obtain tax advantages although incidentally escaping more rigorous forms of regulation applied to banking. Similar observations apply to other cases of failing life insurance companies whose business has been taken over by other companies. Now, following the Policyholders Protection Act, 1975, all proper claims of policyholders from failed companies will be met to at least 90 per cent of their value.

(b) Service quality

In West Germany, where price competition is relatively ineffective due to the form of the premium regulation of life insurance, it may be expected that service competition would replace it. Marketing expenses represent the resources flowing into the sale of policies and into the services provided to consumers. In fact, the sale of policies can be regarded as a service as well. Particularly private firms, as mentioned above, spend more than two thirds of total costs on marketing expenses. One would expect such large expenditure to be positively correlated with consumer satisfaction. The measurement of consumer satisfaction is not possible directly but observations on policyholders' complaints are recorded by the regulatory agency. Using such information a proxy of consumers' satisfaction was developed and the results showed that policyholders complain more often about firms with large marketing expenses than about firms with small marketing expenses. Thus the measure of quality of service adopted is negatively correlated with the level of complaints. It is therefore not apparent that the higher level of expenditure on service provided to German consumers is valued by them.

CONCLUSION

It is difficult to reach a final conclusion following the comparison of the performance of insurance companies in West Germany and the UK. On the question of insolvencies, West Germany clearly has the better record. However, losses to consumers from insolvency in the UK have not been significant in relation to the total business of the industry but now, at least, in the UK policyholders should not suffer too greatly if a company fails. The comparison of cost and price measures betwen the two countries is instructive and, in some cases, clearly shows the UK companies to be performing much better than the German companies. Within Germany, the form of premium and profit regulations cause changes in the operations of private insurance firms so that they operate at a less cost efficient level. Another striking feature is the extraordinarily high level of reinsurance payments made by private insurance firms, though all German insurance companies seem to pass on a much higher percentage of their premiums in reinsurance than do the British insurance companies. This can be accounted for by the fact that reinsurance is one arm of the insurance industry that is unregulated in Germany and private firms can send a high level of premium income to closely affiliated reinsurance companies and thereby evade part of the profit regulation. The principle of 'freedom with disclosure' evidently failed under pressure. If it is preferable to make the decline of unsuccessful and mismanaged financial institutions an orderly one, rather than leaving it to the pressures of competition alone, then some more extensive form of regulation involving solvency monitoring is required. But there is a price to be paid for that degree of regulation, and a higher price to be paid for regulation which, as in Germany, goes well beyond that level. Competitive markets, with adequate safeguards, seem to serve customers better in the long run by promoting efficiency than attempts to protect customer policyholders by strict regulations on all aspects of operation.

ACKNOWLEDGEMENTS

This paper is a preliminary report on a comparative study of insurance regulation in the two countries, undertaken in collaboration with Professor Dr. Jörg Finsinger and supported by the Anglo-German Foundation.

ASYMMETRIC INFORMATION AND CREDIT RATIONING: ANOTHER VIEW OF INDUSTRIAL BANK LENDING AND BRITAIN'S ECONOMIC PROBLEM

John Cable and Paul Turner

1.   INTRODUCTION

British banks have often been attacked for providing inadequate finance for industry. Lever and Edwards (1980) and Carrington and Edwards (1979, 1981), hereafter referred to as L-E-C, are among the more recent critics. In comparisons with more successful countries like West Germany and Japan, they find UK industrial finance 'short-term, dear, unreasonably restricted in amounts, carrying legal risks, and subject to excessive security requirements'. They see the banks' alleged shortcomings as an important cause of Britain's relative decline, but nevertheless a 'remediable defect' in the short run - the required change in lending practice being something 'concrete and copyable which the more successful countries are doing, which we can adopt'.

According to L-E-C the problem is behavioural: 'excessively cautious' bank-lending policies are to blame, rather than a lack of industrial projects which are viable by international standards. Thus they imply either irrationality or undue risk-aversion on the part of the banking system. This paper examines an alternative hypothesis: that the credit-rationing ('unreasonably restricted amounts') and strict collateral requirements ('excessive security requirements') which L-E-C describe may be rational, risk-neutral responses to problems of assymetric information in the loan market, of the kind economists have been examining over the past decade in insurance and credit markets where clients have different risk characteristics known to the individual clients but not to the insurance companies or lending institutions (Rothschild and Stiglitz, 1976; Jaffee and Russell, 1976; Stiglitz and Weiss, 1981).

We build in particular on Jaffee and Russell (hereafter J-R) who demonstrate the rationality of credit-rationing in competitive credit markets lending to personal borrowers.[1] In our case - the UK industrial finance market - borrowers are firms investing funds in industrial projects rather than consumers anticipating future consumption, and lending is oligopolistic rather than competitive.

Our first task is therefore to extend J-R's results to these conditions, and this is done in sections 2 and 3. International differences in lending practice are then explained in section 4, consistently with our theory, by reference to institutional differences affecting the way information is distributed between lenders and borrowers. Finally section 5 considers the implications of our analysis for UK policy.

2. THE OPTIMALITY OF CREDIT RATIONING

In their two period, Fisherian consumption model J-R derive the demand for loans: $L^* = L^*[R]$, (suppressing fixed values of Y_1 and Y_2), where L is loan size and $R = (1+r)$. If the maximised utility function is quasi-concave, they show that the demand curve is the locus of the peaks of indifference curves in L,R space which increase monotonically up to the demand curve and fall thereafter (figure 1). Moving to our industrial credit case, where borrowers are profit-maximising firms investing in fixed capital in period one and earning a return Y_2 in period two, the firm's iso-profit curves will have similar properties provided that projects of various size are feasible and production is subject to first increasing and then decreasing returns.[2] Hence the firm's unconstrained demand curve for loans $L^* = L^*[R]$ is again the locus of their maxima.

In so far as the conditions governing the supply of credit apply in the same way to industrial as to consumer credit markets, J-R's assumptions that lenders are risk-neutral and maximise expected profit, borrowing in a perfect capital market at rate $I = (1+i)$, with no other costs and subject to constant returns, still apply in the industrial credit case. Hence, as in the J-R model, expected profit is contract revenue (LR) times the likelihood of repayment ($\lambda [LR]$) minus opportunity cost (LI): thus $E(\Pi) = LR\lambda [LR] - LI$ and under competition $E(\Pi) = 0$ so that $R\lambda [LR] = I$.

The repayment probability function $\lambda [LR]$ takes account of defaults. J-R consider two cases. In the first there are honest and dishonest borrowers (who cannot be distinguished ex ante by lenders) and first and second period incomes Y_1, Y_2 are certain. Honest borrowers always repay L^*R, but dishonest borrowers choose between $C_2 = Y_2 - L^*R$ and $C_2 = Y_2 - Z$ according to $Z \lessgtr L^*R$, where Z is some default penalty. If Z is the same for all borrowers, dishonest borrowers all default over loan sizes greater than L in figure 2. However, if Z is allowed to vary continuously across borrowers above some level Z_{min} at which no defaults occur, the distribution of Z will determine a no-default function $\lambda [LR]$ as in figure 3. The properties of the no-default function - $\lambda [LR] = 1$ for $LR \leq Z_{min}$ and, more especially, $\lambda' [LR] < 0$ for $LR > Z_{min}$ are the critical input in the J-R model and crucial to the existence of an equilibrium with rationing.

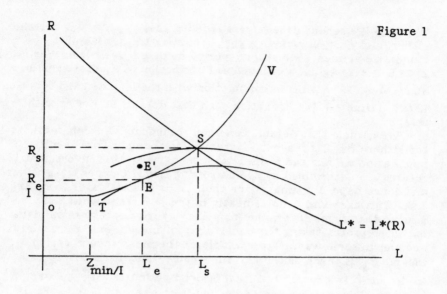

Figure 1

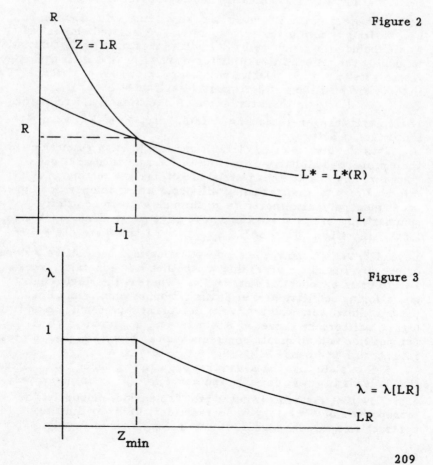

Figure 2

Figure 3

In J-R's second case buyers are identical ex ante, but become either 'lucky' or 'unlucky' ex post according to the size of a stochastic element Z in second-period income. Default now occurs if $Z < LR - Y_2$. Again, a continuous distribution of Z across borrowers above some Z_{min} will, in conjunction with the loan demand function $L^*(R)$, define a λ [LR] function such that default increases with loan size.

We assume that default can occur in industrial credit markets for either of J-R's reasons. Moreover, in the industrial credit application we can add a third case, recognising that investment returns are determined by the borrowing firms' choices and actions, and hence depend ultimately on their skills and attitudes towards risk. This case also handles neatly in the J-R framework. Thus assume that firms determine loan size in period one by maximising expected profit, taking the uncertainty of investment returns into account in some way. (For example, if the mean second period income $\bar{Y}_2$ is taken as the certainty equivalent, L^* is determined as in the basic J-R model.) Actual (second period) returns depend on individual investment strategies, and in this sense $Z = \bar{Y}_2 - Y_2$ is no longer stochastic. However, we can assume a distribution of Z across firms according to firm-specific, risk-related characteristics. These include the firms' skills in finding investment opportunities and in judging the probabilities of different payoffs, and their attitudes towards risk i.e. their relative risk-aversion or risk-preference. Even if there are no dishonest borrowers default must occur if $Z = Y_2 < LR$. Again the distribution of Z (ultimately of the firms' characteristics) generates a no-default function λ [LR] with properties as before.

Thus the loan-demand, default and credit-supply functions and their properties all carry over from the consumer market case considered by J-R to an industrial credit-market setting. J-R's principal results, that rationing will occur under competition but not under monopoly, also therefore go through and can be briefly summarised. in L,R space the competitive supply function is the locus $\overline{OTSV}$ (figure 1). For $L \leqq z_{min/I}$ $\lambda = 1$ and therefore $R = I$. Beyond T, as J-R show, the supply function may be positively sloped or backward bending, according to whether λ is generated from a Pareto or an exponential distribution. Whereas the single contract, no-rationing equilibrium is at S, the rationing equilibrium E will prevail. Borrowers who would not default at S prefer E, which is on a higher indifference curve. If E is offered, S is driven out, and competition will eliminate contracts such as E' with higher interest rates than E and hence $E(\Pi) > 0$.

J-R explain that the advantage of rationing under competition is that it leads to fewer defaults and hence $R_e < R_s$. However, they also show that rationing is never profitable under monopoly; the monopolist's best strategy to decrease defaults is by limiting contract size through higher interest rates. Thus monopoly equilibrium will occur at a point on the demand curve to the left of S in figure 1, vertically above the intersection of the monopolist's marginal cost and expected marginal revenue curves.

We now extend the J-R framework to take account of oligopolistic lending. First we show that, assuming symmetric duopoly for simplicity, the non-collusive Nash equilibrium coincides with competitive equilibrium and entails rationing. There are three steps in this argument. We show that (i) any rationing contract, for which there exists a corresponding non-rationing contract with the same default rate and which makes positive profits, can be beaten out of the market; (ii) any non-rationing contract with positive profit will be beaten out of the market; and (iii) there exists a zero-profit rationing contract which dominates the zero-profit non-rationing contract.

(i)   Consider the rationing contract P in figure 4 on the rectangular hyperbola $LR = k$, which is the locus of all L,R combinations at which the default rate is the same, since loan repayment is constant. If both banks initially offer P then one can obtain the whole of the market for itself by offering a marginally less restrictive contract on the $LR = k$ locus without changing the size of the loan repayment.

If the bank initially had n_1 borrowers and gains n_2 through offering the less restrictive contract then the change in profit is

$$(n_1 + n_2) [LR\lambda(LR) - L_2 I] - n_1 [LR\lambda(LR) - L_1 I], \tag{1}$$

where L_1 and L_2 are the initial and new loan sizes. (1) can be rewritten as

$$n_2 [LR\lambda(LR)] - n_1 (L_2 - L_1) I - n_2 L_2 I . \tag{2}$$

Since an arbitrarily small reduction in the restrictiveness of the loan will secure the whole market we can neglect the second term and (2) becomes

$$n_2 [LR\lambda (LR) - L_2 I]. \tag{3}$$

The condition for the new contract to make more profit than the old is therefore just that the new contract must itself make positive profit.

(ii)   Likewise a non-rationing solution with positive profits will be beaten out of the market under the Nash assumption. Suppose one bank offers Q' instead of Q in figure 4. The change in profit is

$$(n_1 + n_2) [LR\lambda(LR)' - L_2 I] - n_1 [LR\lambda(LR) - L_1 I] \tag{4}$$

$$= n_2 [LR\lambda(LR)' - L_2 I] + n_1 [LR\lambda(LR)' - LR\lambda(LR)] + n_1 [L_1 I - L_2 I],$$

where $LR\lambda(LR)'$ is the average revenue generated by the new contract. Assuming Q' is sufficiently close to Q to neglect the second two terms (4) reduces to

$$n_2 [LR\lambda(LR)' - L_2 I]. \tag{5}$$

The condition for the new contract to make more profit than the old is again simply that the new contract must itself make positive profit.

    (iii)   It remains to show that there exists a zero profit rationing solution which dominates the zero-profit non-rationing solution. This is analogous to the J-R analysis of the competitive case. Consider figure 5. Q is the zero-profit, non-rationing solution. However point E where the bank's zero profit locus is tangential to the firm's iso-profit locus yields higher profit to the borrowing firm. If equilibrium were at Q either bank could offer E' and make positive profit. But non-collusive Nash behaviour drives the equilibrium contract to E which is also the competitive equilibrium.

    Our second extension of the J-R model shows that, at the opposite extreme from Nash behaviour, fully collusive, joint-profit maximising behaviour leads to the non-rationing monopoly outcome as in the J-R analysis. In figure (6) $S(L)$ is now the two-plant monopoly supply curve, i.e. the sum of the duopolists' marginal cost curves defined by the first derivatives of their profit functions with respect to L. A rationing contract such as A cannot prevail since there always exists a more profitable non-rationing contract such as B where revenue $LR\lambda(LR)$ is unchanged but loan size, and hence opportunity cost, is lower. The joint profit-maximising solution therefore lies on the demand curve (at M in figure 6) above the intersection of the marginal cost and expected marginal revenue curves. As in the J-R model there is no necessary relation between the collusive loan size and the competitive (or Nash), rationed loan size. The colluding firms may offer a larger loan though they will of course charge a higher price.

    Between these extremes lie a range of conjectural variations models, which can also entail rationing. Consider for example the asymmetric response pattern where rival new contracts which would be preferred by borrowers (and hence threaten the firm's existence) will be matched, but new contracts which borrowers would reject are ignored. As in the familiar kinked demand curve oligopoly model we obtain a range of possible equilibria which are shown in figure (7). The banks' iso-profit curves here assume an equal division of borrowers between banks. The range of possible equilibria consists of the locus $\overline{MC}$ of tangencies between bank and firm iso-profit curves between the monopoly (M) and competitive (C) contracts. (Bank profits fall and firm profits increase for movements from M towards C.) Rationing occurs everywhere except at the end point M, which will be attained only if there is collusion.

    Taking our results together we see that credit rationing may occur under competitive or Nash-type lending behaviour and under certain conjectural variations assumptions, but not under simple

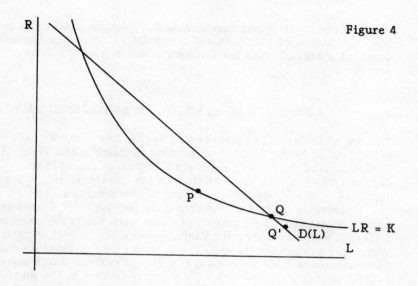

Figure 4

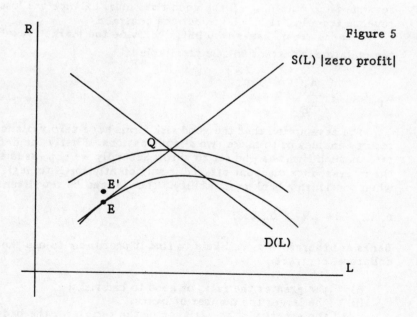

Figure 5

monopoly or joint-profit maximising duopoly. In passing we note that the coincidence of the Nash and competitive outcomes depends on constant marginal costs for the banks, which may not be met in practice.

3.   COLLATERAL REQUIREMENTS AS A SCREENING MECHANISM

The use of collateral as a screening device to counteract adverse selection has been analysed thoroughly by Stiglitz and Weiss (1981). In this section we provide a simple illustrative example to demonstrate that the banks' demands for collateral can be a rational response to the existence of asymmetric information.

Consider a market where there are two types of borrower with normally distributed returns on projects with the same mean but different variances. For simplicity assume that the first group of borrowers has zero variance. The second group or the type two borrowers have positive variance on future returns hence a greater default probability. By making a slight reduction in the interest rate and asking for collateral the bank can offer a contract which will be preferred by type one borrowers (good risks) and rejected by type two borrowers (bad risks). For this to be profitable the increase in revenue from obtaining all the good risks must balance the loss of revenue from bad risks who reject the contract.

If there are n_b banks who initially divide the market evenly then the collateral contract will be profitable if

$$n_1 \ LR \ > \ \frac{n_1}{n_b} \ LR + \frac{n_2}{n_b} \ LR \ \lambda_2. \tag{6}$$

The assumption that the good risk firms have zero variance of returns enables us to make two simplifications. Firstly the default rate on such firms can be set to zero. Secondly we can assume that the interest rate discount offered is sufficiently small to neglect when considering bank profitability. Thus (6) can be rewritten:

$$n_1 \ (n_b - 1) \ LR > n_2 \ LR_2. \tag{7}$$

Banks are therefore more likely to find it profitable to use the collateral contract:

(i)   the greater the ratio of good to bad risks;
(ii)   the larger the number of banks;
(iii) the greater is the variance of the return for the bad risks (and therefore the greater the default rate).

Under Nash behaviour all banks will eventually offer the same collateral contract and again divide the market evenly.

If all firms can meet the collateral requirement and there exists some degree of monopoly profit then there is no net welfare effect

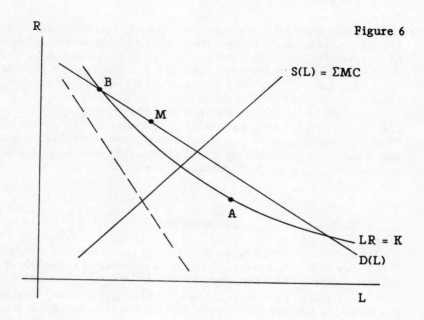

Figure 6

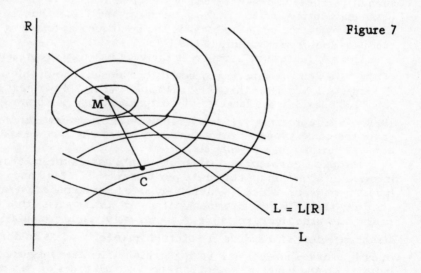

Figure 7

of the new contract. This is because the collateral requirement merely transfers some of the risk which had been borne by the banks to the bad risk firms. In the case where firms operate in a competitive environment, however, the bad risk firms will be driven out of the market and there will be a net welfare loss to the community (and a loss of profitability to the banks).

Another important consideration is that ability to meet collateral requirements may not be distributed evenly across firms. Thus as the collateral required increases some firms (both good and bad risks) are forced to drop out of the market leading to a net welfare loss. This problem is likely to be particularly severe for new firms.

4. INTERNATIONAL DIFFERENCES

On the foregoing arguments credit restrictions and strict collateral terms can arise from rational, risk-neutral lending behaviour in the presence of informational asymmetries between lenders and borrowers, under a range of market conditions.[3] Hence, lending practice in a country may reflect the degree of such asymmetries, so that international differences in lending behaviour such as L-E-C highlight will be associated with structural differences affecting the way information is distributed in the loan market. We suggest that such differences can be observed in the close institutional links between industry and the banks in Germany and Japan that, in L-E-C's own account, are absent in the traditional, arms-length creditor-debtor relationship in the UK.

The key feature in Germany is the very extensive representation of the banks on the supervisory boards of industrial companies.[4] Recent statistics show that the banks hold 145 or 9.8 per cent of the total 1480 seats in the largest 100 companies (Monopolkommission, 1980), with representatives in 61 companies.[5] In no less than 20 cases the banks provided the supervisory board chairman, and the deputy chairman in a further six.

Through their representatives the banks have a direct channel to internal information on corporate performance, strategy and investment plans, which is extensively safeguarded under German company law. Further informational opportunities arise from the banks' two other main roles vis-à-vis industry: as intermediaries or direct suppliers of all kinds of external finance,[6] and as holders of (mostly proxy) shareholders' voting rights.[7] The heavy dependence of industry on the banking system for access to all types of external finance results in a substantial flow of information about corporate plans and performance to or via the banks; in the case of direct bank borrowing the information which legally must be sought and given before substantial loans are given goes well beyond UK practice. And companies are hardly in a position to refuse requests for further information when they come from banks armed with the ultimate sanction of voting power.[8]

In the case of Japan, we focus on the intermarket business groups through which "Zaibatsu and other affiliations link industrial, commercial and financial firms in a thick and complex skein of relations matched in no other industrial country" (Caves and Uekusa, 1976).[9] Significantly, each group contains a number of financial institutions, typically including a commercial bank, a trust bank and an insurance company, enabling the different financial needs of the group to be met (Elston, 1981). Again, it is the informational aspect of the groups which is important for our analysis. Central to this are the weekly meetings of the president-directors of group companies, and the meetings that also take place at lower levels in the managerial hierarchy. The meetings involve, and indeed often take place under the auspices of the banks, who act as group co-ordinators as well as lenders and financial advisors. The exchange of information within the groups is so central to their existence and operation that one Japanese observer has described them as 'information clubs', and proposed that the theory of clubs be used to analyze their behaviour (Imai, 1975). Also significant to our analysis is the group trading company. Financed largely by the group bank this typically provides trade finance to smaller firms in the group "with which it is in more knowledgeable contact and thus provides a buffer to the bank against the riskier end of the lending spectrum" (Elston, 1981, emphasis added).

We conclude that in both countries the banks gain detailed knowledge of the characteristics and policies of individual companies, including their risk characteristics, via institutional arrangements that are not present in the UK. Hence we would argue that a lower degree of informational asymmetry could indeed account for the observed inter-country pattern of lending practices.

5.   IMPLICATIONS FOR UK POLICY

On the L-E-C hypothesis there is a short run policy option, since it is simply the attitudes of bankers which are at fault. All that is required, according to L-E-C, is to exhort the banks to lend more, over longer terms, to more highly-geared companies. If, however, our alternative hypothesis is correct, this would have little effect, since it would involve inducing the banks to depart from current behaviour which is not 'unduly cautious' but privately rational given the circumstances in which they operate. Thus the problem is now not behavioural but structural, centering on an institutional failure in the distribution of information, in the face of which credit-rationing and strict collateral terms are used to minimise default and screen out bad risks.[10] As the problem is structural there are no easy short-run options; contrary to L-E-C, it is no more malleable in the short run than are other preferred explanations of Britain's relative industrial decline, such as inefficient management and obstructive trade unions.

Even in the long term, full-blown adoption of either the

Japanese or the German system is arguably neither feasible nor desirable. In each case the present situation is the product of a long-term historical development,[11] and it is hard to identify a polifically feasible transition path from the current UK position to either of the others. A large scale realignment of existing property rights and/or a major revision of company law would be involved. Then, new patterns of behaviour and new policy conventions would have to evolve, with no guarantee of the desired end-results on industrial lending, especially since the operation of the German and Japanese systems also depends - to an undetermined extent - on cultural factors. There could also be adverse antitrust implications, which have previously caused concern and been discussed in their original, German and Japanese contexts (Brown, 1980; Monopolkommission, 1980; Eckstein, 1980).

Increasing bank representation on existing UK company boards (if the technical problem that directors are elected at shareholders' meetings could be satisfactorily solved) might be seen as moving some way towards the German system. However, the effectiveness of external board members of UK company boards is open to question. It has been argued that, sitting alongside executive directors on unitary boards (unlike their counterparts on the superior level, all-external supervisory boards in the German dual board system) they occupy peripheral and relatively weak positions, hampered in policy discussions by their lack of inside knowledge of the company's activities and often not receiving the information they ask for. Moreover, the UK bank appointees would not enjoy their German counterparts' unique advantage due to the combination of representation, virtual monopoly over the supply of external finance, and voting power. Potential anticompetitive effects acting via increased opportunities for cartel organisation would also require consideration and possible countermeasures.

6. CONCLUSIONS

Credit rationing and collateral requirements can be rational, risk-neutral strategies for lenders in loan markets bearing similarity to the UK industrial credit market, if there is an asymmetry in the way information is distributed between borrowers and lenders. Differences between UK banking practices and those of other countries seem to correspond to institutional differences affecting the way information is held. To the extent that UK lending practice is shaped by structural factors affecting the way information is distributed in loan markets, policies to exhort banks to lend more to more highly geared companies are unlikely to be effective.

NOTES

1.   Rationing is defined as lenders supplying fewer funds than are demanded by borrowers at going interest rates. Stiglitz and

Weiss (1981) consider a different case, where some borrowers are unable to obtain loans while others are.

2.   Firms maximise $\Pi = N_2 - LR$ where LR is the loan repayment, N_2 is (second-period) revenue net of all other costs and $N_2 = N_2$ (L). The iso-profit curves are defined by

$$N_2 (L) - LR = \bar{K}$$

where $\bar{K}$ is constant. Since $\partial LR / \partial L = R$, a constant, their increasing/decreasing shape clearly requires $\partial N_2 /\partial L \gtrless 0$ according to $L \lessgtr L^*$.

3.   Less obviously in the case of stochastic returns, where neither borrowing firms nor lending bank can be better informed about expected returns. However, we regard this as the least important of the four cases considered.

4.   For a more detailed account see Cable (1985a, b).

5.   This is in fact less than the 179 seats held only three years earlier (Monopolkommission, 1978), the decline being due mainly to the extension of co-determination laws requiring increased trade union representation.

6.   Bank borrowing is itself the largest single external source, accounting for around 20 per cent of total enterprise funds, two-thirds or so of which are long-term loans (Samuels and MacMahon, 1978). In addition, the banks are the key to virtually all other sources, since they also handle most new issues of marketable securities (placing substantial proportions directly with their own customers), and provide advisory and brokerage services in securing foreign, government and non-bank loans. As a result, the banking system is "virtually indispensable to companies seeking any form of external finance" (Vittas, 1983).

7.   Resulting in bank control of 36 per cent of voting rights in the top 100 companies, and over 50 per cent, on average, in the ten largest (Monopolkommision, 1978).

8.   The fact that banks can participate in policy in Germany (and also Japan) could well explain their willingness to value the company as a 'going concern' rather than taking its 'carcass value', which L-E-C describe as typical UK behaviour.

9.   See also Cable and Yasuki (1985). Specifically, we focus on the three successors to the pre-war Zaibatsu companies (Mitsui, Mitsubishi and Sumitomo) and the three banking groups (Fuji, Sanwa and Daiichi-Kangin). In 1977 these six accounted for 55 out of 80 companies listed in the top 100, and a total of 178 companies, with over 16 per cent of the assets of all limited companies.

10.   The use of conventional risk screens (e.g. firm size, industrial classification, type of investment) is not a complete solution. As J-R point out, these can be used to allocate particular borrowers among standard risk categories, but credit rationing is then needed to deal with the problem of individual variation within the relevant group. Rationing will be most severe for new firms. Though

our models consider only single contracts, we can imagine a series of loan contracts between individual firms and banks, revealing the firm's characteristics and eroding the initial asymmetry over time. Thus we expect market segmentation according to risk categories and rationing or no rationing according to the degree of asymmetry within each segment.

11. Ironically, both developed as second best options in the absence of established external capital markets like those in contemporary Britain and America, in Germany during the initial, post unification phase of industrialisation and in Japan during the post second world war recovery period.

REFERENCES

Adams, M. (1985) "Ökonomische Analyse der Verschuldens – und
    Gefährdungshaftung", R.V. Decker/C.F. Müller Verlag
    _____ (1984) "Liability for Fatal Accidents in the Law of Torts
    and the Regulation of the German Insurance Industry",
    Discussion Paper No. 22, University of Berne
Akerlof, G. (1970) "The Market for Lemons: Qualitative
    Uncertainty and the Market Mechanism", Quarterly Journal
    of Economics 84, pp. 488–500
Artis, M.J. and Karakitsos, E. (1983) "Intermediate Target Variables:
    their Role in Policy Formation with Special Reference to
    the Money Supply and the Exchange Rate", Fourth Report
    from the Treasury and Civil Service Committee on
    International Monetary Arrangements, HMSO HC (1983-83)
    21-III

    _____ (1984) "Monetary and Exchange Rate
    Targets in an Optimal Control Setting", in J.S. Bhandari
    (ed.) Exchange Rate Management under Uncertainty, MIT
    Press
    _____ and Lewis M.K. (1981) Monetary Control in the United
    Kingdom, Phillip Allan, Oxford
Backus, D., Brainard, W.C., Smith, G. and Tobin, J. (1980) "A Model
    of US Financial and Non-Financial Economic Behaviour",
    Journal of Money, Credit and Banking, Special Issue, May,
    pp. 259–293
    _____ and Driffill, J. (1984a) "Inflation and Reputation",
    Discussion Paper no. 560, Queen's University, Kingston,
    Canada, forthcoming in the American Economic Review
    _____ (1984b) "Rational Expectations and Policy
    Credibility Following a Change of Regime", Discussion
    Paper no. 564, Queen's University, Kingston, Canada,
    forthcoming in the Review of Economic Studies
Barro, R.J. (1974) "Are Government Bonds Net Wealth?" Journal of
    Political Economy 82, pp. 1095–1117
    _____ and Gordon, D. (1983a) "A Positive Theory of Monetary

References

Policy in a Natural-Rate Model, <u>Journal of Political Economy</u>, 91, pp. 589-610

_____ (1983b) "Rules, Discretion and Reputation in a Model of Monetary Policy", <u>Journal of Monetary Economics</u> 12, pp. 101-121

_____ and Grossman, H.I. (1971) "A General Disequilibrium Model of Income and Employment", <u>American Economic Review</u> 61, pp. 82-93

_____ (1976) <u>Money, Employment and Inflation</u>, Cambridge University Press, Cambridge

Begg, D.K.H. (1980) "Rational Expectations and the Non-neutrality of Systematic Monetary Policy", <u>Review of Economic Studies</u> 47, pp. 293-303

_____ (1982) "The Rational Expectations Revolution in Macroeconomics: Theories and Evidence", Phillip Allan, Oxford

_____ (1984) "Modelling the Term Structure with and without Certainty Equivalence", <u>Economic Journal</u>, Conference Proceedings, Vol. 94 Supplement, pp. 45-58

Benassy, J.-P. (1975) "Neo-Keynesian Disequilibrium Theory in a Monetary Economy", <u>Review of Economic Studies</u> 42, pp. 69-91

Blanchard, O.J. and Kahn, C.M. (1980) "The Solution of Linear Difference Models under Rational Expectations", <u>Econometrica</u> Vol. 48, No. 5, pp. 1305-1311

Blinder, A.S. and Solow, R.M. (1973) "Does Fiscal Policy Matter?", <u>Journal of Public Economics</u> 2, pp. 319-338

Bohm, V. (1978) "Disequilibrium Dynamics in a Simple Macroeconomic Model", <u>Journal of Economic Theory</u> 17, pp. 179-199

Bosman, H.W.J. (1980), "De Monetaire Politiek in Nederland", <u>Maandschrift Economie</u>, 44, No. 9, pp. 340-365

_____ (1984) <u>Monetary Policy in the Netherlands in the Post-Smithonian Era</u>, SUERF Series 43A, Tilburg

Brainard, W.C., and Tobin, J. (1968) "Pitfalls in Financial Model Building", <u>American Economic Review</u>, pp. 99-149

Branson, W.H. (1976) "The Dual Roles of the Government Budget and the Balance of Payments in the Movement from Short-Run to Long-Run Equilibrium", <u>Quarterly Journal of Economics</u> 90, August, pp. 345-368

_____ and W. H. Buiter (1982) "Monetary and Fiscal Policy with Flexible Exchange Rates" in Bhandari, J. & Puttnam, B. (eds.) <u>Economic Interdependence and Flexible Exchange Rates</u>, MIT Press, 1983

Brock, W.A. (1974) "Money and Growth: The Case of Long-run Perfect Foresight", <u>International Economic Review</u> 15, pp. 750-777

Brown, C.J.F. (1980) "Industrial Policy and Economic Planning in Japan and France", <u>National Institute Economic Review</u> 93, August, pp. 59-75

References

Budd, A., Dicks, G., Holly, S., Keating, G. and Robinson, B. (1984) "The London Business School Econometric Model of the UK", _Economic Modelling_ Vol. 1, No. 4, pp. 355-420

Buiter, W.H. (1980) "Crowding Out of Private Capital Formation by Government Borrowing in the Presence of Intergenerational Gifts and Bequests", _Greek Economic Review_ 2, pp. 111-142

Buiter, W.H. (1984) "Fiscal Policy in Open, Interdependent Economies", CEPR Discussion Paper No. 28

_____ and Miller, M. (1981a) "The Thatcher Experiment: The First Two Years", _Brookings Papers on Economic Activity_ 1, pp. 315-367

_____ (1981b) "Monetary Policy and International Competitiveness: the Problems of Adjustment", _Oxford Economic Papers_, reprinted in "_The Money Supply and the Exchange Rate_", (Eltis, W.A. and Sinclair, P.J.N. eds.) Oxford University Press, Oxford 1981

_____ (1983) "Changing the Rules: Economic Consequences of the Thatcher Regime", _Brookings Papers on Economic Acticity_ 2, pp. 305-365

Butter, F.A.G. den, Fase, M.M.G. and Huijser, A.P. (1979) "Het Netto Buitenlands Actief van de Handelsbanken", _Maandschrift Economie_, 43, No. 4, pp. 161-190

Cable, J.R. (1985a) "Capital Market Information and Industrial Performance: The Role of West German Banks", _Economic Journal_ Vol. 95, No. 377, pp. 118-130

_____ (1985b) "The Bank-Industry Relationship in West Germany: Performance and Policy Aspects", in Schwalbach (ed.) _Industry Structure and Performance_, Edition Sigma, Berlin, forthcoming

_____ and Yasuki, H. (1985) "Internal Organisation, Business Groups and Corporate Performance: An Empirical Test of the M-form Hypothesis in Japan", _International Journal of Industrial Organisation_, forthcoming

Carrington, J.C. and Edwards, G.T. (1979) _Financing Industrial Investment_, Macmillan and (1981) _Reversing Economic Decline_, Macmillan

Caves, R.E. and Uekusa, M. (1976) _Industrial Organisation in Japan_, Brookings Institution

Chiang, A.C. (1974) _Fundamental Methods of Mathematical Economics_ (2nd edition), McGraw-Hill Kogakusha, Tokyo

Christ, C.F. (1968) "A Simple Macroeconomic Model with a Government BudgetConstraint", _Journal of Political Economy_ 76, pp. 53-67

_____ (1979) "On Fiscal and Monetary Policies and the Government Budget Restraint", _American Economic Review_ 69, September, pp. 539-552

Cockwell, H.A.L. and Green, E. (1976) _The British Insurance Business 1547-1970_, Heinemann

Colenutt, D. W. (1977) "Determinants of Expense Ratios in UK Life

References

Assurers", Journal of Risk and Insurance, March
Corker, R. (1985) "Exchange Intervention: An Alternative Strategy",
    Economic and Financial Review Vol. 1, pp. 78-81
    _____ and Holly, S. (1984) "The Effect of Interest Rate Changes
    in the LBS Model", London Business School Centre for
    Economic Forecasting, Working Paper No. 6, November
Department of Trade and Industry (1985) U.K. Government White
    Paper Financial Services in the UK, Cmnd 9432, HMSO,
    January
    _____ - Insurance Annual Report, HMSO
    (various editions)
Diamond, P. (1965) "National Debt in a Neoclassical Growth Model",
    American Economic Review 55, pp. 503-511
Dixit, A.K. (1976) Optimisation in Economic Theory, Oxford
    University Press, Oxford
Dornbusch, R. (1976) "Exchange Rate Dynamics", Journal of Political
    Economy 84, pp. 1161-1176
    _____ and S. Fischer (1980) "Exchange Rates and the Current
    Account", American Economic Review 70, December, pp.
    960-971
Dunnen, E. den (1973) "Monetary Policy in the Netherlands", in
    Holbik, K. (ed.) Monetary Policy in Twelve Industrial
    Countries, Boston, pp. 282-328
    _____ (1979) "Postwar Monetary Policy", De Economist,
    127, No. 1, pp. 21-57
    _____ (1981) "Dutch Economic and Monetary Problems in
    the 1970s", in Courakis, A.S. (ed.) Inflation, Depression and
    Economic Policy in the West, London/Oxford, pp. 181-202
Eckstein, W. (1980) "The Role of the Banks in Corporate Concentra-
    tion in West Germany", Zeitschrift für die gesamte
    Staatswissenschaft, 136, pp. 465-482
Elston, C.D. (1981) "The Financing of Japanese Industry", Bank of
    England Quarterly Bulletin, 21, pp. 510-518
Fama, E.F. (1968) "Risks Return and Equilibrium: Some Clarifying
    Comments", Journal of Finance, March, pp. 29-39
Finsinger, J. (1982) "Die Auswirkungen der steuerlichen Bevorzugung
    des Lebensversicherungssparens", Finanzarchiv, Band 40
    Heft 1, pp. 99-108
Fischer, S. (1977) "Long-Term Contracts, Rational Expectations, and
    the Optimal Money Supply Rule", Journal of Political
    Economy 85, pp. 191-205
    _____ (1984) "Contracts, Credibility and Disinflation", NBER
    Working Paper No. 1339, April
Fisher, P., Holly, S. and Hughes-Hallett, A. (1985) "Efficient
    Solution Techniques for Dynamic Non-Linear Rational
    Expectations Models", London Business School Discussion
    Paper No. 145
Francis, J.C. (1976) Investments, McGraw Hill.
    _____ and Archer, S.H. (1979) Portfolio Analysis,
    Prentice-Hall (2nd Edition)

References

Gale, D. (1983) <u>Money: In Disequilibrium</u>, Cambridge University
    Press, Cambridge

Gallais-Hamonno, G. (1970) <u>Les Sociétés d'Investissement à</u>
    <u>Capital Variable, SICAV</u>, PUF, Collection SUP

A. Giovannini (1984) "Fiscal Policy, the Capital Stock and the
    Exchange Rate" Columbia University

Gower Report (1982) <u>Review of Investor Protection</u>, Cmnd 9125,
    HMSO, January

Green, C. (1984) "Preliminary Results from a Five Sector Flow of
    Funds Model of the UK 1972-77", <u>Economic Modelling</u> Vol.
    1, No. 3, pp 304-306

_____ and Keating, G.B. (1985) "Market-Clearing Asset Prices in
    Mean Variance Models", London Business School Centre for
    Economic Forecasting Working Paper

Hahn, F.H. (1980) "Monetarism and Economic Theory", <u>Economica</u>
    47, pp. 1-17

Hall, S. (1984) "An Improved Solution Technique for Large Economic
    Models with Consistent Expectations", mimeo, National
    Institute for Economic and Social Research.

HM Treasury (1982) <u>Macroeconomic Model Technical Manual and</u>
    <u>Equation Listing</u>

Hodrick, R.J. (1980) "Dynamic Effects of Government Policies in an
    Open Economy", <u>Journal of Monetary Economics</u> 6, April,
    pp. 213-240

Hoggarth, G. (1984) "Recent UK Monetary Policy - Is the
    Government's Monetary Strategy Impotent?", Henley
    Centre Discussion Paper No. 14

Holly, S. and Zarrop, M. (1983) "On Optimality and Time Consistency
    when Expectations are Rational", <u>European Economic</u>
    <u>Review</u>, February, pp. 23-40

Imai, K. (1976) Gendai Sangyo Soshiki

Jaffee, D. and Russell, T. (1976) "Imperfect Information and Credit
    Rationing", <u>Quarterly Journal of Economics</u> 90, pp. 651-666

Kay, J.A. (1982) "The Price of Mixed Life Business", mimeo

Keating, G. B. (1985) "The Macroeconomic Impact of the British
    Telecom Flotation" <u>Economic and Financial Review</u> Vol. 1
    pp. 49-54

Kessler, G.A. (1981) "De Invloed van het Nederlandse Monetaire
    Beleid en Wisselkoersbeleid op de Ontwikkeling van de
    Werkgelegenheid", <u>Maandschrift Economie</u>, 45, no.2, pp.
    53-80

Korteweg, P. (1980) "Monetair Beleid in Nederland", <u>Economisch</u>
    <u>Statistische Berichten</u> 65, 12 and 19 November, pp.
    1256-1264 and 1284-1291

_____ and Loo, P.D. van (1977) <u>The Market for Money and</u>
    <u>the Market for Credit. Theory, Evidence and Implications</u>
    <u>for Dutch Monetary Policy</u>, Leiden

Kouri, P.J.K. (1976) "The Exchange Rate and the Balance of
    Payments in the Short Run and in the Long Run: A
    Monetary Approach", <u>Scandinavian Journal of Economics</u> 2,

pp. 280-304

Kreps, D. and Wilson, R. (1982) "Reputation and Imperfect Information", Journal of Economic Theory 27, pp. 253-279

Kydland, F. and Prescott, E. (1977) "Rules Rather than Discretion: the Inconsistency of Optimal Plans", Journal of Political Economy 85, pp. 348-352

Laidler, D. (1984) "The 'Buffer Stock' Notion in Monetary Economics" Economic Journal, Conference Papers Supplement, pp. 17-34

Lever, H. and Edwards, G.T. (1980) "Why Germany Beats Britain" and "How to Bank on Britain", The Sunday Times, November

Loo, P.D. van (1980-1) "On the Microeconomic Foundations of Bank Behaviour in Macroeconomic Models", De Economist 128, No. 4, pp. 474-495

_____ (1980-2) Interest Arbitrage and the Exchange Rate Regime: Some Reduced Form Evidence for the Netherlands, Working Paper 8063, Money and Banking Workshop, Erasmus University Rotterdam, revised version of a paper presented at the Konstanzer Seminar on Monetary Theory and Monetary Policy, June 1980

_____ (1983) A Sectoral Analysis of the Dutch Financial System, Leiden/Antwerpen

Malinvaud, E. (1977) The Theory of Unemployment Reconsidered, Blackwell, Oxford

Markowitz, H. M. (1952) "Portfolio Selection" Cowles Foundation Monograph No. 16, New York

Marston, R.C. (1984) "Stabilization Policies in Open Economies", in R.W. Jones and P.B. Kenen (eds.) Handbook of International Economics Vol. 2, North-Holland

Merton, R.C. (1973) "An Intertemporal Asset Pricing Model", Econometrica, Vol. 41, pp. 867-889

Metzler, L.A. (1951) "Wealth, Saving and the Rate of Interest", Journal of Political Economy LIX, April, pp. 93-116

Mishkin, F.S. (1980) "Is the Preferred Habitat Model of the Term Structure Consistent with Financial Market Efficiency?" Journal of Political Economy Vol. 88, pp. 406-411

Monopolkommission (1976, 1978, 1980) Hauptgutachten I-III, Nomos Verlag, Baden-Baden

Mundell, R.A. (1963) "Capital Mobility and Stabilization under Fixed and Flexible Exchange Rates", Canadian Journal of Economics and Political Science 29, pp. 475-485

Mussa, M. (1982) "A Model of Exchange Rate Dynamics", Journal of Political Economy 90, February, pp. 74-104

National Institute of Economic and Social Research (1983) National Institute Model 6, London

Nederlandsche Bank, De (1979) Report for the Year 1979, Amsterdam

Okun, A. (1978) "Efficient Disinflationary Policies", American Economic Review 68, pp. 348-352

Ott, D.J. and Ott, A. (1965) "Budget Balance and Equilibrium Income", Journal of Finance, pp. 71-77

Parkin, M. (1970) "Discount House Portfolio and Debt Selection", Review of Economic Studies Vol. 37, pp. 469-497

Pauly, M. (1982) "Further Notes on Computing Rates of Return on Mixed Life Insurance Policies", mimeo

Rabohypotheekbank (1978) Jaarverslag 1978, Utrecht

Rankin, N. (1984) "Fiscal Policy in Quantity-Constrained Equilibrium", D.Phil thesis, University of Oxford

Report of the Tribunal appointed to inquire into certain issues in relation to the circumstances leading up to the cessation of trading by the Vehicle and General Insurance Co. Ltd. HL80 HC133, HMSO 1972

Rodriguez, C.A. (1980) "The Role of Trade Flows in Exchange Rate Determination: A Rational Expectations Approach", Journal of Political Economy 88, December, pp. 1148-1158

Rothschild, M. and Stiglitz J. (1976) "Equilibrium in Competitive Insurance Markets: The Economics of Imperfect Information", Quarterly Journal of Economics 90, pp. 629-649

Rustem, B. (1983) "Rival Models: Min-Max Problems and Algorithms", in T. Basar and L.F. Pau (eds.) Dynamic Modelling and Control of National Economies, Pergamon Press, Oxford

Sachs, J. (1980) "Wages, Flexible Exchange Rates and Macroeconomic Policy", Quarterly Journal of Economics 94, June, pp. 731-748

_____ and Wyplosz, C. (1984) "La Politique Budgétaire et le Taux de Change Réel", Annales de l'INSEE 53, Janvier-Mars, pp. 63-91

Samuels, J.M. and McMahon, P.C. (1978) Saving and Investment in the UK and West Germany, Wilton Publications

Sharpe, W.F. (1964) "Capital Assets Pricing", Journal of Finance, September, pp. 425-442

Sidrauski, M. (1967) "Rational Choice and Patterns of Growth in a Monetary Economy", American Economic Review 57, (papers and proceedings) pp. 534-544

Spencer, P.D. (1981) "A Model of the Demand for British Government Stocks by Non-Bank Residents 1967-77", Economic Journal, Vol. 91, no. 364, pp. 938-960

_____ and Mowl, C. (1978) "The model of the Domestic Monetary System", Government Economic Service Working Paper No. 17

Stiglitz, J. and Weiss, M. (1981) "Credit Rationing in Markets with Imperfect Information" American Economic Review 71, pp. 393-410

Taylor, J. (1983) "Aggregate Dynamics and Staggered Contracts", Journal of Political Economy 88, pp. 1009-1021

_____ (1983) "Union Wage Settlements During a Disinflation", American Economic Review 73, pp. 981-993

Thanheister, H.T. (1976) "Strategy and Structure in Germany", in Dyas, G.P. and Thanheister, H.T. The Emerging European Enterprise, Macmillan, London

References

Timmerman, P.C. (1977) <u>The Intervention Policy of the Netherlands Bank in the Money Market</u>, Reprint 33, The Netherlands Bank, Amsterdam

Tobin, J. (1980) "Government Deficits and Capital Accumulation", in Tobin, J., <u>Asset Accumulation and Economic Activity</u>, Blackwell, Oxford

_____ and Buiter, W.H. (1976) "Long-run Effects of Fiscal and Monetary Policy on Aggregate Demand", in Stein, J.L. (ed.), <u>Monetarism</u>, Amsterdam: North-Holland

_____ and Buiter, W.H. (1976) "Long-run Effects of Fiscal and Monetary Policy on Aggregate Demand", in Stein, J.L. (ed.), <u>Monetarism</u>, Amsterdam, North-Holland, pp. 273-309

Turnovsky, S. (1976) "The Dynamics of Fiscal Policy in an Open Economy", <u>Journal of International Economics</u> 6, pp. 115-142

Vittas, D. (1983) "Banks' Relations with Industry", <u>Committee of London Clearing Banks</u>, Research Group

Wallis, K.F. (1980) "The Econometric Implications of the Rational Expectations Hypothesis", <u>Econometrica</u>, Vol. 45, 1, pp. 49-73

Wessels, R.E. (1982) "The Supply and Use of Central Bank Advance Facilities", <u>Journal of Monetary Economics</u> 10, July, pp. 89-100

Wickens, M.R. (1984) "Rational Expectations and Exchange Rate Dynamics" mimeo, University of Southampton

Williamson, O.E. (1970), <u>Corporate Control and Business Behaviour</u>, Prentice Hall, Englewood Cliffs, N.J.

_____ (1975) <u>Markets and Hierachies</u>, Macmillan, New York

Wilson, C.A. (1979) "Anticipated Shocks and Exchange Rate Dynamics", <u>Journal of Political Economy</u> 87, pp. 639-647

Zijlstra, J. (1979) <u>Central Banking, A Moderate Monetarist's View</u>, Jerusalem